EUI – Series A – 4

Daintith and Hancher, Energy Strategy in Europe:
The Legal Framework

European University Institute
Institut Universitaire Européen
Europäisches Hochschulinstitut
Istituto Universitario Europeo

Series A

Law/Droit/Recht/Diritto

4

Badia Fiesolana — Firenze

Energy Strategy in Europe: The Legal Framework

by

Terence Daintith and Leigh Hancher

1986

Walter de Gruyter · Berlin · New York

Library of Congress Cataloging in Publication Data

Energy strategy in Europe.
(Series A--Law / European University Institute = Series A--Droit / Institut universitaire européen ; 4)
Includes index.
1. Power resources--Law and legislation--European Economic Community countries. 2. Energy policy--European Economic Community countries. I. Daintith, Terence. II. Hancher, Leigh, 1956– . III. Series: Series A--Law ; 4.
KJE6698.E54 1986 343.4'092 86-3158
ISBN 0-89925-173-0 (U.S.) 344.0392

CIP-Kurztitelaufnahme der Deutschen Bibliothek

Energy strategy in Europe: the legal framework / ed. by Terence Daintith ; Leigh Hancher. – Berlin ; New York : de Gruyter, 1986.
(European University Institute : Ser. A, Law ; 4)
ISBN 3-11-010646-9

NE: Daintith, Terence [Hrsg.]; Istituto Universitario Europeo ⟨Fiesole⟩: European University Institute / A

Dust Cover Design: Rudolf Hübler, Berlin. – Setting and Printing: Arthur Collignon GmbH., Berlin.
Binding: Verlagsbuchbinderei Dieter Mikolai, Berlin.
Printed in Germany

Foreword

This book is a product of our collaboration within the framework of research at the European University Institute, Florence, on the theme of legal implementation of economic policy in Europe. The general concern of the project with the way in which economic policies are translated into law, and with the dual role of law as both instrument of, and constraint upon, policy is here focussed on the field of energy policy in the Community and, in particular, on the new energy strategy of the Commission and the legal context in which it must operate. In preparing this study we have profited greatly from the holding of a colloquium at the Institute in September 1982 on the theme "Legal Implementation of Energy Policy in Europe 1973–80". A full list of papers read at that colloquium, and available on file at the Institute, will be found in Appendix III to this volume. A substantial part of the material in this study was first presented by us at the colloquium and has been revised and developed in the light of discussion there; and papers from other contributors, particularly on national energy laws and policies, have enabled us to correct and supplement our factual data and to develop a better understanding of different approaches to legal implementation. The text presents the state of our knowledge as at end-January 1984, though in some places we have been able to take account of developments occurring after this date.

Special mention should be made of the contribution to this work of Mr. R. De Bauw, now Head of the Oil Policy Division within the Energy Directorate-General of the Commission, and formerly Head of its Energy Policy-Division and as such, associated with the preparation of most of the Commission's energy policy papers since 1973, who has generously allowed us to draw heavily on his colloquium paper "La Communauté Européenne et la Politique de l'Energie" in our description of the energy strategy, in sketching the history of Community energy policy and in discussing the strategy's likely impact. Mr. De Bauw has also been kind enough to read and comment upon the entire work in draft form, leading to improvement of the text at a number of points. In view of the importance of his contribution, we would like to make it clear that save where express reference is made to his writings in text or footnotes, the responsibility for the opinions expressed herein is entirely ours, and not that of Mr. De Bauw.

Our thanks go also to Mr. C. J. Audland, Director-General for Energy, and to the officials of the Directorate-General for their friendly encouragement and practical help. Within the Institute, we should like to express our gratitude to Peter Versteeg for help with statistical information and to Anne-Lise Strahtmann for efficient secretarial support.

Terence Daintith
Leigh Hancher

San Domenico di Fiesole
January 1984

Table of Contents

List of Tables

Chapter I

A Legal Perspective on Energy Policy

I. Introduction

Not many people, we would guess, could be found to say that the energy sector offered a good example of positive and effective European integration. The general consensus, in which senior Community officials participate no less than outside observers, is that the Community's performance in this field has been inadequate. Repeatedly, the European Council has called for Community action; the Commission has offered proposals for action; the Council of Ministers has resolved to act: and yet, in the words of the Commission itself:

> The inadequacy and inconsistency of the action taken in the wake of these expressions of political will can only be deplored.[1]

Naturally, a wide variety of reasons has been offered for this disappointing performance in a vital sector. The division of energy matters among three separate Treaties (and, initially, three separate executives) has undoubtedly been a handicap. So too, perhaps, has been the failure of the framers of the Rome Treaties to perceive the need for an energy policy as such, or any need at all for an oil policy different from that applying to the general run of manufactured products. Comparable specific reasons can be adduced in relation to coal (the inherent difficulty of managing the rundown of the industry in a period of great uncertainty about the availability of other fuels) and nuclear energy (conflicting expectations among the signatories of the Euratom Treaty; misperception by the framers of the nature of the problems of nuclear development).[2] Rehearsed at intervals over the quarter-century of the existence of the Rome Treaties, these arguments diminish in conviction: twenty-five years is surely long enough to adapt inappropriate structures or even to build new ones. More recently, the emphasis in explanation has changed, and structural, rather than institutional, impediments to common action have been emphasised. Our attention is

[1] The Development of an Energy Strategy for the Community, COM (81) 540 final, para. 1.

[2] Lucas, N. J., *Energy in the European Communities* (1977).

directed to the differences between Member States which, it is suggested, may be too great to permit them to develop a common energy policy, or at least a policy of the type which involves a significant degree of centralisation of decision-making power and means of action in the hands of Community organs. Among differences mentioned are the energy endowments, and hence degree of dependence on imports, of Member States; their differing predilections for free market, or dirigiste, solutions to energy policy problems; the importance of the public sector in the energy markets of some, of the private sector elsewhere; and member States' differing approaches to relations, with third countries, and different particular links with them.[3]

Obviously such divergences are neither new, nor peculiar to the energy sector. As early as 1958, it was clear that differences of interest between coal-producing and coal-importing States in the original Six were a major obstacle to the implementation of a Community solution to the difficulties of high-cost Community coal production; so they have remained to the present day.[4] What is new, perhaps, is acceptance of the fact that such divergences are here to stay; that there is no Community dynamic which will inexorably bring about a convergence of the economies of its Member States, either in performance or in methods of management. In the energy sector, the Commission appears to have accepted the essence of this analysis, and to have drawn the conclusion that a more successful energy policy must accept, and in some way manage, the diversity of Member State situations, attitudes and policies in the energy sector.

This is reflected by the publication of the Commission's communication of October 1981, entitled "The Development of an Energy Strategy for the Community"[5], which we here call the 'strategy document'. As well as examining energy policy issues, this communication is in part the result of a more general exercise of reflection on new Community policies – the so-called May 30th Mandate exercise – in which the Council requested the Commission to seek a better balance between community policies.

Having recalled the challenge which the energy problem poses to the Community, along with the problem of effecting some alteration in patterns of supply and demand, the Commission's document underlines the need for continued action, based on the combined efforts of all interested parties, including producers, consumers, the Member States and the Community itself.

It begins by drawing attention to the fact that the energy situations of the Member States are divergent, both in terms of their natural resource

[3] See *E. g.* EC Commission. Progress in Structural Change – The Main Findings of The Commission Review of Member States' Energy Policies, COM (84) 87 final, para. 8.

[4] Proposals for a Balanced Solid Fuels Policy, COM (83) 309 final.

[5] COM (81) 540 final. The text of the document is reproduced as Appendix 1.

endowments and in their institutional frameworks. Thus it would be pointless, in these circumstances, to envisage the centralisation of energy-related decisions in the hands of the Community. Member States do, however, have a certain amount of shared interest, direct and indirect, in energy matters and hence the pursuit of common objectives should be feasible. Once agreement has been reached on a common objective, it should be sufficient that it be adopted by Member States in their national policies, with some equivalence of effort:

> Equivalence of effort does not require any substantial centralisation of energy policy instruments, nor does it require the pursuit of uniformity in the diversification of energy supply, which must vary according to national circumstances. But it does call for collective discipline going beyond mere expression of common agreement. The policies of each Member State must reflect a willingness to pursue common goals.[6]

The Commission will undertake periodic reviews to determine the extent to which common goals have been incorporated into national policies and to ensure that in the pursuit of a common interest a collective discipline is respected, without prejudice to legitimate divergences in institutional structure and national interest. The Commission will not hesitate to point out gaps and weaknesses in Member States' policies.

National action alone, however, will not ensure the attainment of common goals. In certain areas, the Treaty has specifically reserved competence to the Community for example in commercial policy matters (Art. 110 et seq.) or on crisis management (Art. 103(4)). In other cases, even although there is no express competence to act on the part of the Community, reasons of efficacity might compel it to take action, where, for instance, action on the part of Member States might lead to a duplication of effort, or where that effort might only have a limited effect. Research and development (beyond the explicit provisions of the ECSC and Euratom Treaties) might be one conceivable area, as might relations with third countries (i. e. relations which do not fall within the terms of the common commercial policy, *stricto sensu*). The need for Community action could arise where national initiatives were lacking or were insufficient or where such initiatives did not extend throughout the Community, for instance through the enforcement of measures taken to implement the directives on the restriction of the use of hydrocarbons in electricity production or by issuing recommendations to encourage measures to facilitate investment in the rational use of energy.

Within this framework of general principles, the Commission has identified, in the strategy document, five main operational priorities for action on all energy sources. These priorities do not replace earlier objectives of

[6] *Ibid.*, para. 6.

energy policy,[7] but indicate those areas in which action is most urgent. In each case there is scope for both Community and national action, the role of the one or the other being defined according to the criteria indicated above. In the first two instances, the Community will be confined to an essentially co-ordinating role, while in the other three, there is potential for some intervention.

The first is to raise the level of *investment* in the more rational use of energy and in alternatives to oil, such as coal. Despite the fact that an investment may appear viable, economic uncertainty and other constraints affect the decisions of producers and consumers alike.

The second priority is more rapid progress in ensuring a common approach to *energy pricing and taxation.* So far as they intervene in the formation of energy prices, public authorities must take account of the objectives of energy policy.

The third concerns measures to mitigate the instability of the oil markets. The problem of security of supply, however, affects all energy sources: coal, gas and uranium.

The fourth priority concerns the reinforcement and refinement of common action in support of *research and development* and technological demonstration in the energy sector. Emphasis is put on a better co-ordination of national programmes and an improved dissemination of the results, the consequences for industrial planning being self-evident.

Finally, attention is turned to a more co-ordinated approach *to external energy relations.* The Community must establish a framework of relations which guarantees security and stability of supply. The Community has also an important role to play in energy co-operation with the less developed countries who have been disproportionately affected by the high level of oil prices.

These priority areas and general principles express the essence of the new strategy. The pace of the Community's decision-making process is such that measures presently being taken, three years after the publication of the document, were originally proposed some time before its formulation. It is perhaps premature, therefore, to attempt a judgment on its significance for the future of the Community energy sector, though we offer some comments on subsequent events in our final chapter. Our purpose here is not to undertake a comprehensive analysis and critique of the new approach: rather, we intend to look at it, and at the divergence thesis which it appears to reflect, from a specific perspective: that of the legal framework, and implementation, of energy policy. Our view is that there is a legal dimension to divergence which, while closely linked with economic and political dimensions, is something more that a mere reflection or expression of

[7] *E.g.* Guidelines and Priorities for Action under the New Community Energy Programme, SEC (1973) 1431.

these latter differences. Even where policies are similar, differences in legal structure or in ways of using law to implement policy may create difficulties in the way of operation of common Community rules, in the energy sector as in other areas. From the legal perspective, therefore, one specific question we may ask about the new strategy is how it reflects, and how it will accommodate, the legal dimension of divergence between Member States. This involves looking at the legal structure of energy markets, and energy industries, in Member States, and at the legal implementation of energy policy in those States; and attempting to relate the differences that emerge both to the Community performance in energy policy over the years to 1981, and to the new approach of the strategy. This will be the main focus of the present study.

There is a second, quite different kind of question which the lawyer might pose in relation to the new energy strategy. This has to do not with national legal structures, but with Community law itself. Can an energy strategy which is flexible enough to accommodate the range of national divergences already mentioned be faithful to the general and basic principles of the European Community Treaties, in particular to the commitment to a free and uncompartmented energy market? We shall also attempt an answer to this question, by briefly reviewing the Commission's approach to the enforcement of free trade principles in the energy sector and the difference that the strategy could make.

II. The Legal Dimension of Diversity

The first requirement for discussion of diversity between Member States in their approach to energy questions is, paradoxically, a common framework of analysis which can be applied to each State's experience. The basic element of the framework to be used here is the analysis of State — and for that matter Community — policy in sectors such as energy in terms of the employment of a range of instruments for the purpose of attaining specified policy objectives. This simple differentiation of objectives and instruments is a first step in analysing diversity.

Every national government has a range of instruments available to it for the achievement of its economic policy objectives: information, exhortation, regulation of the behaviour of private economic agents, the offering of incentives, intervention as a participant in the market. Some kinds of instrument may be more apt for the achievement of particular objectives, or types of objective, than others. Kenneth Boulding offers a simple example:[8] if a government wishes to maintain a fixed price for gold in

[8] Boulding, K., *Principles of Economic Policy* (1958), at pp. 176–177.

terms of its own currency, a prohibition on sales at other prices is unlikely to work effectively. Gold transactions are, as a practical matter, hard to police, so that if the market price for gold diverges much from the fixed price, black markets are likely to develop. A much more effective course is for government to announce its readiness to buy and sell gold, as offered and demanded, at the price fixed. So long as buyers and sellers remain convinced of government's willingness and capacity to meet all offers and demands at this price, third party transactions will take place at, or very close to, this level.

Examples of this kind suggest that there may exist some pattern of association between policy objectives and the instruments chosen for their achievement. Some support for this supposition is to be found in the international surveys of economic policy carried out by Kirschen and his associates in 1964 and 1974,[9] at least so far as Western Europe is concerned. Here we have broadly followed the basic terminology of these studies, describing energy policy in terms of objectives (quantifiable goals of policy), instruments (means employed by government for the pursuit of objectives) and measures (here used, with a sense a little different from that of Kirschen, to refer to the acts of government through which instruments are brought into operation). Kirschen specifies policy objectives in broad terms (full employment, price stability, expansion of production etc.), and is able to show certain regularities in the employment of instruments for these ends across a range of eight states, including six present members of the European Communities. For example, over the period 1949–60, government investment and manipulation of direct taxes on enterprises were used in all states examined to encourage expansion of production, while direct controls and exchange rate adjustments were hardly used at all for this purpose.[10] Such regularities are, however, rather limited: what appears perhaps more strongly from Kirschen's work is the diversity of approach to be found, in states with broadly similar political principles and economic circumstances, to common policy goals.[11] It is the exception, rather than the rule, for a given type of instrument to be preferred by all the states surveyed for the achievement of a particular policy objective.

This diversity in the implementation of economic policy is the starting point of this legal study. For lawyers to set out to examine such a subject

[9] See Kirschen *et al.*, *Economic Policy in Our Time* (1964, 2 vols): Kirschen *et al.*, *Economic Policies Compared: West and East* (1974, 2 vols). The economic climate has of course, changed considerably since Kirschen's work was published, but this change has not detracted from the relevance of his findings.

[10] Kirschen (1964), p. 350 (Table XIII. 2).

[11] Thus it appears, from the table cited in note 10, supra, that while money and credit policy was a significant instrument of production expansion in Belgium and Italy, and a dominant one in West Germany, it played only a minor role, or no role at all, in the other five states.

may at first sight seem a little odd: do not the causes of diversity lie in political, social and economic, rather than legal factors? Certainly such causes do operate. In relation to the major macro-economic policy objectives (high and stable level of employment, external balance, economic growth, stable prices) this diversity reflects the fact that conflicts between the objectives may be resolved in different ways as between one state and another (and, indeed, in different ways over a period of time within a single state). Different priorities among conflicting objectives may naturally be reflected in a different choice of instruments.

Conflicting objectives, however, can provide only a part of the explanation. Even if we restrict our attention to the European Economic Community, and consider more precise and limited objectives of policy where conflicts are less likely to provoke instability in the choice of instruments, we find significant variations in the way the same policy objective is approached in different states. The objective of securing a minimum wage, for example, has been approached in the United Kingdom largely through the extension, via compulsory arbitration, of collectively-bargained wage rates; in France, a national minimum wage is set by government. In this case, we might look first for an explanation to socio-economic divergences between the two societies: to the greater strength of trade unions in the United Kingdom, and the consequent emphasis placed on collective bargaining as the preferred means of setting all remuneration levels. In other cases, differences of trading pattern might be more relevant: thus the different systems of agricultural price support used in the United Kingdom (prior to 1973) and in the EEC reflect the former's position as a major food importer and the latter's substantial self-sufficiency.

Few of these varied policy instruments can be carried into operation without resort or reference to legal measures of some kind. The role of the legal measure may be purely formal or technical, as where the chosen policy instrument is the provision of information and advice and a government advisory body requires to be set up by decree; at the other extreme the instrument may be wholly expressed by way of a legal rule or rules, as occurs when the instrument selected is the prohibition, sanctioned by legal penalties, of particular courses of private conduct. As an example of an intermediate position we may cite cases in which the legal rule provides authority for governmental action (for example, the payment of subsidies to farmers) but does not itself specify the details of the scheme of action, this being left for informal rules or individual discretionary decisons.

In all these employments, the content and shape of the legal rules will be largely determined by the nature of the instruments they are designed to render operative; and the choice of such instruments may, as we have seen, be dictated, or at least suggested, by a wide variety of economic and social factors, some of which may be peculiar to a given State, others commonly or universally encountered. These considerations might seem to suggest a purely instrumental role for law in relation to policy: that is to say, that law is significant merely as a machinery through which the process of policy implementation is carried on. One does not need to be a professional lawyer to feel that such a picture of the relationship between law and policy distorts by omission. Ultimately it may be true that all legal rules are called into being by societal needs and that the content and structure of the legal system are thus wholly dependent on more fundamental social needs and relationships. At any given time, however, government policy is being formed and executed within a social and economic framework of which the state constitution, the legal system as a whole, and specific legal rules, all form important elements. Moreover the constitution, the legal system, and individual rules of law, all operate as constraints on government action, independently of the social and economic forces that brought them into being and sustain them. Such forces may indeed – particularly in relation to individual rules of law – be spent, but if the law survives it cannot be ignored: in the design of a policy instrument a relevant legal rule must either be respected, altered, or breached, and each of these courses entails a set of costs and benefits which would not have been the same had no rule existed. Law, therefore (including the constitution) should be seen as shaping the instruments of policy (and, *a fortiori*, the measures which operationalise those instruments) as well as serving them.

These considerations suggest that just as some divergences in national energy policies are explicable by reference to economic or social circumstances, others will find their explanation in differences in the legal circumstances surrounding policy-making in different Member States. A successful Community policy will therefore require to deal in some way with such differences: either attempting their removal, or seeking to render them irrelevant by creating new, alternative instruments of policy on the Community level, or by accepting and incorporating them. Hence the interest in relating national legal structures both to the Community's energy policy effort over the years to 1981, and to the new strategy then announced with its emphasis on the acceptance of diversity.

The kinds of legal circumstances which may possibly bear upon national policy choices are many and varied, but a fourfold classification will sufficiently indicate the kinds of legal provision we have had in mind in selecting salient examples from the vast range of material which could fall under the rubric of national energy laws.

(i) Legal rules which have constitutional status are obviously of great significance, if only because these are the rules that are hardest to alter. Constitutional provisions may, for example, completely exclude the use of particular kinds of instruments in a given State, or subject their use to conditions so severe as to render them unattractive.

(ii) Also important are rules which attach procedural and other incidents to particular legal forms and techniques: for example, rules determining the capacity (if any) of third parties to sue on a provision of a contract designed for their protection; or requiring the taking of decisions which have certain effects only after the hearing of affected parties; or allowing (or disallowing) suits by private parties to enforce statutory duties also enforceable by criminal process. Such provisions, even if not formally "constitutional", are usually deeply entrenched in the general structure of the legal system. Their effect on economic policy implementation may perhaps be considerable, in that they may affect the capacity of government to control fully the effects of certain kinds of economic instruments which require the use of particular legal forms.

(iii) In addition to these two fairly specific types of legal circumstances, we may also need to allow for effects and influences which, while properly labelled "legal", may yet be much more indeterminate. The historical evolution of a given legal culture may dictate or encourage certain choices – in terms of "ways of doing things" – which are not easily referable to the effects of rules of the types above-mentioned. An example might be the Anglo-Saxon preference for procedural rules and safeguards as a guarantee of fair administrative action, contrasted with the French reliance on judicial review of administrative action on substantive grounds.

(iv) Finally, another kind of legal circumstances are those created by the existence, at the time when policy is being formulated, of relevant bodies of substantive law, whose adaptation or development may furnish one means of achieving the objective at hand. In such a situation the policy-maker may be more likely to resort to an instrument which draws on such a body of law than to one which requires the creation of quite new legal arrangements. In so far as such substantive norms are seen as accidental, as responses to past policy needs rather than as core elements of the legal system, this fourth set of legal circumstances may tell us less about the capacity of a given legal system to respond to policy-makers' demands than do the others; but a demonstration of the relevance of existing substantive provisions to the policy-maker's choice of instruments would provide new support for incrementalist theories of policy formation and implementation.[12]

III. Organisation and Limits of the Study

In the light of these general ideas, we have structured this study in the following way. In Chapter II, we undertake a general review of the conduct

[12] Leading exponents include Braybrooke and Lindblom: see their *A Strategy of Decision* (1970), especially chapter 5.

of Community energy policy up to the reappraisal of 1980–81. This is familiar ground, but we need to traverse it in our own way in order to point to elements in this history which are of particular significance from the legal point of view: whether, for example, particular measures, or unsuccessful proposals for measures, involved transfers of competence to the Community, legal restrictions on Member State behaviour, or neither. Chapter II is therefore a partial history, and the fact that certain aspects of the story receive little or no mention (administrative organisation within the Commission, for example, or the general state of Commission-Council relationships at different times) does not mean that we necessarily think them less important, as factors contributing to the problems of Community energy policy, than the legal issues on which we concentrate.

Chapters III to IV are devoted to energy situations, institutions, market structures and policies in the Member States. Chapter III deals with the energy situation of Member States, in terms of dependence on imports, and patterns of domestic fuel availability and overall fuel use, and with their national energy policy objectives. Chapter IV describes the legal organisation of national energy institutions and markets. Chapter V considers the energy policies adopted by Member States, with particular reference to their legal expression and implementation.

Any attempt at analysis of Member State energy policies, even if solely from the legal perspective, encounters the problem of the vast mass of legislative and other official material that could be of relevance, coupled with the fact that in most countries little systematic work has been done on the collection, arrangement or analysis of national energy law. Some specific topics have attracted quite a substantial literature, either internationally (for example, the siting of nuclear and other types of power plants[13]) or in individual countries (for example, in Germany, regulated competition in electricity supply),[14] but comprehensive analyses on which we could draw directly are lacking. To make the task manageable, therefore, we have set two kinds of limit on our inquiries.

First, we have confined our attention to the four largest members of the Community, France, Germany, Italy and the United Kingdom, and among the smaller Member States, have considered only the position in the Netherlands. The large States and their problems obviously carry the greatest weight in the Community policy-making process (or in obstructing it), but this is not the sole, or even the most important reason for their selection. In addition, they are representative of energy diversity in the Community (a very high degree of import dependence in Italy, a low one in the United Kingdom; a strong commitment to nuclear power in France,

[13] O.E.C.D. The Siting of Major Energy Facilities (Paris 1980).

[14] Groner, H., "Regulated Industries" in Zeitschrift für die gesamte Staatswissenschaft, Band 136, Heft 3, (1980) p. 360.

a much weaker one elsewhere), and *prima facie*, of other kinds of diversity too, this group of four States manifesting strong contrasts in such matters as the preference for dirigiste versus market solutions, centralised versus regional government, public versus private energy enterprises. Some of these stereotypes, as we shall see, tend to break down a little upon closer examination — for example Germany shows quite a high percentage of public ownership in some energy sectors — but not to the point where these essential contrasts are lost. Likewise, the inclusion of the Netherlands is suggested not so much as a representative of the smaller Member States, but rather because of its distinctive position as a major energy producer and exporter, and one which is having to cope with foreseeable decline in production of its main fuel, natural gas, at a time when other Member States are converting to that fuel. The special position of Rotterdam in the international oil and petroleum products trade likewise distinguishes the Netherlands' situation from that of other Member States.

Second, we have concentrated, in our examination of these Member States' policies, on the period since the oil crisis of 1973—74. Information about this period is both more easily obtained, and more easily compared — as between one State and another — than in relation to earlier periods, because of the clarification and convergence of Member State policies that began at this time.

The crisis itself, comprising the Arab oil embargo and the four-fold increase in crude oil prices created within the Community a profound 'energy shock' and caused a major re-appraisal of energy policies hitherto in force, or of the absence of such policies. A major result was to engender a degree of solidarity among oil-importing countries sufficient to sustain the founding, within the framework of the OECD, of an International Energy Programme and Energy Agency (IEA)[15], and thus to create a forum for the discussion and development of common energy policies among such countries. This effort of co-ordination was with some hesitation taken up, as we shall see in Chapter II, within the Community, whose faltering energy policy efforts were spurred by the realisation of a common and serious danger.

At all events the emergence of the IEA has ensured that the shared impulsion to new energy policies has followed a common direction. There is a high degree of similarity between the policy objectives espoused by the five states under study. Subject to appropriate caution about possible disparities between proclaimed and real objectives, this similarity provides a baseline from which we can begin to explore differences in the instruments chosen by States for the attainment of objectives, and to consider the extent to which such differences may be attributable to that legal dimension of

[15] See *e.g.* Evans, A. C., "The International Energy Agency" (1981) Journal of World Trade Law 440.

diversity which is a major concern of this study. By identifying the objectives which Member States have made the subject of international or Community commitment, and examining in detail the national policy objectives they have formulated for themselves, we disengage a scheme of national objectives, which is used as the organising framework for the discussion of national energy policies, in the period since 1973, in Chapter V.

This concentration on the post-crisis period does not, of course, imply neglect of everything that went before. Inherent in our conception of "legal circumstances" is the idea that existing legal structures and substantive legal rules condition, maybe strongly, the ways in which States set out to achieve new policy objectives. It becomes important, therefore, to understand the background of energy law – that is to say, the legal rules expressing and regulating energy institutions and energy markets in the States we are examining – against which decisions about the implementation of post-crisis policies have been taken. This is the object of Chapter IV, which is in the nature of a brief survey, industry by industry and country by country, highlighting features of the legal organisation of the energy industries and markets which may have a particular influence on the choice of instruments for policy implementation. Frequently we shall find that it is necessary to look back a number of years, to a time when conditions and objectives may have been very different, to trace the origins of particular elements in the organisation of energy markets.

Chapter VI takes up the second of our main questions, the commitment of the EEC Treaty, as of the other two Treaties, to a free and uncompartmented energy market – or markets. It looks at the enforcement practice of the Commission under the Treaties with a view to seeing what derogations from free movement of goods principles it has been prepared to tolerate. Ground covered in Chapter II (for example, the difficulties experienced in bringing oil within the general regime of the common commercial policy) will not be retrodden here: together, however, the two chapters should give some idea of how far basic common market principles have been respected in the energy sector and the extent to which any shortfall stems from inconsistencies between those principles and the specific goals of energy policy.

Finally, in Chapter VII, we return to "The Development of an Energy Strategy for the Community" and drawing together the key elements of the material presented in our substantive chapters, we pose anew our two central questions.

Chapter II

The Community's Record in the Energy Sector

I. Introduction

In this chapter we examine the performance of the Community in the energy sector. Our perspective is legal, in the sense that we are concerned with the way in which the basic Community legal framework has operated in this field, and with the degree to which the Community has succeeded in equipping itself with, and operating, the specialised rules or competences which have appeared necessary to meet the particular circumstances of this sector. It is such specialised rules and competences, which may involve vigorous steps towards integration but also derogations from general Community free trade principles, to which the EEC Treaty attaches the phrase "Common Policies" – referring in particular to agricultural policy and transport policy. While no such status was envisaged by the framers of the EEC Treaty for energy policy, the Commission strove over a long period ending only in 1980–81 to develop and implement a common energy policy, which would provide solutions to the European energy problem going beyond those offered by general Treaty principles.[1] One important part of that policy has always been the achievement of a genuine common market in energy, through the enforcement of common market principles; another, the development and operation of a coherent specialised set of instruments to meet the particular problems of the energy sector. Both elements in the history of energy policy (or attempts to make energy policy) up to 1981 may be better understood if we begin by clarifying the basic Treaty framework within which this process has been carried on.

II. The Energy Common Market

Legally speaking, there is no energy common market. Rather, there are separate common markets: one for coal and coke, one for nuclear power, one for other energy sources, including oil and natural gas. Processes of

[1] For a list of Commission initiatives, see the bibliography cited in Appendix 2, below.

energy production and distribution cannot of course be neatly compartmentalised according to this system: all the fuel sources mentioned contribute to electricity generation within the Community, and are in competition in this and other uses. The lawyer, however, has to remember, when discussing energy policy issues, that the competences of the Community institutions, Commission, Council and Parliament, to deal with such issues, stem not from a single constituent document, but from three separate treaties which continue in existence, notwithstanding the merger of the institutions of the three Communities effected for the Court and Parliament in 1958 and for the Council and Commission in 1967.[2] The point is one of substantive, and not merely formal importance, because the three treaties, establishing respectively the European Coal and Steel Community (ECSC) in 1951, the European Economic Community (EEC) in 1957 and the European Atomic Energy Community (Euratom) in 1957 differ significantly in scope, style and effect.

The following brief examination of the principles of the three Treaties highlights the more fundamental differences and may be helpful in understanding the legal context in which the Community energy markets are supposed to operate.

The Treaty of Paris, signed in 1951, provides for a common market, involving the abolition of duties and quantitative restrictions on trade in coal and steel between Member States, the removal of discrimination in prices, the prohibition of state subsidies, and the removal of restrictive practices tending towards the collusive sharing of markets. It also endows the Commission, as the executive organ under the Treaty, with quite extensive emergency powers to deal with situations of glut or of scarcity in the supply of coal or steel which might arise in the Community. The Treaty does not establish a true customs union, with a common external tariff and unified customs procedures. Indeed, it expressly reserves competence in matters of commercial policy to the Member States, stating that

> the powers of the governments of Member States in matters of commercial policy shall not be affected by this Treaty, save as otherwise provided therein.[3]

The following provisions of the Treaty do, however, envisage substantial potential restrictions on the powers of national governments.[4] Minimum and maximum rates of customs duties as against third countries may be

[2] Convention on Certain Institutions common to the European Communities (Rome, 25 March 1957); Treaty establishing a single Council and Commission of the European Communities (Brussels, 8 April 1965).

[3] Article 71, first para. This freedom, and the conclusions drawn from it by the Court of Justice in Cases 9 and 12/60, *Vloebergbs* v. *High Authority* [1961] E.C.R. 197 have led at least one commentator to suggest that the ECSC partakes more of the character of a free trade area than of a customs union. Samkalden, S.E.W. 1961. 150, at p. 154.

[4] Articles 72–75.

established; the Commission has a limited right of supervision in relation to the administration by Member States of import and export licences and the conclusion of commercial agreements, with powers to ensure that licensing arrangements are not unnecessarily restrictive and that such agreements do not hinder the implementation of the Treaty; and the Commission is also given limited special powers to combat dumping, subsidised imports, and imports "in relatively increased quantities and under such conditions that these imports cause or threaten to cause serious injury to production within the common market of like or directly competing products." In fact, however, if not always in form, the principle of freedom has prevailed over the detailed mechanisms of collective action.[5]

The Euratom Treaty, signed in 1957, gives the Community the task of creating the conditions necessary for the speedy establishment and growth of nuclear industries in Europe by granting powers in respect of research and development, health and safety, environmental protection, and the promotion of the use of nuclear energy for peaceful purposes. However, in Euratom, in contrast to the ECSC and EEC the idea of a common market appears as a subsidiary one. Member States agreed to create a nuclear common market and to make provision for the free movement of goods, but in relation to the raw materials of nuclear energy, the mere removal of barriers to free movement was not seen as sufficient to ensure one of the objectives of the Treaty, that all users receive a regular and equitable supply of ores and nuclear fuels.[6] The special conditions of the nuclear industry led the drafters of the Treaty to take the view that this objective could only be achieved through the creation of a monopoly supply agency, on a centralised basis. This body, the European Supply Agency, a Community organ under the supervision of the Commission, was entrusted with the task of matching users' needs with producers' capabilities and with the availability of supplies from outside the Community, and of concluding contracts for the purpose of furnishing such supplies. To enable it to discharge these functions, the Agency was given an exclusive right of importation of nuclear materials into the Community, and a monopoly right of purchase from producers within it.

In contrast the *EEC Treaty*, also of 1957, contains no specific provisions on energy policy in general, nor any policies for the fuels not covered by the other Treaties: oil, gas and electricity.[7] The belief of the framers of the Treaty appears to have been that the application of its general principles in these sectors would be sufficient and appropriate to deal with any problems that might arise. The general mechanisms for the construction

[5] Reuter, *La Communauté Européenne du Charbon et de l'Acier* (1953) Ch. IV.

[6] Euratom Treaty, arts. 92—100 and Annex IV.

[7] See Evans, A.C. "The Development of a Community Policy on Oil", (1980) 17 C.M.L. Rev. 371.

of a single internal market are more fully and clearly stated than in the ECSC Treaty, and there is no indication in the Treaty that the basic range of rules – the prohibition of import and export duties and duties of equivalent effect, of quantitative restrictions and measures of equivalent effect, of restrictions on freedom of establishment and personal movement, and of certain other State measures distorting the pattern of intra-Community trade such as discriminatory internal taxation, State aids, and manipulation of the behaviour of State enterprises – should not be applicable in the energy sector as in all others covered by the Treaty. The desire to tackle problems of specific sectors through an appropriate application of general provisions is further seen in the limited attention paid to problems of glut and scarcity which, as we have just seen, were treated as a primary issue to be addressed by the Euratom Treaty, and as the subject of quite elaborate emergency powers in the ECSC Treaty. Outside the agricultural sector, problems of glut are referred to only obliquely, in provisions on dumping[8], on deflection of trade,[9] and on protective measures for the transitional period[10] while problems of shortage receive passing mention[11] in the framework of an article on the co-ordination of short-term economic policy.

The generalising approach of the EEC Treaty applies also in its provisions on external commercial relations. These merit particular attention here, both because the major sources of EEC energy supply continue, notwithstanding North Sea oil discoveries, to be third-country imports, and because the Treaty, in this respect, is a good deal more rigorous and centralising than Euratom or ECSC. The EEC Treaty sets up a customs union, involving the adoption both of a common external tariff and of a common commercial policy "based on uniform principles, particularly in regard to changes in tariff rates, the conclusion of tariff and trade agreements, the achievement of uniformity in measures to protect liberalisation, export policy and measures to protect trade such as those taken in case of dumping or subsidies."[12] Under this scheme, Member States abandon the essence of their commercial policy competences to the Community, and have no freedom to take unilateral measures such as the imposition of temporary national quotas or tariffs on third country imports, save in exceptional circumstances closely defined by the Treaty.[13]

The reader in the 1980's may well ask how, in 1957, the framers of the EEC and Euratom Treaties can have contemplated with equanimity the

[8] Article 91.
[9] Article 115.
[10] Article 226.
[11] Article 103(4).
[12] Article 113(1).
[13] See Article 115.

division of energy-related natural resources among three largely separate sets of institutions applying three separate Treaties. Central to an answer to this question are a failure, some would say a wilful failure, on the part of the framers to perceive the growing importance of oil imports to Western Europe, and an excessive faith in the rapid development of cheap nuclear energy supplies.[14] What shaped the Rome Treaties was the desire to find concrete expressions of the will to European unity in vital domains. Nuclear energy was seized upon as being the most vital of all, a sector of unlimited future potential in which co-operation and integration were essential if the countries of Western Europe were to have any chance of escaping the hegemony of the United States and the threats and challenges of the Soviet bloc. The Messina conference of Foreign Ministers of the Coal and Steel Community, which formally initiated the process of developing the Rome Treaties, concluded with a resolution one of whose explicit aims was the "creation of a joint organisation having the responsibilities and the facilities for ensuring the development of atomic energy for peaceful purposes".[15] From the beginning, therefore, the integration of the nuclear energy sector was seen as a project separate from, though parallel to, the development of a general common market. It was treated separately in the Spaak Report[16] and it was not surprising that it should finally have culminated in the agreement of a separate treaty.

Less easy to understand is the treatment of conventional energy sources in 1957. The Messina Conference had devoted considerable interest to conventional as well as nuclear energy, and the Spaak Committee established an expert Commission on the subject and devoted a section of its report to it. Yet there was no amendment to the ECSC Treaty. Neglecting the impact of continuing supplies of low-cost oil, the Committee saw only the problems of coal-based electricity and gas supply industries, in particular their need for co-ordinated investment planning in the period of transition to nuclear energy as the main primary energy source. As monopolistic public utilities, they fitted with difficulty into the competitive framework designed by the EEC Treaty; and yet they were not placed under the explicit tutelage of the more dirigiste ECSC. The interest and experience of the ECSC in relation to the coal-based energy industries was recognised

14 On the treatment of these questions in the development and drafting of the Rome Treaties, see generally, Lucas, N., *Energy and the European Communities* (1977) at pp. 11–29.

15 Resolution of the Foreign Ministers of the ECSC at the Messina Conference, 2 January 1955: Cmd. 9525 (1955).

16 Rapport des Chefs de Délégation aux Ministres des Affaires Etrangers (Comité Intergouvernemental créé par la Conférence de Messina) Bruxelles, 21 avril 1956.

only by the conferment by governments on the High Authority of the ECSC of responsibility for convening a mixed committee composed of representatives of the executives of the EEC and Euratom.[17]

III. The Growing Dependence on Imported Energy

An account of the development of policy in the period from 1957 must begin by considering the evolution of the Community's supply situation. In this respect, it did not take long for the assumptions of the framers to be falsified.

In 1957 coal production of OECD European members was 501.5 million tonnes, while net crude oil imports stood at 108 million tons. By 1960 net oil imports had almost doubled to 172 million tonnes while coal production declined slightly to 456.6 million tonnes.[18] In 1960 these oil imports accounted for 32.5 per cent of the primary energy needs of the nine countries which were to be members of the Community in 1973; by 1973 that figure was 63 per cent. The clear price advantage of oil over coal which brought about this penetration was due to a combination of factors, a combination whose short life was not fully foreseen by European policy makers in the sixties. First, the restriction of the American market by the Eisenhower import quota, introduced in 1959, effectively turned Western Europe into the main market for the huge oil reserves of the Middle East. Second, the very high profits of the majors in the decade following the Second World War attracted substantial numbers of new companies to the search for concessions in the Middle East and elsewhere, with a consequent increase in the rate of exploration and discovery. Third, the concession system then regulating oil production throughout the Middle East left producing companies free to respond to increased competitive pressures by lowering or discounting prices, to the detriment of the producer States, who saw their resources being depleted rapidly and their per barrel tax and royalty take diminishing.[19]

Oil demand rose very rapidly in the sixties in response to these favourable supply conditions, while Community coal mines, handicapped by ever-increasing production costs, were closed in large numbers, and the development of nuclear energy was substantially slowed down, thus rendering the Community extremely vulnerable to disruptions in supply.

In these circumstances, it was not surprising that, when the opportunity offered, the oil exporting nations, irritated by the deterioration of their

[17] See Lister, *Europe's Coal and Steel Community* (1960) at 335–336, and J.O. (C.E.C.A.) 1957, p. 574 (7 December 1957).

[18] Figures from O.E.C.D., *Energy Balances, 1959–1973* (1979).

[19] Hossain, K., *Law and Policy in Petroleum Development* (1979), at p. 11.

financial and resources position, should seek and obtain major changes in the exploitation regime. Following the example of Libya, which in 1970 used the threat of restriction of production to secure better financial terms first from one of its concessionaires, then from all the rest, other OPEC members collectively negotiated with the oil companies a series of agreements securing higher taxes and posted prices, and a commitment to the progressive introduction of state participation in the companies' concession interests. All these arrangements represented a forcible renegotiation of existing contracts on a massive scale. Experience of their capacity for collective action in the negotiation of these new agreements, and enjoyment of their fruits, paved the way for the more spectacular actions of OAPEC members of October 1973 to Spring 1974.

However, while it was the OAPEC embargoes and supply reductions that created the oil crisis of 1973–74, it was the fourfold price rise accompanying these OAPEC actions, and which was not confined to OAPEC production, that prompted a fundamental Western re-thinking of the energy problem. Oil, which for Western countries had since the mid-nineteen-fifties become steadily cheaper, both in relation to other products generally and to other fuels in particular, was suddenly a high cost fuel.

IV. Initial Attempts at Policy Formation 1957–73

Intimations of insecurity had been received by Member States in the nineteen-sixties and even before. The closure of the Suez Canal in 1956 led the Oil Committee of the OEEC (now the OECD) to recommend agreement on emergency oil-sharing arrangements, and attempts had been made within the ECSC, Euratom and the EEC, at Inter-Executive level, to establish a system of reference pricing. This latter attempt failed due to inability to agree either on choice of fuel on which to base the reference system, or on the price levels to be adopted.[20]

With the re-opening of the canal in 1957 and the resumption of low-cost oil supplies, difficulties in disposing of the Community's coal production reached a level serious enough for the Commission to seek to invoke the Treaty's emergency mechanisms.[21] The attempt failed: Member States preferred to rely on national controls on third-country imports, and national subsidies for domestic production, even at the cost of a degree of re-partitioning of the common market for coal.

This was a sombre lesson, particularly when viewed against the background of hope with which the new enterprises of Euratom and the EEC

[20] See Lucas, *supra*, note 14, pp. 34–35.

[21] Article 59. For detailed analysis of this article, see Gori, in Quadri, Monaco, Trabucchi, *Commentario C.E.C.A.* (1970), vol. II at pp. 759–760.

were being got under way. Its positive result was the initiation of the Community's first series of studies of energy policy as such within an Inter-Executive Working Party on Energy.[22] In June 1962, in response to a call from Ministers, the Inter-Executive Group produced a memorandum based on two fundamental principles: a common market for energy and security .of supplies.[23]

In pursuit of the first principle, the Group recommended a policy of encouraging investment in sectors other than energy, on the basis that exports from these sectors would pay for oil imports. This was judged to be a more effective way of dealing with increased energy demand than subsidising costly and uncompetitive coal production.

Security of supply was to be achieved through diversification of suppliers, thus attenuating the risk of sudden or accidental disruption on the part of one major supplier. If the oil companies failed to achieve this measure of diversification, the Community would take an interest in maintaining or developing production from Middle Eastern oil wells, which although more costly to run, would assure a greater level of security. In this respect attention was turned to the role of Community oil companies and recognition was given to the need to place these companies on an equal footing with the majors.

Finally there was to be a common policy on the stockpiling of reserves, to ensure that a temporary oil shortage would not cause excessive disruption to the economies of Member States, and that disparities in stocking levels would not produce any distortions in competition.

Support for this oil policy and the proposed means of implementing it was expressed by the governments of the Member States in a Protocol of Agreement of April 1964. Its adoption, however, resulted in only two concrete measures — a Council Directive of 1968 obliging Member States to maintain emergency stocks of crude and petroleum products corresponding to 65 days consumption[24] and a Decision of the High Authority authorising Member States to grant financial aid to their coal industries.[25] That Decision has been renewed on succesive occasions, and in its present version, is applicable until the end of 1985. Despite its advantages (i. e. the maintenance of Community coal production) the Decision bears witness to the impossibility of drawing up a common coal policy deserving of the name, due to the inability to reach agreement between coal-producing and coal consuming countries. In all other respects, the recommendations contained in the 1964 Protocol were largely ignored.

[22] Ninth General Report of the ECSC (1961).

[23] Memorandum sur la politique énergétique, 25 June 1962 (ECSC Luxembourg, August, 1962).

[24] Council Directive 68/414, J.O. 1968, L308/14.

[25] Decision 3—65 of February 17, 1965, J.O. 1965, p. 480: see also Fifteenth General Report ECSC (1969) Ss. 89—91.

With the fusion of the three Executives in 1967, it was hoped that a new impetus would be given to the formulation of a common energy policy now that a single Commission and Council would be able to take an overall view of the problems posed by the different forms of energy. In its First Guidelines for a Community Energy Policy, the new Commission proposed that the development of community action be undertaken in three directions:

- the construction of a common framework of action based on forecasts, general and sectoral guidelines in the event of a supply shortage
- the establishment of a common market
- the continued provision of cheap and secure supplies.[26]

We have already mentioned the stocks Directive of 1968 in connection with the first of these three aims, but as for the remaining two, little progress was made, the numerous Commission proposals relating to such matters as the harmonisation of energy pricing and taxation failing to win Council support.

In 1972 the Commission renewed its attempts at drawing up a common energy policy. In its communication entitled "Necessary Progress in Common Energy Policy"[27], it recommended, on the basis of a number of sectoral analyses, new guidelines to be followed by the Member States: an immediate solution to the environmental problems posed by energy use; a sustained effort to achieve a more rational use of energy, irrespective of an eventual increase in prices; the adoption of a programme of research and development and improvement in the general levels and conditions of production, refining, transport, stockage and use of energy; the development of alternative sources of energy and renewables and new uses of traditional energy forms. Emphasis was also placed on external relations: co-operation with other consumer countries and co-operation between the Community and producing countries. On the domestic front, the Commission submitted several proposals to ensure the cohesion of the market, insisting once more on the need to adopt a permanent mechanism to deal with oil supply shortages.

Similar recommendations had been made by the Oil Committee of the OEEC (now OECD), following the closure of the Suez Canal in 1956.[28] The further closure of the canal in 1967 in consequence of the Arab–Israel War brought widespread disruption to oil movements, prompted emergency national legislation and led European members of OECD to agree to improve their oil stock-piling arrangements and their emergency procedures for the apportionment of supplies. In 1969 the TAPline, the main pipeline

[26] EC Commission, Prémières Orientations pour une politique énergétique communautaire (Brussels, 1968).

[27] COM (72) 1200.

[28] *Oil – the Outlook for Europe* (OEEC, Paris, May 1956).

from the Gulf to the Mediterranean, was blown up by Palestine guerillas, intensifying reliance on tanker transport, strengthening the position of the Libyans and enabling them to begin the process of upsetting oil production and trade arrangements to which we have already referred. Again a response to this threat came from the OECD, whose Council, by a Recommendation of June 1971 and a Decision of November 1972 introduced new arrangements for oil stock-piling and for tackling temporary shortages, including a system for the equitable sharing of oil within Western Europe in the event of a serious shortage.[29]

The most the European Community was able to do in response to these insecurities was to translate OECD initiatives into binding – though not very demanding – EEC measures for crisis management. The emergency stocks requirement[30] was raised to 90 days' consumption by a Directive of 1972.[31] A further Directive in 1973 required Member States to equip themselves with powers appropriate to deal with an energy crisis (compulsory deployment of stocks, restriction of energy consumption, allocation of supply, control of prices), and set up a consultative crisis machinery within the Community framework.[32] The fact that these measures were, in a sense, only restatements of commitments made within the intergovernmental forum of OECD should not be taken to mean that they merely gave formal expression, at EEC level, to national policies whose implementation was already in hand: five Member States, in fact, found themselves unable to comply with the 1972 stocks Directive until the Commission, in 1975, threatened enforcement proceedings under article 169. Within the framework of the present study, moreover, their significance is quite considerable, for their effect was to identify a set of crisis objectives for all Community members and, indeed, to give those objectives legal force. The 1973 Directive corresponds closely in its terms with what we here call objectives for short-term management of disturbances in energy supply.[33] Outside the area of emergency measures the Community's energy policy record, viewed in 1973, was negative, both in regard to the development of specific solutions to energy problems and even with respect to the regular application and development of the general community regime as it affected the energy sector.[34]

29 Evans, A.C. "The International Energy Agency" (1981) Journal of World Trade Law 440.

30 Council Directive 68/414, *supra* note 24.

31 Council Directive 72/425, O.J. 1972, L291/154.

32 Council Directive 73/38, O.J. 1973, L228/1.

33 See Chapter III, p. 38 below.

34 On Commission thinking at this time (and later) on security of oil supply, see De Bauw, "The European Community: Economic Security and Energy Supply." in Alting von Geusau and Pelkmans, eds., *National Economic Security: Perception, Threats and Policies* (1982) Ch. 6.

In the coal sector, the ECSC provided little more than a mechanism for the oversight of Member States' coal pricing and subsidy policies, and permitted the maintenance of divergent national policies towards third country coal imports and the maintenance of internal barriers to trade in such imported coals, a position endorsed by the Court of Justice in the *Vloebergbs* case.[35]

Euratom was in a state of total disarray. The centralised supply arrangements which were at the centre of the scheme of the Treaty had not operated. Member States were required by the Treaty to review these arrangements at the end of 1964 and either confirm them or adopt new ones. By 1973 they had succeeded in doing neither. France, brought before the Court in 1971 accused by the Commission of regular and systematic breach of the supply rules, was able to claim, not without some justification, that the activities of the Supply Agency had become "unreal" – though the Court did not accept the French argument that they had lost all legal foundation.[36] This breakdown may be linked to a general weakness of Euratom stemming from an early failure of the will of the Member States to co-operate effectively in the nuclear sector, but it has more specific roots in the development of the supply situation. In the first place, the feared dearth of supplies of source materials which was a principal cause of the specific design of the Treaty did not materialise. The Agency has always operated under simplified procedures for the exercise of its rights which effectively left parties to conclude their own contracts, subject only to a right of supervision by the Agency which has been of little practical significance.[37] This situation still obtains. Second the Treaty has never had any practical effect on the disposition of the Community's own uranium supplies. Workable supplies have hitherto been found only in France and have never been effectively subjected to the Treaty regime, being employed partly for French defence purposes,[38] partly for the fuelling of French nuclear power stations, which enjoyed an initial derogation under article 223 and which have since benefited from the 'connected undertakings' provision of article 62. Third, and in the opinion of one commentator, most important,[39] Member States have not always observed the spirit, and perhaps not even the letter, of the provisions which sought to complete

[35] Cases 9 and 12/60, [1961] E.C.R. 197, *supra*, note 3.

[36] Case 7/71 *Re The Euratom Supply Agency*: *Commission* v. *France* [1971] E.C.R. 1003. The Court held that the ESA was operating lawfully under the existing arrangements, and that France was in breach of its obligations under the Treaty. On the operation of Euratom generally see Polack, *Euratom: Background, Issues, Economic Implications* (1964).

[37] See Commission Decision of 5 May 1960, J.O. 1960, p. 774 and the Rules of the ESA of 5 May 1960, J.O. 1960, p. 777 as amended by O.J. 1975, L. 193/37, esp. art. 5.

[38] And thus exempted from the regime of the Treaty under article 84, para. 3.

[39] See Polack, *supra*, note 36.

the Community's effective control of supplies by securing that it take the place of Member States in agreements for nuclear co-operation negotiated with third countries.[40]

In the EEC framework, certain advances had been made. Member States were obliged, by Directives of 1964[41] and 1969[42], to grant freedom of establishment and freedom to provide services in mining and in oil production and drilling activities. A system of central information collection on energy markets was in course of construction: under a Regulation made in 1972 Member States were obliged to report to the Commission on investment projects in the oil, gas and electricity sectors (enterprises in the nuclear sector had been required since 1958 to report investment projects directly to the Commission).[43] Member States were also obliged, by Regulation of 1972, to notify the Commission of imports of crude oil and natural gas (an obligation later extended to imports of petroleum products, and to corresponding exports).[44]

This positive achievement in the sphere of information was counterbalanced by the inability of the Community to bring into effective operation, in the energy sector, the external trade regime of the Treaty. Petroleum products were the last for which levels of duty were agreed in the negotiations on the common customs tariff, in 1964, four years after the level of the great majority of duties had been settled.[45] Nine years later, neither the common regime for imports from third countries under the common commercial policy, nor the common regime for exports, was in operation in relation to crude oil, natural gas, and petroleum products.[46] Nor had Member States been able to agree on a common definition of origin for petroleum products, though a Regulation covering virtually all other products had been passed in 1968.[47] The causes of this remarkable

40 Article 106. In recent years the Commission has been more successful in enforcing this principle.

41 Council Directive 64/428, J.O. 1965, p. 1871.

42 Council Directive 69/82, J.O. 1969, L. 68/4.

43 Council Regulation 1056/72, O.J. 1972, L. 120/7.

44 Council Regulation 1055/72 on imports of crude oil and natural gas, O.J. 1972, L120/3, applied by Commission Regulation 1068/73, O.J. 1973, L113/1; Council Regulation 388/75 on notifying the Commission on exports of crude oil and natural gas to third countries, O.J. 1975, L45/1, applied by Commission Regulation 2678/75, O.J. 1975 L275/8, and Council Regulation 3254/74 on petroleum products, O.J. 1974, L349/1, applied by Commission Regulation 2677/75, O.J. L275/1; Council Regulations 649/80, O.J. L73/1, and 713/80, O.J. L81/1 on the importation of petroleum products – individual notification requirement.

45 Council Decision 64/303, J.O. 1964, p. 1209.

46 Council Regulation 2603/69, J.O. 1969, L325/25.

47 A proposal of July 1974 (O.J. 1974, C124/1) would have extended Regulation 302/68 (J.O. 1968, L148/1) on the common definition of the concept of the origin of goods so as to cover petroleum products, and a proposal of October 1972 (J.O. 1972

failure to bring a group of products fully within the regime of the Treaty are to be found both in the degree of importance attached by all Member States to oil as a strategic product, and in the strongly divergent approach of Member States to questions of oil policy, best exemplified by the contrast between the dirigiste attitude of the French, manifested particularly through their strenuous adherence to their monopoly import regime, and the free market philosophy pursued in this field by the Dutch and the West Germans. Some legal expressions of this contrast are documented in Chapter IV; here we need only record that by 1973, in the face of French unwillingness to abandon their monopoly unless the Community adopted the kind of dirigiste import policy that would be anathema to the Dutch and Germans, the Commission had failed to obtain significant adjustments of the monopoly, and was, indeed, still authorising the French to maintain consequential barriers to intra-Community trade on the basis of article 115.[48]

So much for Treaty implementation.[49] On the side of specialised policy initiatives, the fate of the Commission's proposals contained in the communication entitled "Necessary progress in Community energy policy" illustrates the vicious circle which became characteristic of the common energy policy, and which may be taken as a major reason for the failure to develop a common approach. The Council considered it dificult to arrive at an agreed position in respect of such a wide range of analyses and of the large number of – more often than not – general measures which had been proposed. The preparatory work did in fact show that the actual scope of most of these measures could generally only be assessed in the light of specific proposals which the Commission might decide to make in the future. Hence, the Member States asked the Commission to propose a cohesive set of measures to form the basis of the common energy policy. As soon as the Commission complied with the request and submitted formal proposals, item by item, the Council found itself unable to arbitrate successfully between the various interests of the Member States and the adoption of the measures was obstructed on the pretext that a decision could not be taken unless they were viewed in the context of a set of broader measures.

In April 1973, in an attempt to break this deadlock, the Commission presented to the Council a new communication, "Guidelines and priority

C 134/21) would have extended Regulation 1025/70 (J.O. 1970 L124/6) on common rules for imports from third countries so as to cover all hydrocarbon imports from third countries.

48 Commission Decision of March 6, 1974, O.J. 1974, L143/15 authorising the French Republic to maintain its quota system until the end of 1975.

49 The remaining paragraphs in this section are drawn directly from De Bauw, "La Communauté Européenne et la Politique de l'Energie", referred to at p. V *supra*.

actions under the Community energy policy",[50] the content of which included both guidelines to inspire future activity by the Community institutions and sufficiently detailed principles for specific proposals to be made to the Council without delay. This document obviously contained no particularly new proposals but it did concentrate discussion on a number of what were felt to be important points:

- relations with other energy-importing countries
- relations with energy-exporting countries
- the organisation of the oil market
- the development of nuclear energy.

While reaffirming the pressing need to draw up a Community energy policy, and recognising that the priority guidelines and actions constituted, in their broad lines, the appropriate basis of discussion for the Community measures intended to ensure security of energy supply, the Council did not specifically agree on any of the proposals put forward and in particular could not agree on the priorities to be selected.

V. The 1973 Crisis

First reactions of EEC Member States to the embargo and cutbacks of 1973 did not augur well for Community solidarity or for the preservation even of such minor elements of common policy as already existed. The United Kingdom and France, which had been singled out for favourable treatment by OAPEC states because of their "positive" attitude, sought to prevent the equalisation of hardship by oil companies and in particular the diversion of supplies to the embargoed Netherlands: within the OECD framework they also refused to permit the activation of the oil-sharing programme. The Netherlands responded with implicit threats to cut off natural gas supplies to its Community partners. It took United States leadership, in the Washington energy conference of February 20, 1974, to bring all the EC countries, with the exception of France, to a common accord with other OECD nations on the creation of an International Energy Agency (IEA) within the OECD and the joint acceptance of an International Energy Programme (IEP) under which supplies would be shared among member nations in the event of a supply shortfall, either collective or individual[51]. This Programme requires Member States, in given circumstances, to restrict consumption and to make transfers of oil and petroleum products between themselves. It thus specifies conditions

[50] Guidelines and Priority Actions under the Community Energy Policy, SEC (73) 1481, (April 1973).

[51] Cmnd. 5826 (1975); 14 I.L.M. 1.

and purposes for the instruments with which Member States are required to equip themselves under the EEC's 1973 directive, but does not imply the adoption of new national policy objectives or the creation of additional national instruments.

As in the pre-crisis period, the OECD here gave a lead which the European countries were eventually to follow by setting up comparable arrangements as a matter of mutual obligation within the EEC framework. Such steps were, indeed, more necessary than before, since the self-exclusion of France from the IEA on grounds of its "confrontational" character was quite likely to create for other Member States conflicts between their EEC and IEP obligations in the event of activation of the Programme. By 1977, therefore, the Community had laid the bases for its own emergency system, providing for the setting by the Commission, in the case of supply difficulties, of consumption reduction targets, and the switching of oil saved between Member States[52]. While the scheme can be argued to be somewhat more flexible and sophisticated than that of the IEA (for example it distinguishes between substitutable and non-substitutable consumption), it is designed to work in conjunction with the IEA scheme and is likely to depend for its effective operation on co-operative links with oil companies developed within the IEA framework. In addition to these positive measures for crisis management, the EEC also introduced in 1977 arrangements for the relaxation of free trade obligations within the Community where Member States experienced supply difficulties or abnormal increases in trade in products in the hydrocarbons sector: under the supervision of the Commission Member States may use export licences to monitor, and if necessary to restrict, exports of such products from their territory to that of other Member States.[53] Again neither these relaxations nor the EEC emergency regime abovementioned necessarily imply the adoption by Member States of objectives or instruments beyond those agreed upon in 1973; and both sets of measures utilise the 1973 consultation arrangements.

VI. Energy Policy Objectives 1973–80

The 1973 crisis had the great merit of dramatising the need, long since perceived by the Commission, for Member States individually, and for the Community as a whole, to formulate and carry into action longer-term policies for the reduction of oil dependence. This made it somewhat easier

[52] Council Decision 77/706, O.J. 1977, L292/9 and Commission Decision 79/639, O.J. 1979, L183/1.

[53] Council Decision 77/186 O.J. 1977 L61/23, amended by Council Decision 79/879, O.J. 1979 L270/58, and applied by Commission Decision 78/896, O.J. 1978, L311/13.

for the Council to take positive steps towards a Community energy policy on the basis of the stream of energy objectives, plans, recommendations and proposals for legislative measures which the Commission continued to address to it.[54]

The basic Community statement of general energy planning objectives is still to be found in the Council's Resolution of September 17, 1974.[55] Here the Member States committed themselves to:

– reduce the rate of increase of internal consumption of energy through rational use and economy measures, but not so as to compromise objectives of social and economic development;
– increase security of supply by:
  accelerating the development of nuclear energy supplies (the Dutch and the Danes issued a note of reservation on this point);
  fully using the Community's own hydrocarbon and solid fuel resources;
  diversifying sources of external supply;
  efforts in research and technical development;
– consider problems of environmental protection relating to the production and use of energy.

These anodyne statements did at least express a certain degree of consensus among the Member States on the basic guidelines and priorities to be adopted as part of the common energy policy and which were to be taken account of in the formulation of national policies. They were given a little more content by further Council Resolutions of December 17, 1974[56] and February 13, 1975.[57] In the first, the Council attempted some quantification of objectives, proposing for 1985 a reduction in imported energy dependence to 50 per cent (or, if possible, 40 per cent) involving increased reliance on solid fuel, natural gas and, in particular, nuclear energy[58], and reduced reliance on oil, all as compared with earlier 1985

[54] For example, COM (74) 1960 (final) on energy objectives for 1985, EC Bull. 9/74, at p. 24; COM (74) 10 (final) on implementation of guidelines and priority actions, EC Bull. Supplement 4/74; COM (74) 550 (final) on a new energy strategy for the community, EC Bull. Supplement 4/74; COM (74) 1970 (final) on medium term guidelines for electricity; COM (74) 1963 (final) on nuclear fuel policy; COM (74) 1961 (final) on a common policy for the hydrocarbons sector; COM (74) 1962 (final) on support for common projects in the hydrocarbons sector; COM (74) 1964 (final) on oil supply difficulties; COM (74) 150 (final) on common action programmes and a draft Council Resolution on rational utilisation of energy: COM (75) 691 (final) on Community financing of energy policy; COM (75) 692 (final) on the implementation of energy policy guidelines; COM (76) 508 (final) on Community energy policy.

[55] O.J. 1974, C.153/1.

[56] O.J. 1975, C153/2.

[57] O.J. 1975, C153/6.

[58] The Dutch expressed reservations on the nuclear energy targets at paras. 4 and 5 of the Council Resolution of December 17, 1974.

projections, a reduced growth of energy demand and a change in the consumption structure so as to make increasing use of electricity as more nuclear capacity came on stream. The second resolution offered a little more detail on modes of implementing these objectives, though rather in terms of defining Community actions to be taken than of making national policy objectives or instruments more precise. Three successive reports on the realisation of the 1974 priorities show that in fact forecasts of total energy consumption have steadily declined[59] but this can largely be attributed to forecasts of slower overall economic growth. Moreover one can observe a shortfall in production of nearly all energy sources in most of the Member States, above all in the case of nuclear, but also in the coal and oil sectors. This does not call into question the good intentions of governments in their pursuit of common objectives, but rather their capacity to manage the contraction of their coal industry and to overcome the external and internal difficulties standing in the way of increased oil and nuclear production.

In May 1980 the Council, this time with 1990 as its target date, adapted its 1974 objectives.[60] The Resolution shows a significant change of tone. In 1974, the Council *approved* quantified *objectives*; in 1980, it asked the Commission to *measure the convergence* of Member State policies by reference to certain defined *orientations*. In the longer term there appears here to be a weakening of commitment; in the shorter term, however, we should note a contrary tendency, in that only a few months earlier, Member States had for the first committed themselves internationally and within the Community context to specific national energy policy targets. In 1979 the "sub-crisis" caused by the change of regime in Iran led to a series of meetings of the European Council and of the leading Western importing nations, in the course of which the Community committed itself to global oil import targets for 1980 and 1985. A subsequent meeting of the Council of Ministers in December formally approved the breakdown of these targets into national import ceilings for 1980 and 1985 which individual Member States expressed themselves "determined" to respect; the Council also approved procedures for the monitoring of oil imports.[61]

VII. Energy Legislation 1973–1980

Between 1973 and 1980 the Community's effort in energy legislation was concentrated in two main fields: energy demand, and information. In the

[59] Review of Energy Policy Objectives for 1990, COM (81) 64 final; The Energy Situation in the Community, COM (81) 60 final; Community Energy Strategy, Progress and Guidelines for Future Action, COM (83) 305 final.

[60] O.J. 1980, C.149/1.

[61] See Bull. EC. 6/79 pts. 1.1.7, 1.2.2., 9/79 pt. 2.1.9. and 12/79, pts. 2.1.140, 2.1.141.

field of energy demand, the main Community-level activity until 1977 consisted in a series of Recommendations to Member States from the Council, urging them to take large numbers of eminently sensible, and highly detailed, steps to promote the saving of energy.[62] Really these non-binding recommendations constitute no more than a checklist of energy-saving measures, such as fitting boilers with thermostats, telling motorists how to save fuel when driving, encouraging the use of public transport by the provision of bus shelters, and arranging domestic hot water systems so as to avoid temperatures over 60 °C and ensure that "dead legs are as short as possible." Of greater real significance, because legally binding on Member States, are the Directives, all of 1975, limiting the use of natural gas and petroleum products as fuel for electricity generating stations, and requiring the maintenance of minimum stocks of fuel at thermal generating stations.[63] First Directives in the energy-saving field did not appear until 1978, when the Council adopted a Directive on performance standards for new heat generators (boilers etc.) in new or existing non-industrial buildings and on insulation in new buildings of this type.[64] A Directive relating to energy consumption labelling appeared in May 1979.[65] It has been applied to electric ovens,[66] and the Commission has subsequently proposed its application to other electrical appliances with a high level of energy consumption and market penetration.[67]

This period also saw the elaboration of the Community's information system on energy markets. Notification of imports and exports was, as we have already seen, extended to petroleum product imports and to exports

[62] Council Recommendations 76/492 on the rational use of energy by promoting thermal insulation of buildings, 76/493 on rational use of energy in the heating systems of existing buildings, 76/494 on the rational use of energy consumed by road vehicles, 76/495 on rational use of energy for urban passenger transport, 76/496 on the rational use of energy for electrical household appliances, O.J. 1976, L140/11–18: 77/712 on the regulation of space heating, the production of domestic hot water and the metering of heat in new buildings, 77/713 on the rational use of energy in industrial undertakings, 77/714 on the creation in the Member States of advisory boards or committees to promote combined heat and power production and the exploitation of residual heat, O.J. 1977, L295/1–5.

[63] Council Directive 75/339, O.J. 1975, L153/5 on maintenance of minimum stocks of crude oil and/or petroleum products at power stations: Council Directive 75/404 on restriction of use of natural gas in power stations, O.J. 1975, L178/24; Council Directive 75/405 on the restriction of the use of petroleum products in power stations, O.J. 1975, L178/26.

[64] Council Directive 78/170, O.J. 1978, L52/32, see also the Commission's draft directive of April 1980 on the performance of heat generators, COM (80) 108 final.

[65] Council Directive 79/530, O.J. 1979 L145/7.

[66] Council Directive 79/531, O.J. 1979, L145/7.

[67] See Commission proposal COM (80) 193 final; Council Directive 82/885, O.J. 1982 L378/19.

of crude oil, natural gas, and most products.[68] A general obligation on Member States to provide information relevant to the formation of energy policy was imposed in 1974.[69] Information on pricing was an issue peculiar to the EEC regime. Under the ECSC Treaty, pricing is a matter of direct concern to the Commission, which may lay down rules directly binding on enterprises on the publication and alignment of prices, and may, indeed fix prices in certain circumstances.[70] The Euratom regime likewise transfers competence over pricing to the Community, providing that prices should normally be determined by the balancing of supply against demand, with which national regulations may not interfere, but that they may also be fixed by the Council.[71] For prices of crude oil and petroleum products, therefore, both on import and in the internal market, a Directive[72] of 1976 imposed on the Member States the obligation of reporting to the Commission, leaving it to them to secure that they receive sufficient and appropriate information from enterprises covering shares of the market specified in the Directive to enable them to discharge this obligation.[73]

VIII. Conclusion

Besides these advances we should note some things that did not happen in the post-crisis period. A Community coal policy was not agreed; there was no reform of the supply chapter of the Euratom Treaty; the common origin rules, and the common import and export regimes, were not extended to oil and gas; no progress was made on harmonisation of energy taxes within the Community. A crisis management system, and joint commitment to some common, if loose, energy policy objectives, seemed by 1980 to be the only insignia of Community solidarity available to set against the persistence of a defiantly unintegrated energy market.

With equally defiant optimism, the Commission in 1980, sought to reopen the debate with what has been called the 'new initiative'.[74] This set

68 See references at note 44, *supra*.

69 See now Council Regulation 1729/76 concerning the communication of information on the state of the Community's energy supplies, O.J. 1976, L.198/1, repealing and replacing the original Reg. 293/74.

70 ECSC Treaty Articles 61–64.

71 Euratom Treaty, Arts. 67–69.

72 Council Directive 76/491, O.J. 1976, L140/4, applied by Commission Decision 77/190, O.J. 1977, L61/34.

73 For Community legislation on pricing and other matters since 1981, see Chapter VII below.

74 See De Bauw, *supra* note 49: the relevant documents are: Energy Policy COM (80) 130 final; Economic Aspects of a Community Initiative on Energy, COM (80) 151 final; Energy Price and Tax Harmonisation in the Community, COM (80) 152 final;

of proposals shows marked similarity of substance to the priority areas of the strategy document: they included the adoption of measures designed to reduce disparities in pricing and taxation levels within the Community, one of the aims of such harmonisation being the encouragement of energy conservation. Emphasis was also placed on the need to accelerate the level of investment in projects which would lead to sizeable reductions in dependence on imported energy. Financial assistance from the Community was to be made available to encourage this sort of investment. Finally, attention was turned to the question of making available the necessary resources at Community level, to finance such investment. Suggestions on various types of energy taxes were made with a view to supplementing the existing Community budget, but which would not impose too high a charge on the final consumer. The Council was reluctant to act on these propositions, and without entering further investigation of their feasibility, judged that there was little opportunity at that time of achieving the necessary degree of political consensus.

This further rebuff caused the Commission to review its whole approach to energy policy. The result, as presented in the strategy document, signifies a change, not of substance – for the Community's problems had not changed – but of approach. The key to the change, signalled by the substitution of "strategy" for "policy", is that the Community can rely on an energy policy which is diversified and decentralised (i. e. made and carried out by Member States) so long as there is "equivalence of effort", "collective discipline", and "a willingness to pursue common goals". At the same time, centralised Community action still has a place: "where this is required by the provisions of the Treaty or where it will be more effective than the sum of national measures even where these are properly co-ordinated."[75] To provide a basis for evaluating this approach, whose originality lies in its explicit acknowledgement of diversity within the Community, we propose to review some of the significant differences between Member States, with particular reference to those that find expression in legal form.

Fiscal instruments for raising Community revenues from energy, COM (80) 153 final; A Community Programme for the Promotion of Investment in Energy, COM (80) 220 final.

[75] COM (81) 540 final, paras. 6, 7.

Chapter III

National Energy Objectives

I. Oil Dependence: Import Dependence

To understand the policy objectives that Member States adopted during the nineteen-seventies we need to sketch, if only in outline, the energy problem they faced. Naturally, no two of the five States we are considering showed exactly the same pattern either of energy supplies or of energy demand. We look at some of the differences in a moment. What they all shared, what made the behaviour of OAPEC in late 1973 and of OPEC countries in 1974 into a crisis of European proportions, was heavy dependence on energy imports, and heavy dependence on oil. By 1972, over the whole EEC, crude oil imports, at 567.58 million tonnes of oil equivalent (mtoe), by themselves covered 63.8 per cent of energy demand. The collective exposure of EEC countries to political and economic pressure, in terms of the source of these imports, was considerable. Taking the Nine together, 70.35 per cent of these imports came from OAPEC countries (23.3 per cent from Saudi Arabia alone), and a further 24.45 per cent from other OPEC countries. These levels of oil dependence were, moreover, associated with a fast rundown in the coal industries of the Member States and hesitations and delays in their nuclear power programmes.

If we now look at the five States, it is hard to see any significant difference in terms of oil reliance. France, in 1972, depended on imports for over 97 per cent of the crude it used, Germany for over 93 per cent, Italy for 97 per cent, the Netherlands for over 96 per cent and the UK for over 98 per cent. We would, however, reach a different conclusion by looking at figures for overall import dependence in all energy sources. Here the figures are: France, 72 per cent; Germany, 52 per cent; Italy, 79 per cent; Netherlands, 17 per cent; UK, 51 per cent.[1]

To appreciate the likely significance for policy formation of these similarities and divergences, we need to consider how, in the different States, energy demands were being met in 1972. The contribution of the various

[1] Details of the development of import dependence for the different energy sources will be given in Chapter IV.

primary energy sources to the satisfaction of total internal demand was, in 1972, as follows:[2]

Table 1
Internal Energy Demand, 1972

	Total demand (mtoe)	Solid fuels %	Oil %	Gas %	Primary elec. (nuclear, hydro, geothermal, imports) %
France	164.6	17.8	67.3	7.1	7.8
Germany	248.6	32.5	55.2	8.8	3.1
Italy	121.1	6.6	73.9	10.6	8.7
Netherlands	57.7	5.2	49.6	45.6	−0.5
UK	214.6	35.1	49.8	11.1	4.1

These figures are not to be explained by differences in the pattern of energy use in these countries. While there are certainly variations in such patterns, attributable to such factors as the size and shape of the country (consumption for transport), the extent and nature of industrial activity (industrial consumption), and climatic factors (domestic consumption), the shares of final consumption going to the different sectors are broadly similar, as the following table shows:[3]

Table 2
% Shares of Different Sectors in Total Final Consumption, 1972

	Industry (including non-energy uses)	Transport	Other (commercial, domestic, agricultural)
France	44.5	19.6	36.0
Germany	45.6	17.0	37.5
Italy	50.8	18.6	30.6
Netherlands	42.7	15.3	42.0
UK	44.6	19.8	35.6

We may note that while transport is the sector most heavily dependent on oil as an energy source, the United Kingdom, with the highest transport demand for energy, still managed the lowest total reliance on oil. This suggests considerable potential for diversification away from oil, in all States.

One might therefore expect diversification, in the sense of the substitution of other fuels for oil in suitable employments, to be one of the common

[2] *Eurostat: Overall Energy Balances (1973—1977)* (1977).
[3] O.E.C.D., *Energy Balances 1959—1973* (1979).

themes of national post-1973 energy policies. We should not however expect uniformity of policy in this regard: the starting points for diversification, and its direction (that is, the mix of substitutes aimed for) were too different. Oil not only held different shares in overall internal demand in different States; it also held different shares in the specific uses most apt for substitution. Below, for example, are the shares of oil in electricity generation in 1972.[4]

Table 3

Shares of Oil in Electricity Generation 1972

	%
France	49.3
Germany	12.7
Italy	54.0
Netherlands	21.3
UK	27.9

Other things being equal, the Italians appear to have had by far the largest scope for switching to other fuels. Other things are of course never equal: factors such as the age of the existing facilities, the strictness of pollution regulations, the rate of growth of demand, and the capacity to generate the necessary capital funds, all need to be considered. The direction of substitution will also vary according to what alternative fuels are available, the price at which they can be obtained, and the alternative uses to which they can be put. Substitution of one imported fuel for another offers fewer attractions than substitution of domestically produced fuels: one might therefore expect France and Italy, which are poor in such fuels, to be more inclined towards the nuclear option than Germany, the Netherlands and the United Kingdom. Even within this latter group, important differences exist: Netherlands natural gas, for example, is a premium fuel and reserves were declining soon after 1972; in the United Kingdom, the prospect of freedom from oil import dependence was already beckoning as a distraction from any substitution efforts.

On the demand side, no State, one would think, would neglect, as an element of its post-crisis energy policy, the need to have mechanisms available for meeting new disturbances by the restriction of demand: indeed, as we have seen, all Member States of the Community committed themselves to this, as a matter of legal obligation, in 1973.[5] In regard to the evolution of demand in the longer term, Member States likewise committed themselves, politically if not legally under the Council's Resolu-

[4] *Ibid.*

[5] Council Directive 73/238 O.J. 1973, L228/1.

tion of December 17, 1974[6], to work for reduced growth of energy demand, but we should expect the translation of this and subsequent similar commitments into national policy objectives and, thereafter, into instruments for achieving them to vary according to the faith of different governments in the capacity of the price system to accomplish this reduction efficiently. A failure to state specific conservation objectives should not therefore be taken to imply an absence of commitment to energy saving; nor, of course, does the explicit adoption of this objective necessarily mean that a government will not implement measures which tend to weaken the energy-saving impacts of the price mechanism.

II. Energy Policy Objectives

Any comparative account of national energy policy objectives must cope with the different ways in which national governments approach the relationship between the planning and execution of policy. While "planning" is an important expression of governmental activity in France, and to a lesser extent in Italy and the Netherlands, United Kingdom and West German governments have been less concerned about being seen to plan: indeed, for quite a long period up to the late nineteen-sixties the Germans appear to have felt that to plan explicity could not be compatible with their conception of a social-market economy, with limited steering mechanisms. In the United Kingdom the reason for this relative abstinence from public planning has been less ideological, more the operation, in relation to major public policy constructions, of what the British philosopher Antony Quinton has recently described as the British qualities of "all pervasive doubt and scepticism" and of "rather carefully thought out inaction".[7] In consequence, we may find that sometimes policy objectives have to be deduced from the measures taken to implement them. While in this process ambiguity and uncertainty as to objectives could arise, in practice we shall see that a sufficient variety of sources of information exists to make national policies tolerably clear.

We should also be aware that there is an inherent ambiguity in the very term "energy policy", in the sense that policy-makers do not conceive of energy issues in isolation from other policy goals which may extend across the energy sector as well as other sectors. Differences as between Member States in these trans-sectoral policy goals may influence the vigour with which, or the instruments through which, the energy policy goals themselves are pursued. A government whose general policy goal is to remove all barriers impeding the free functioning of markets is hardly likely to pursue

[6] Resolution of December 17, 1974, O.J. 1975, C 153/1.
[7] Quoted in The Sunday Telegraph, February 7, 1982.

its energy goal in the same way as one whose overriding priority is to secure State control of all strategic sectors of the economy. Hence we should be aware not only of different approaches to planning, but also that despite an espousal of seemingly common objectives, Member States could be seeking to achieve divergent non-energy goals through their plans, a point which could have implications for co-ordination of policy at Community level.

Analysis of the content of national plans and policy statements, mostly issued since 1973, and on the EEC and IEA commitments of 1973 and 1974, suggests a classification of national policy objectives which we may use to describe their contents in a little more detail, and to organise our account, in Chapter 5, of national policy measures. A list of such plans and statements will be found in Appendix 3. Objectives may be grouped into three broad categories:

- management of short-term disturbances in energy supply;
- alterations in the structure and level of energy demand;
- alterations in the pattern of energy supply.

While these categories will suffice for a description of national policies, we can in some cases break them down into more detail for the purposes of analysing policy implementation. While the first group can be treated as a whole, within the second group it is useful for some purposes to distinguish between

- promotion of economy in energy use; and
- alteration of energy consumption patterns.

The first of these heads includes most of what we call "energy conservation" measures, while the second is more concerned with inter-fuel substitution in such applications as power station firing, industrial boilers, domestic heating, and so on. In the third group, we can distinguish

- the development of domestic energy supplies (with particular reference to nuclear energy); and
- the diversification of supplies of imported energy.

These headings represent a way of classifying the energy objectives that are actually announced by the governments of the Member States. The scheme is in no sense normative: it only represents what governments have said they will try to do, not what agencies like the EEC Commission or the IEA have said they should be trying to do. However, in view of the process of decision making in the IEA and EEC alike, there is in fact a close correspondence between international prescriptions and national ambitions.

The division of these objectives into broad groups is partly temporal, partly material: the first main category represents the aims of government in the face of supply crises and disturbances, both external and internal — for instance the miners' strike in 1973 caused the United Kingdom government to have resort to emergency legislation. The second and third categories differ essentially in that instruments deployed in pursuit of the second (adjustment of demand) will be directed to the wide body of energy consumers whereas instruments under the third (adjustment of supply) could be restricted to a numerically smaller group of energy suppliers, some of whom may be owned by, or subject to some other form of proprietary control by the national governments.

III. Management of Short-term Disturbances in Energy Supply

States' commitments in this sphere have been expressed, as already noted, in the form of a Directive of the Council of the European Communities[8], and we find little mention in national energy plans, strictly so-called, of these essentially responsive policy objectives. Measures actually adopted by Member States[9] attest to the acceptance in practice by States of the objectives implicit in the Directive. Differences of approach of course exist, notably in the much greater reliance in Germany than elsewhere on market forces as the means of securing a satisfactory new equilibrium between energy demand and supply. Among these objectives of "adequate response" the only one which figures significantly in national energy plans and policy documents, doubtless because it takes time to accomplish and has a more positive sound than have controls or taxes, is that of preserving the level of supply in emergency by the constitution of appropriate stocks of energy resources. While the Italian Donat-Cattin Plan of 1975 refers only to oil stocks[10], the Dutch Energienota and German First Programme Revision of 1974 refer respectively to the creation of natural gas reserves[11] and to the establishment of coal stocks for emergency and counter-cyclical purposes.[12] These additional stocking objectives (for it will be remembered that all EEC Member States are committed by Directives of 1968 and 1972 to the constitution of oil stocks)[13] clearly reflect the different resource endowments of the states in question. These resource endowments have also, as we shall see, been quite influential in shaping plans for the alteration of patterns of energy supply.

8 Council Directive 73/238, O.J. 1973, L 228/1.

9 For a detailed account of these measures see Chapter V, Part I.

10 See summary in "Italy's National Energy Plan," Petroleum Economist, November 1975, at p. 414.

11 Bijl Hand. TK 1974–75, 13122 nr. 2, at p. 125–6.

12 See Bundeswirtschaftsministerium, Erste Fortschreitung des Energieprogramms der Bundesregierung, November 4, 1974, and comment in Hrbek, "Coal Policy of the Federal Republic of Germany," in Ionescu, ed., *The European Alternatives* (1979), p. 157, at 163.

13 See Chapter II, pp. 20–22 above.

IV. Alterations in the Structure and Level of Energy Demand

Following the onset of the crisis, most governments committed themselves sooner rather than later to a policy of active promotion of energy saving and conservation. Such a commitment appears in the 1974 Dutch White Paper[14], in the French Messmer Proposals (1974), and in the Italian Donat-Cattin Plan (1975)[15]. In Germany, research into energy saving appears as one of the subjects of the 1974–77 research programme[16], but the First Revision of the Energy Programme (1974) simply revises energy use projections downward[17]: a specific policy commitment in this regard does not appear until the Second Revision[18] and is re-inforced in the Third Revision. In the United Kingdom, specific energy saving measures appear from 1974–75 onwards, but without any new general policy commitment until 1976.[19] The methods adopted or recommended for achieving energy savings are too diverse to permit detailed treatment here, but reference may perhaps be made to two significant and individualistic elements of national policy: the creation by the French Government of the specialised Agence pour les économies d'énergie in 1974[20] and its subsequent merger with other specialised agencies to form a single Agence pour Maîtriser l'Energie, and the far-reaching proposals of the Pandolfi Plans in Italy to achieve energy savings by the gradual conversion of industrial capacity to activities involving lower energy consumption[21], a radical approach which, if fully implemented, would require instruments and measures rather different from those of energy conservation generally.

One area where one might expect complete unanimity of national policy is in respect of changes in consumption patterns, especially the substitution of other fuels for oil in appropriate uses. It is true that all national programmes envisage, in the long term, some degree of such substitution. They vary, however, in regard to time-scale, amount of substitution, and preferred substitute fuels. In the Netherlands, to take the really special case, the problem was seen in 1974 as one of excessive employment of domestic natural gas in non-premium uses, and in the short term substitu-

14 *Supra*, note 11, at p. 126.
15 *Supra*, note 10, at p. 413.
16 See comments by Simeons, C., *Energy Research and Development Programmes in Western Europe* (1978), at p. 149.
17 *Supra*, note 12.
18 Bundeswirtschaftsministerium, Guidelines and key figures for the extension of the Energy Programme (1977) 30 Bundesregierung 269.
19 See Energy Policy: a Consultative Document, Cmnd. 7101 (1978), ch. 5 and para. 14.31.
20 Decret 74–1003, of November 29, 1974, Journal Officiel, Lois et Décrets 1974, p. 12014. See further below, Chapter V, pp. 104–105.
21 See Mondo Economico, July 22, 1981, pp. 38–9.

tion of oil for this gas, and hence an increase in oil consumption, was seen as the solution[22]. Only in the longer term was it thought that coal or nuclear power could fill the gap. Elsewhere the emphasis was on nuclear energy as the preferred substitute for oil, in such employments as electricity generation. As we have seen, the scope for such substitution varied considerably in 1972. Only France has adopted and maintained a policy of replacing oil with nuclear power so far as possible.[23] In Germany, Italy and the United Kingdom a pre-existing commitment to the growth of nuclear power generation was initially reinforced by the events of 1973–74, but political and technical obstacles to rapid nuclear development had by 1977 provoked reappraisals which saw a continuing or even increasing role for domestic coal in the United Kingdom[24] and Germany[25], and, remarkably, an increased emphasis in Italy on imported coal as opposed to nuclear energy.[26] In rather similar fashion the Netherlands, now not a coal-producing country, gave greater prominence to coal than to nuclear power as an oil substitute in its 1979–80 Energy Report.[27] France, by contrast, even in the VIIIth Plan (1979)[28], was prepared to offer only weak encouragement to coal substitution in industry.

V. Alterations in the Pattern of Energy Supply

The uncertain commitment of all States except France to the development of nuclear energy will have appeared from the previous paragraph. Nonetheless, it needs to be remembered that with the possible exception of the Netherlands, some increase in nuclear generating capacity has been an objective of all states throughout the period under examination. In relation to other domestic energy sources, we find in all states a commitment to comprehensive programmes of research and development, in which the emphases vary according to the natural possibilities of the different localities. The Italians, for example, have accorded a higher priority to the

22 Energienota, *supra* note 11, at p. 127.

23 The so-called Messmer Programme of March 4, 1974, see Faberon, *Politique et Moyens Juridiques des Economies d'Energie en France* (1979) at p. 64. There has been recent controversy on the current overcapacity of the nuclear industry, and it is likely that downward modifications of earlier projections will be incorporated in the IXe Plan. Le Monde, May 6, 1983.

24 Cmnd. 7101, *supra*, note 19, chs. 6 and 10 and paras. 14.27 and 14.28.

25 The Second Revision of the Energy Programme, *supra*, note 18, at p. 268. Third Revision, (1981) Bundesregierung, November 5, 1981.

26 Pandolfi Plan, *supra*, note 21, at p. 39.

27 Notaenergiebelied, Bijl Hand. TK 1979–80, 15802 nr. 6–7, at pp. 5–8.

28 Commission de l'énergie et matières premières, *La Relève du Pétrole*, (1980), p. 106.

development of solar energy than have the British[29]. Those countries with coal resources – France, Germany, the United Kingdom – have sought to stabilise coal production rather than allow it to run down, though long-term decline is still envisaged by the French VIIIth Plan[30] and the weak financial position of the United Kingdom coal industry continues to make for an uncertain future.

Some specific national objectives in the field of domestic resource development which are not generally encountered should also be mentioned. In Italy, the Donat-Cattin Plan (1975) put some emphasis on the improvement of refinery efficiency[31], while later plans have referred rather to increasing levels of refinery utilisation[32]. In the United Kingdom and the Netherlands, producers of potentially highly mobile hydro-carbon resources, there has been concern to ensure the employment of those resources in ways most favourable to the public interest. In the Netherlands this has come to mean the domestic use of natural gas, rather than its exportation (1974 White Paper)[33]; in the United Kingdom, the domestic refining of offshore oil production rather than its export in the crude state.[34] Such issues have not arisen in relation to coal, where transport costs make exports difficult.

Finally we turn to States' objectives in relation to the diversification of imported energy supplies. Such an objective does not appear to be a significant element of United Kingdom energy policy. Elsewhere it is, and the differences between States are of emphasis rather than substance. Three elements in a policy of diversification may be distinguished. There is first the opening up of new sources of imports: this is referred to generally in the Italian Plans and the Dutch 1974 White Paper[35], and with particular reference to gas by the German Energy Programme of 1973[36] and its First Revision in 1974[37], and with reference to oil and coal in the French VIIth[38]

[29] See Pandolfi Plan, *supra*, note 21 at pp. 48–49 and the UK Energy Policy Review, *supra*, note 19, paras. 11.10, 11.14, 11.15.

[30] *Supra*, note 28, at p. 114.

[31] *Supra*, note 10, at pp. 414–415.

[32] *Supra*, note 21, at p. 49.

[33] Energienota, supra note 11, at p. 127. Limited natural gas exports are now (1984) being once more encouraged by the Dutch government.

[34] Offshore Oil and Gas Policy, Cmnd. 5696 (1974). In fact, however, substantial exports of crude to EEC and IEA countries have taken place.

[35] *Supra*, note 11, at p. 126.

[36] Bundeswirtschaftsministerium, Das Energieprogramm der Bundesregierung, September 26, 1973, and comment in Hrbek, *supra*, note 12, at 163.

[37] *Supra*, note 12.

[38] Commissariat générale du Plan: Rapport de la commission de l'energie. Rapport preparatoire du VIIème Plan, at pp. 26–27.

and VIIIth Plans.[39] Second, there is the overlapping idea of having a variety of sources of supply for any given imported energy source, which is stressed particularly by the Italian Plans and by the French VIIth Plan[40], which quantifies maximum permissible dependence on any one supplier. Third, there is the idea of having effective control over one's external sources of supply, for example, through exploration and exploitation by national companies. This long-standing feature of British[41], Dutch[42], French[43] and Italian[44] oil policy was in course of adoption by Germany[45] when the crisis broke and has been reaffirmed elsewhere: particular note may be taken of the suggestion of the French VIIIth Plan that French companies should be encouraged to acquire coal-mining interests abroad.[46]

This brief description of national energy policies should have shown that while there is a fundamental similarity of direction and objectives, there nonetheless exist significant differences of content and of emphasis. While these differences are certainly not so great as to make it impossible to compare the process of legal implementation and State choices among policy instruments, they need to be borne in mind when reviewing the instruments that given States have used by reference to the common schema

[39] Rapport sur les principales options du VIIIe Plan, Projet soumis par le gouvernement à l'avis du Conseil Economique et Social (1979), IIIe Partie: "Les six options du VIIIe Plan; Reduire notre dépendence en energie et matières premières", at pp. 51–52.

[40] See note 38 and Loi 76–670, of July 21st, 1976, Journal Officiel. Lois et Décrets, (1976), p. 4462.

[41] Under the Anglo-Persian Oil Company (Acquisition of Capital) Act 1914, the British government was entitled to acquire a participatory shareholding in that company, founded in 1909.

[42] The N.V. Koninklijke Nederlandsche Maatschappij tot Exploitatie van Petroleumbronnen in Nederlandsch-Indie, later to become known simply as "Royal Dutch" was founded in 1890. The merger of Royal Dutch and the English firm, the Shell Transport and Trading Co. Ltd. in 1903 led to the creation of the Royal Dutch/Shell companies.

[43] The Compagnie Française des Pétroles (CFP) was founded in 1924 on the French government's initiative for the purpose of exploiting and processing Mesopotamian oil.

[44] The Ente Nazionale Idrocarburi (ENI) was formed in 1953, (Law No. 183, February 10, 1953) and charged with "promoting and carrying out enterprises of national interest in the field of hydrocarbons and natural gas". The same law also transferred to ENI the rights and moveable property of the State, including the State shareholdings in the Azienda Generale Petroli Italiani, (AGIP), a company formed in May 1926 with the object of prospecting for, purchase and exploitation of, petroliferous deposits, and the acquisition of shareholdings in similar companies.

[45] Following a meeting in May 1973 between the head of Veba AG and the Economic Minister, Hans Friderichs, it was announced on June 18, 1973 that Veba would take over the exploration company Gelsenberg.

[46] *Supra*, note 39.

of policy objectives. Likewise to be borne in mind when assessing the significance of differences in instruments and measures are the structure and organisation of energy institutions and markets in the various States. It is to an examination of such institutions and markets that we now turn.

Chapter IV

Legal Structuring of National Energy Industries and Markets

I. Introduction

We referred earlier to the existence of factors which might affect the selection and operation of instruments for the pursuance of energy policy objectives.[1] These factors include the existing legal structures and rules which constitute and regulate energy institutions and markets in the States we are examining. To understand what features of the legal apparatus may have this effect, we need to look more closely at the concept of a policy instrument, which we introduced at the very beginning of this study.

The essential question is how law serves as an instrument of policy. Such an instrumental function is not the only or perhaps even the most significant function performed by law in a modern society; that it is nonetheless important can hardly be denied.

Any government can utilise two modes of action in pursuit of policy objectives: direct and indirect. By direct action is meant changes in government's own behaviour, that is in the behaviour of persons and things under the direct and hierarchical control of leaders of government. By indirect action is meant action which operates through changing the behaviour of people outside government, and thus outside its general command structure. Such people, on the view of the relationship between government and society shared by all members of the Community, do not have general duties of obedience to the wishes of government: they must be persuaded or, if persuasion is insufficient and compulsion is needed, specific legal authority must be obtained. The mode of operation, and the results, of direct and indirect action may not in practice differ greatly – implementation studies have taught us not to assume that hierarchical control assures the mechanical implementation of orders[2] – but the distinction is of capital importance for lawyers. In the countries we are examining the government's

[1] See Chapter I, pp. 8–9.

[2] For a review of recent studies on implementation theory, see Dunsire, A. *Implementation in a Bureaucracy* (1978).

capacity for direct action is very limited. This reflects the fact that, even within the public sector, there is diffusion of activity and responsibility among large numbers of bodies with separate legal existence which, in the legal sense, are thus external to the central organs of government, in just the same way as are private persons and corporations. Such bodies, whose competence may be restricted by reference to territory (Laender, Regions, communes) or by reference to functions (e. g. State industrial corporations, including energy corporations like the British National Coal Board, Gaz de France, or Italy's national electricity board ENEL), or in both ways (e. g. local or municipal energy utilities), cannot be controlled by directions of an intra-organisational type; if they are to be directed by central government, law must provided for this, either in their own legal constitution, or under more general legal powers.

In the sphere of indirect action, when the behaviour of others has to be changed if policy is to have effect, government's essential choices are between confining itself to the provision of information for the guidance of behaviour, or acting more vigorously so as to increase costs of behaviour contrary to its policy (as by prohibition, cost-adding regulatory requirements, or taxation) or reduce costs of behaviour in line with its policy (as by the granting of subsidies). None of these approaches to the changing of behaviour *necessarily* involves legal measures; but in fact, the nature of the constitutional orders of all the countries under examination is such as to require that most of these actions normally be supported by, or expressed, in, a legal measure. It will thus be helpful to classify indirect policy instruments in a way which makes it possible to relate specific legal rules to instrument-types, according to the following table:

Table 4

Classification of Policy Instruments

1. Unilateral regulation
2. Taxation
3. Consensual constraints, i. e. control of activity through contractual and other agreements with government
4. Removal or relaxation of unilateral regulations
5. Removal of taxation or the granting of tax exemptions
6. Other public benefits, e. g.
   subsidies and other financial assistance, provision of public services, and other forms of assistance in kind
7. Public sector management
8. Information

In this Table, no attempt is made to break down the ways in which legal rules may be employed in the management of the public sector. Management of the activity of public bodies distinct from central government may rely heavily on the general or special legal rules through which they were constituted – for example, in Great Britain, government's power as a shareholder over a body constituted as a public limited company, or its explicit power of direction of a body constituted as a statutory public corporation. Such constitutive rules may perform functions of cost alteration which, in the private sector, would have to be effected by regulation, taxation or public benefits; but in addition, these latter kinds of instrument may also be extended to the public sector. The interweaving of these different kinds of instruments makes it dangerous to be too dogmatic about the control role played by each one individually. A further particularity of measures of public sector management is that they may be no more than a transmission mechanism for instruments designed to operate primarily on private sector activity. Such would be the case, for example, with a direction to state banks to grant 'soft' loans for private energy saving projects.

As we have already seen, a substantial amount of substitution between instruments may be possible in relation to the same policy objective.[3] In briefly sketching the institutional background to the national policies adopted in the post-crisis period, we should therefore try to focus on elements which may have had a particular influence on the choice of instruments by Member States, that is to say, on differences in their modes of seeking to attain their broadly similar policy objectives.

Three broad hypotheses about choice of instruments, which we can test in the next chapter against choices actually made by Member States in the pursuance of their energy policy objectives since 1973, seem to us to be, *a priori*, sufficiently plausible to act as guidelines for the selection of material.

First, the smaller (or more highly organised) the population whose behaviour the government wishes to influence, the less likely is government to resort to regulatory instruments of type 1 above. Rather, it will prefer to take advantage of the possibilities of direct contact, and of negotiation, afforded by these small numbers, by using instruments of the consensual type, either to constrain (type 3), or to promote (type 6), or both.

Second, when governments stand in a proprietary relationship whether as owners, part-owners or major creditors, effective guarantors etc.) with enterprises whose behaviour they wish to influence, they are more likely to use the powers flowing from that relationship to accomplish this objective than to employ instruments which operate independently of that relationship. This suggests, in most cases, a reliance on the tools specific to public sector management, or on those of type 6.

On the basis of these two ideas we look in the first main division of this chapter at the structure of the different energy markets – electricity,

[3] See Chapter I, pp. 6–7.

nuclear energy, coal, gas and oil and petroleum products — in the countries under study. Relevant information will include the degree of concentration, as expressed in the number of enterprises in the market and their vertical and horizontal links with other stages in the energy production and distribution chain, and with other energy markets; the degree of organisation of markets, for example through representative bodies which can deal directly with government and thus permit the creation of bargaining as opposed to regulatory situations even where market participants are numerous; the extent of public ownership and the levels (national, regional, local) at which public enterprises operate; and the existence and nature of legal controls on market entry, such as statutory monopolies, licensing and concessionary regimes. Obviously the financial considerations involved in such highly capital-intensive industries as nuclear power generation or oil production and refining also restrict the possibility of market entry and make for concentration, but here we can only be concerned with legal factors governing entry to the market.

A third hypothesis is that governments will prefer, wherever possible, to utilise existing instruments and measures to achieve their objectives in this sphere, rather than to create new ones.[4] We assume that new problems will be faced, at least initially, by using or adapting existing means. In the second main division of the chapter, therefore, we look at permanent controls which might be used in this way: that is, which are applicable, but not necessarily confined, to energy markets. We look in particular at controls on imports and exports, price controls, and subsidy arrangements. It should also be remembered that controls on market entry, such as licensing, are likely to be a source of continuing control which can be used as an instrument for the achievement of new energy policy objectives.

II. Market Structures

A. Electricity

In the *United Kingdom*, electricity was brought under public ownership by the Electricity Act 1947, and a later Electricity Act of 1957 introduced a tripartite structure, comprising a Central Electricity Generating Board (CEGB) which generates and sells bulk electricity to 12 Area Boards who retail electricity in England and Wales. (A separate structure exists for Scotland and Northern Ireland). An Electricity Council is responsible for advising the Secretary of State for Energy on matters concerning supply, finance, demand forecasting, investment planning and pricing. Certain minor exceptions to the state monopoly on generation have existed since

[4] See Chapter I, p. 9.

1957, but were slightly enlarged in 1976[5] and more recently by the Energy Act of 1983. There is no horizontal or vertical integration with other energy industries.

In *France* the law of April 8, 1946, as amended by the Armengaud law of 1948[6], gave Electricité de France (EDF) a complete monopoly of production, transportation, distribution, importation, and exportation of electricity, although as with the United Kingdom, certain minor exceptions to the monopoly on production were made, the most important being the continued production of hydro-electricity by the Compagnie Nationale du Rhone.

The behaviour of publicly owned enterprises in France, especially following the 1973 oil crisis, has been in marked contrast to their European counterparts. Martin[7] states that the essential principle of their behaviour is to control the environment in which they operate and this has meant that they have sought to extend their control upstream to secure supplies and downstream to secure markets, as well as attempting to secure control of alternative energies which could either use or which could threaten them. Finally they have attempted to secure financial independence from the State. EDF has perhaps been the leader in this development, and while it is not possible here to cover in any detail its involvement in the wide variety of activities in which it is now engaged, a brief outline of those links should be sufficient to support the above argument relating to the control of EDF's operating environment.[8] EDF has numerous subsidiaries involved in the development and marketing of new uses of electricity designed to promote its policy of "tout Electrique". EDF is also engaged in the construction of central solar heat engines in collaboration with CNRS (Centre National de Recherche Scientifique) and others. EDF has made attempts, so far unsuccessful, to infiltrate the nuclear reactor construction industry, for instance in its efforts to buy part of the Westinghouse holding in Framatome, now 30 per cent owned by the CEA. In order to achieve financial independence, EDF participates in international finance markets with the backing of French banking consortia.

In the *Netherlands*, in contrast, there is no single, central body responsible for the distribution or production of electricity, but instead we find a number of independent provincial and municipal companies[9], whose activi-

[5] Electricity Act 1957, s.2; Local Government (Miscellaneous Provisions) Act 1976, s. 11.

[6] Law of August 2, 1948. The CNR is a société d'économie mixte.

[7] Martin, J. M., "Les industries de l'énergie en France," Chronique sociale de France, April—May 1975.

[8] A list of the major subsidiaries of the French energy industries can be found in Chevalier, J. M. "Les entreprises publiques en France", La Documentation Française (1980).

[9] There are 11 Provinces ("Provincies") and 800 Municipalities ("Gemeenten") constituting the second and third tier of administration in the Netherlands. The functions

ties are in part regulated by the Electriciteitswet[10] 1938. All the electricity production companies are members of the SEP, a co-operative which owns and operates the transmission grid. The different production companies co-operate with each other on the basis of a general SEP agreement which regulates the buying and selling of electricity between SEP and its members. The VEEN, on the other hand, is an association of both producers and distributors, which aims to promote the interests of the public electricity suppliers through research, policy formulation, and co-ordination of activities, as well as negotiating with the Minister of Economic Affairs on pricing and consumer policy. It formulates an annual Electricity Plan, dealing with changes in production capacity, and although in principle every undertaking can determine its own tariff and pricing structure, in practice tariffs and prices are organised by the VEEN.[11] This high degree of organisation of the electricity market through representative bodies would lend support to our second hypothesis, that in less concentrated markets, such organisations act as surrogates. The Dutch electricity companies do not appear to have links with other energy sectors.

In *Italy* the Ente Nazionale d'Elettricita (ENEL) a State owned company, was created in 1962[12] to produce import, export, distribute, and sell all electrical energy from whatever source, over the national territory. However a considerable number of exceptions were made in the case of private generators and municipal companies. It should be noted that these concessions were only granted by the Minister of Industry after consultation with the ENEL.[13] These companies are required to provide information to ENEL on request. Hence that organisation is described as an administrative monopoly as opposed to a *de facto* or *de iure* one.[14]

The particular interests of the municipal electricity utilities are represented by the Federelettrica (Federazione Nazionale delle Aziende e dei

of the provinces tend to be limited to town and country planning, while the municipalities play a more important role in local administration. The legal limitation on the activities of both province and municipality derives from a general rule concerning their capacity as "legal persons'. The creation of, and participation in, foundations or limited companies by the provinces needs prior approval by the central government, and this approval will only be granted when this initiative appears to be in the public interest. (Article 93 (1) of the Provinciewet 1962). The creation of or participation in foundations, limited liability companies or associations by the municipalities is subject to the approval of the "Gedeputeerde Staten" (the Provincial executive) in accordance with Article 228(A) of the Gemeenwet of 1851. The powers vested (to issue concessions) in the Minister of Economic Affairs under the 1938 Electricity Act, appear never to have been used.

10 Samenwerkende Electriciteits Produktiebedryven.

11 Vereneiging van Exploitanten van Electriciteitsbedryven in Netherland.

12 Law No. 1634 of December 6, 1962 in Gazz. Uff. December 12, No. 316.

13 Art 2 of Law No. 452 of June 27, 1964 in Gazz. Uff. July 3, 1964 No. 161.

14 Quadri, G., *Diritto Pubblico dell'economia* (1977), at pp. 80–81.

Servizi Elettrici degli Enti Locali). Unipace (the Unione Nazionale Aziende Produttrici Auto Consumatrici di Energie Elettriche) is the representative organisation for large self-generators.

The two distinguishing features of the structure of the electricity supply industry in *Germany* are the high degree of concentration within the industry and the high level of self-generation.[15] Public utilities, i. e. bodies whose share capital is held either by central, Länder or local governments currently account for about 85 per cent of production and 90 per cent of distribution. Although there are currently some 1,200 electricity supply undertakings (EVU's) a small number of large firms dominate, and many of the smaller companies are viable only because they are able to exploit favourable hydro-electric power generation possibilities. Moreover, the different stages or production, i. e. generation, transmission and distribution, are highly integrated vertically, as the following table illustrates:

Table 5

Concentration According to Market Stages in the Electricity Sector in Germany (%)

Electricity Utility Sector	Gross Generation	Sales to others	Total Production	Special Contract Customers	Tariff Customers
9 vertically integrated grid companies (a)	58	55	41	48	32
12 producing companies (b)	21	27	4	7	–
20 regional companies	6	10	20	17	25
9 municipalities	6	1	10	10	9

(a) Verbundgesellschaften
(b) including power plants of the hard coal mining industries, feeding into the transmission system and large power stations owned by several companies.
Source VDEW 1976

It has been estimated that about 20 per cent of electricity in Germany is self-generated, mainly by coal mines, the Federal Railways and the iron and steel industry. If one discounts the coal sector, industry generates one third of its own electricity demand.[16]

[15] Mueller, J., 'Industrial Self Generation of Electricity in a Public System." in Mitchell, B. and Kleindorfer, P. (eds.), *Regulated Industries and Public Enterprise* (1980), pp. 229–239.

[16] *Ibid.*

Over 700 of the utilities involved in electricity production and distribution are members of the VDEW (Vereinigung Deutscher Elektrizitätswerke). Those companies producing electricity for their own needs and for public distribution, are grouped in the Verband Industrielle Kraftwerkswirtschaft (VIK). Most of the municipal enterprises in the fields of electricity and gas, and more recently, district heating, are members of the Verband Kommunaler Unternehmen (VKU).

As noted, one of the distinguishing features of the German electricity sector is its high degree of concentration. The 1976 Report of the Monopolkommission[17] found that in the energy sector in general there had been a shift in the last decade to vertical and conglomerate forms of concentration, as well as horizontal concentration. Companies with dominant positions in other energy sectors thus have interests in the electricity sector. The oil company Veba[18] still retains considerable interests in coal mining and electricity production. Ruhrkohle in turn participates in other parts of the energy industry, including electricity. Lignite production is primarily undertaken by the electricity concern RWE a company which is also heavily involved in the nuclear industry. In the opinion of the Monopolkommission the substitutional element of competition is threatened by the rise of conglomerate mergers. Recent action by the Federal Cartel Office to prevent this will be examined below.

Controls which restrict entry to the electricity market would appear to have contributed to the degree of concentration, and the activities of the electricity supply undertakings (EVUs) are subject, to a limited extent, to the operation of general competition law. Concessions to EVUs are based on the Street Law, which makes the laying of cables subject to the permission of local authorities and which has given rise to zonal monopolies as the local authorities tended to grant concessional agreements exclusively to one EVU and accepted the obligation to refuse permission to any other EVU to do the same.[19] However, as these concessional agreements could not completely eliminate competition, zonal boundaries were determined by the so-called "Demarkationsverträge" – demarcation agreements between the EVUs. When the Gesetz gegen Wettbewerbsbeschränkungen (GWB) was passed in 1957, the electricity industry was exempted from the operation of competition policy and permitted to continue operating its restrictive practices with the aim of guaranteeing the final consumer a cheap and secure supply of electricity. Hence section 103 GWB, in operation until February 1980, exempted the zonal agreements in the electricity sector

17 Monopolkommission Report, Hauptgutachten I, "Mehr Wettbewerb ist möglich" (1976).

18 See pp. 75–76 *infra.*

19 Gröner, H. "Regulated Industries", in Zeitschrift für die Staatswissenschaft Band 136, Heft 3, September 1980, p. 360.

from the fundamental prohibition on cartels (section 1), as well as from price-fixing (section 15) and exclusivity arrangements (section 18). All other provisions of the GWB are applicable to the electricity sector. Section 104 gives the cartel authorities the power to intervene if the agreements themselves or the way in which they are administered constitutes an abuse of the market position which is otherwise exempted under section 103.[20]

Table 6 provides a breakdown of the nature of ownership of the electricity supply industries and their respective market shares in each of the Member States under study.[21]

Table 6

Electricity: Concentration

Country	Organisation	Control	Share of Market
UK	CEGB	100% State owned	99% conventional production 100% nuclear production Monopoly of distribution
France	EDF CNR	100% State owned Societe d'économie mixte	87% of production 6% of production
Holland	11 producing companies owned by municipal or provincial authorities 94 distribution companies owned by municipal or provincial authorities		
Italy	ENEL	100% State owned	78% conventional production 74% hydro-electric production 100% nuclear production
Germany	RWE VEW VEBA	mixed enterprise companies	45% production 30% distribution

CEGB – Central Electricity Generating Board; EDF – Eléctricité de France; CNR – Compagnie National du Rhône; ENEL – Ente Nazionale d'Energia Elettrica; RWE – Rheinisch-Westfälische Elektrizitätswerke; VEW – Vereinigte Elektrizitätswerke Westfalen.

[20] The GWB was amended in February 1980, strengthening the role of the Federal Cartel Office.

[21] The market shares given in tables 6–12 are compiled from the following sources: Germany: Monig, Schmitt, Schneider and Schurmann, *Konzentration und Wettbewerb in der Energiewirtschaft* (1977). Grayson, L., *The National Oil Companies* (1980), Chapter 6. Metra, *Public Enterprise in the European Communities* (1977), pp. 335–518. Petroleum Economist, April 1982. Italy: Metra, *op. cit.*, pp. 627–800. Grayson, L., *op. cit.* Chapter 5. France: Lucas, N., *Energy Policy in France* (1978). Grayson, L., *op. cit.*, Chapters 3 and 4. Metra, *op. cit.*, pp. 169–323. Netherlands: Metra, *op. cit.*, pp. 857–899 asnd 900–1109. United Kingdom: The Monopolies and Mergers Commission: Petrol, A Report on the Supply of Petrol in the UK, Cmnd. 7433 (1979).

B. Nuclear Generation

In the *United Kingdom* the CEGB owns and operates nuclear plant. In 1981 nuclear power contributed 13.6 per cent to electricity generation. The principal body engaged in nuclear power development is the United Kingdom Atomic Energy Authority (UKAEA) established in 1954 under the Atomic Energy Act, and this statutory corporation is responsible for research into atomic energy and the production, distribution, and acquisition of radioactive substances. The UKAEA may produce, use and dispose of nuclear energy and process or treat radioactive materials but it is not permitted to take part in any defence related programmes. It does, however, have powers to carry out research and other activities relating to waste disposal. The manufacture and supply of fuels for nuclear plant is the responsibility of British Nuclear Fuels Limited, a trading company formerly owned by the UKAEA whose shares are now held by the Secretary of State. Until 1980, the design and construction of reactors was conducted by the National Power Company, which was owned by the National Nuclear Corporation, itself owned jointly by the government and private industry, and managed by the General Electric Company (GEC), a non-governmental concern. This latter, rather curious arrangement did not function well, especially during the late 1970's when considerable disagreement broke out between the participants as to the type of reactor upon which the new generation of nuclear power stations should be based, the CEGB and GEC preferring the American-designed pressurised water model and the government favouring the British-designed advanced gas-cooled reactor. Following a ministerial statement of 1979 the somewhat haphazard structure of the nuclear construction industry was modified. The boards of the National Nuclear Corporation and of the Nuclear Power Company were amalgamated in the hope that a focussing of responsibility for all aspects of the undertaking's involvement in the design and construction of nuclear installations would produce an effective vehicle for the supply of these facilities, both in the UK and elsewhere.

Control over most aspects of nuclear power generation is vested in the Secretary of State for Energy. He has powers to issue directions to the UKAEA[22] and his permission is required before any irradiated material may be treated in order to extract plutonium or uranium from it or to enrich any of the uranium contained in the material in the isotope 235. The Secretary of State for the Environment also has functions impinging on the nuclear industry, through the system of registration of those using radioactive materials and the requirement that accumulations and disposal of radioactive waste must be authorised by him.

[22] Atomic Energy Act 1954 s. 3(2).

The installation and operation of nuclear plant are controlled under the Nuclear Installations Acts 1965 and 1969, and a site licence must be issued by the Nuclear Installations Inspectorate (NII) before any nuclear installation may be constructed or operated, except by the UKAEA.[23] In addition, permits are required under the Town and Country Planning Acts[24] and under the Electricity Acts.[25]

As we have noted in Chapter III, in *France* the development of nuclear power has been made a priority and in 1981 nuclear power contributed 13.1 per cent to electricity generation. The share of nuclear power is expected to grow to 30 per cent by 1990, according to the projections of the Ninth Plan. France is the only Member State with substantial uranium reserves: in 1979 these reserve stood at 154,000 tonnes with total annual production in French mines amounting to 3,000 tonnes.[26] The Commissariat à l'Energie Atomique (CEA), via its wholly owned subsidiary COGEMA, participates in joint enterprises with private firms and foreign capital and now controls the entire nuclear industry in France, from uranium prospecting, mining, ore processing, enrichment, fuel element fabrication to reprocessing.

Not long before the energy crisis, relationships between the State and the two public enterprises involved in the nuclear industry — EDF and CEA — were adjusted to allow greater autonomy to those enterprises, at least for certain aspects of their activities. As a result of the recommendations of the Rapport Cristofini in 1969, a decree of September 1970 introduced a number of organisational reforms, placing the research and scientific development aspects of the CEA more closely under the control of the Ministry of Industry, while its commercial functions were transferred to EDF as far as reactor construction was concerned, and to COGEMA, as far as the commercialisation of uranium exploration, production and reprocessing was concerned. The latter now has a monopoly of fuel-cycle processes. In 1975 the government authorised the CEA to take a 30 per cent shareholding in FRAMATOME which is the sole manufacturer in France of nuclear steam supply systems. When EDF chose exclusively PWR's following the report of the Commission PEON in 1968[27], Framatome effectively became the monopoly supplier of nuclear plant in France.

The 1970 decree had favoured the diversification of CEA activities, and hence that organisation set up a number of subsidiaries to undertake its new activities. This trend gathered momentum in the seventies, and in

[23] Nuclear Installations Act 1965 (Repeals and Modifications) Regulations 1974, regulation 1(3), applying the Health and Safety at Work Act 1974 (Schedule 1).

[24] Town and Country Planning Act 1971, s. 40.

[25] Electricity Acts 1974—1961.

[26] Les Perspectives de l'energie. Avis et Rapports du Conseil Economique et Sociale, J.O.R.F. No 16 (1979) at p. 920.

[27] Commission sur la production d'électricité d'origine nucleaire.

1976 a further re-organisation took place, to ensure that some uniformity between government directives and CEA policy was preserved.[28]

While the CEA is involved in every aspect of the nuclear industry and has also extended its interests into solar technology, via its subsidiary Sofrates, EDF has been unsuccessful in its attempts to infiltrate the nuclear reactor construction industry.

The legal controls on the exploration for and production of uranium, and the strict licensing requirements for the construction of nuclear reactors ensure that the EDF and CEA have a monopoly over every aspect of nuclear electricity generation. The French mining regime is a highly centralised one, with regional and local bodies playing no part whatsoever. Uranium mining is covered by the Code Minier.[29] The Ordonnance of 1945 (now incorporated in Article 6 of the Code) establishing the CEA gives that body special responsibilities for the organisation, control, exploration and production of uranium deposits in France. Although the CEA does not have a legal monopoly on the use of atomic substances, as defined by a decree of 1956,[30] Article 81 of the Code gives it a prerogative to have put at its disposal, after due compensation, all substances necessary for the production of atomic energy. De Laubadère refers to this as a "véritable monopole de l'acquisition".[31]

Until 1954 the CEA was the sole prospector for uranium in France, but subsequent to that date, it offered technical aid to all private persons or companies wishing to undertake prospecting, with a guarantee that all minerals discovered would be purchased. This led to the creation of several private consortia to engage in the exploration for and production of uranium, including CMFU, SIMO and SOGEMA, in all of which the CEA took a shareholding. Since 1976 these shareholdings have passed to COGEMA, the wholly owned subsidiary of CEA.[32] Exploration and production of uranium are governed by a system of *permis de recherche* (permis M), *permis d'exploitation*, and *concessions*, similar to that in force for hydrocarbons. *Permis de recherche* and *permis d'exploitation* are granted by the Minister of Industry and *concessions* are granted by decree of the Conseil d'Etat. Article 54 gives the State complete discretion in the fixing of conditions imposed via the *cahiers des charges*. Although the legislation provides that any company having its headquarters in France or in the European Community may apply for a *permis* or a *concession*, in practice, only French companies have been engaged in uranium production and

[28] Decree no. 76–1250 of December 12, 1975, creating the CEA; Decree no. 76–591 of October 22, 1976, creating COEGMA.

[29] The various laws and decrees relating to mining were codified by a decree of August 16, 1956.

[30] Decree no. 56–992 of September 28, 1956, in J.O.R.F., October 5, 1956, p. 9489.

[31] De Laubadère, A., *Traité Elémentaire de Droit Administratif* (1979) at para. 1205.

[32] *Supra*. note 28.

prospecting. It has been suggested that foreign companies stand a better chance of success if they participate in a French holding company.[33]

Licensing procedures for constructing and operating nuclear plant are governed by a decree of December 1963[34] and a decree of March 1973.[35] Under section 3 of the latter decree, large nuclear installations can be set up only after authorisation from the Ministry of Industry had been granted. Applications for authorisation are subject to local inquiry unless the installation has already been the subject of an enquiry prior to being classed "d'utilité publique".

The development of nuclear energy in the *Netherlands* remained essentially in private hands until the aftermath of the 1967 Suez crisis when two government policy documents outlined the two main tasks of government in this sector as the co-ordination and stimulation of the activities of the various institutions, universities and private companies.[36] A central research institution, and budgetary provision — the so-called Nuclear Development Fund — were established.

The electricity utilities are responsible for the operation of nuclear plant, and a common undertaking, the Gemeenschappelijke Kernenergiecentrale Nederland NV (Common Nuclear Energy Plant in the Netherlands Ltd) was responsible for the exploitation of the first nuclear plant, opened in 1969, while another provincial electricity company is responsible for the operation of a slightly larger plant at Borsele. While direct State control on the operation of the nuclear industry is thus excluded, on the basis of the 1964 Kernenergiewet every stage of the nuclear cycle is subject to licensing and regulation. The necessary license is granted by a committee especially constituted for that purpose.[37] However this Act does not provide for a solution to the problem of the disposal of nuclear waste, a problem which has recently become a major issue in the debate on nuclear energy.[38]

Despite the targets set by the various plans and programmes outlined in Chapter III, *Italian* nuclear production remains amongst the lowest in the Member States, contributing only 1.3 per cent to total electricity

[33] Rapport définitif de Recherches de l'Université de Lille II, *Etat du Droit Minier et de la Fiscalité des Actinides dans les Pays Membres de la Communauté* (1980), at p. 113.

[34] Decret 63—1228 of December 11, 1963.

[35] Decret 73—405 of March 26, 1973 in J.O.R.F., April 4, 1973.

[36] Bylage Handelingen T.K. 1955/56, no. 4026 and 1956/57, no. 4727.

[37] In 1965 the Wet Aansprakelijkheid Kernenergie (Nuclear Energy Liability Act) was adopted (Stb 546). Treaty obligations resulted in the adoption of the Wet Aanspraklijkheid Nucleaire Schepen (Nuclear Ships Liability Act) in 1973 (Stb 410) to implement the Treaty of Brussels of 1962, and the Wet Aanspraklijkheid Kernongevallen (Nuclear Accidents Liability Act) in 1979 (Stb 225). This Act replaced the 1965 Act.

[38] I. Lambs-Hacquebard, "Recht en radioactief afval-een jurisdische terreinverkenning," Ars Aequi 1980, pp. 668—675.

generated in 1981. The Comitato Nazionale della Energia Nucleare (CNEN) was formed in 1960.[39] to promote applied nuclear research on the peaceful use of nuclear energy. However this organisation did not exercise much influence until its reorganisation in 1971 when it was given power to undertake directly, subject to the approval of the CIPE (Comitato Interministeriale per la Programmazione Economica), the construction and development of prototype reactors as well as a major role in assessing safety and radiation protection in planned nuclear installations.[40]

In 1968 the CIPE allocated to ENI, the State hydrocarbon company the responsibility for the procurement and processing of nuclear fuels and the operating company Agip-Nucleare was formed. The nuclear plant construction sector has recently come to be dominated by Finmeccanica, a subsidiary of the IRI which controls 50 per cent of the licence for PWRs, the type of reactor now favoured by the CNEN. Prior to 1980 SIGEN and SOPREN, two subsidiaries of the FIAT concern, were involved in the consortium which planned to construct PWRs under the Westinghouse licence, but FIAT has recently relinquished these companies to Finmeccanica in exchange for a favourable agreement in the aviation manufacturing sector.[41]

As for control of entry to the business of nuclear power generation, the Basic Law no. 1860 of 1962[42] excluded nuclear installations for the purpose of electricity generation from its ambit, and hence the only regulations applying to such installations were contained in a later Presidential decree governing radiation protection and safety.[43] However in 1975 a new system was introduced, primarily designed to surmount local opposition to the siting procedure.[44]

In 1981 nuclear power accounted for 10.4 GWE of total electricity generation in *Germany*, a figure considerably below the projections made in the various Energy Programmes. There are at present 20 companies either operating or engaged in the building of nuclear power stations in the Federal Republic, although several regional and municipal companies participate in the operation of the AVR (Arbeitsgemeinschaft Versuchsreaktor GmbH) and in KWO (Kernkraftwerk Obrigheim GmbH), accounting for 340 MWe out of a total 2290 MWe produced. Once again RWE is the largest producer of nuclear generated power.

39 Law no. 933 of August 11, 1960 in Gazz. Uff., September 6, 1960, no. 218.

40 Law no. 1240 of December 15, 1971, in Gazz. Uff., January 24, 1972 no. 20. The organisation of the CNEN has recently been modified and that agency, now known as the ENEA, has been given wider powers, including the provision of technical and consultation services. Law no. 84 of March 5, 1982. See Chapter V *infra*.

41 See Mondo Economico, March 1981.

42 Law No. 1860 of December 31, 1962, in Gazz. Uff., January 30, 1963, No. 27.

43 Presidential Decree No. 185 of February 13, 1964, in Gazz. Uff., May 3, 1964, no. 112.

44 Law no. 393 of August 12, 1975, in Gazz. Uff., August 23, 1975, no. 224.

Three companies dominate the German nuclear reactor construction industry, and they are all entirely privately owned. Kraftwerk Union (KWU), a wholly owned subsidiary of the Siemens Corporation, dominates the industry and Hochtemperatur Reaktorbau (HRB) and Babcock Boveri Brown Reaktor (BBR) play a minor role. Research and development of nuclear technology is primarily carried out by the two government-financed centres at Jülich and Karlsruhe.

A distinctive feature of the German nuclear energy regime is that there is no single central organisation responsible for nuclear energy. The Basic Law, Article 74, no. 11, attributes legislative competence regarding nuclear matters to the Federal and Land governments concurrently, implying that the Länder have legislative competence only insofar as the Federal Government has not acted on the relevant matter. The Basic Law also stipulates that the Land, with the consent of the Bundesrat, will administer federal laws.

The 1959 Atomgesetz is based on article 74, attributing hybrid competence on matters relating to nuclear strategy. The use of nuclear fuels in privately owned plants is subject to authorisation under article 7 of the Atomgesetz. Detailed provisions on the authorisations needed for each stage of development — siting, construction, commissioning or alteration of plans — are laid down in the 1977 Decree on Licensing Procedure for Nuclear Installations, issued pursant to article 7.[45] Although the Land authorities are responsible for giving final approval to the siting and construction of nuclear installations, the Federal, district and municipal authorities are engaged in the planning process, and the Federal Government has a 'right of instruction' as regards the construction of commercially operated nuclear plant.

C. Coal

The structure of the coal industry in the various countries under study owes much to post-war attempts to rationalise the industry and to later efforts to deal with the over-production crisis of 1957 when coal could no longer compete with cheap oil imports.

In the *United Kingdom*, the National Coal Board (NCB) was created in 1946 with a virtual monopoly of coal production. The CEGB and the British Steel Corporation are however substantial importers of cheaper foreign coal. Initially the NCB had some involvement in other energy sectors, notably in exploration for oil and gas in the North Sea. In 1976 its oil interests were transferred to BNOC,[46] and the NCB's activities

[45] February 18, 1977, BGBl—I 280.

[46] Petroleum and Submarine Pipe-lines Act 1975, s. 13. However the Coal Industry Act 1977, s. 59, extends the scope of petroleum-related activities that the NCB may undertake.

Table 7

Concentration in the Nuclear Sector

Country	Organisation	Control	Share of Market
UK	CEGB	100% State owned	100% production
	BNFL	100% State-owned	manufacture of reactors monopoly of research
France	Cogema	Wholly owned subsidiary of CEA	monopoly of fuel cycle process
	CEA	100% State owned	research, and control of all nuclear activities
	Framatome	34% owned by CEA	sole French manufacturer of nuclear steam supply system
Holland	–	–	–
Italy	Agip Nucleare	100% owned by ENI	monopoly on acquisition of fuels
	Finmeccanica	Subsidiary of IRI	sole licensee for PWRs
Germany	see text		

BNFL – British Nuclear Fuels Limited; Cogema – Compagnie Générale des Matières Nucléaires

are now limited to coal distribution, and the production of coal based chemicals.

In *France* coal production was placed in the hands of a newly-created state monopoly, CDF, in 1946. Coal importation is undertaken by another state owned monopoly, ATIC.[47] As CDF has always been less financially strong than its counterpart in the electricity sector, EDF, its possibilities for diversification have been limited, although it is engaged in some overseas coal mining, and has formed a subsidiary, CDF-Chemie, to take charge of its chemical interests.

In the *Netherlands* coal mining had been predominantly the responsibility of the DSM until 1975 when the last mines in Zuid Limburg were closed. Although these mines were not technically exhausted, it was considered that production was too costly.

In *Italy* the State hydrocarbon company ENI has exclusive prospecting rights on the national territory and at present its subsidiary, Agip-Carbone is engaged in the development of low-grade coal at Sulcis in Sardinia. The 1981 Pandolfi Plan forecasts a massive increase in the utilisation of imported coal; responsibility for its implementation has been divided between ENEL, ENI and Finsider, the State steel company, all of which are represented on

[47] See pp. 78–79 *infra*.

a newly formed coal commission, within the Ministry of State Participation. The same Plan has allocated ENI the role of State energy corporation and it has thus sought to consolidate its position in all the major energy sectors.

Since the merger of 24 Ruhr mining companies to form Ruhrkohle in 1969, the *German* hard coal industry has consisted of six undertakings, of which four are private companies, namely the Gewerkschaft Auguste Victoria, the Eschweiler Bergwerksverein, Preussag AG Kohle and the Gewerkschaft Sophia Jacob. The Ruhrkohle AG, which is by far the largest organisation (accounting for 87 MT of a total of 101.5 MT in 1974) has sixteen shareholders, being companies which put their mining assets into the holding company in accordance with the "Grundvertrag zur Neuordnung des Ruhrbergbaus" – Outline Agreement on the Reorganisation of the Ruhr mining industry – of July 18, 1969.[48] Most of the shareholders are linked with Ruhrkohle by long-term agreements on the supply of coke and power station coal. The second largest company, the Saarbergwerke (1974 production: 9 MT) is under public ownership. The degree of concentration in the brown coal or lignite mining industry is still higher with Rheinische Braunkohlenwerke AG accounting for 85 per cent.

As Germany is the only Member State where there are a number of enterprises engaged in the production of coal, we find several representative organisations: the Steinkohlenbergbauverein is an association of the six main hard coal mining companies in West Germany, established to promote that group's special interests, while the Deutscher Braunkohlen Industrie Verein e. V. is concerned with mining and exploitation of brown coal. Finally the Verein Deutscher Kohlen-Importeure e. V. is a trade association for companies involved in importing coal into West Germany.

Attention has already been drawn to the high level of conglomerate concentration which exists at present in the German energy sector.

D. Gas

The pattern of concentration in the gas industry is similar to that found for the electricity supply industry, and in most countries the legislation applying to the gas industry was enacted at the same time as that for electricity. An exception must however be made for the activity of domestic exploration for and production of natural gas, access to which is normally regulated by legislation applying alike to natural gas and to oil, which will be treated, save for its provisions specific to gas, in the latter section on oil.

The *United Kingdom*: The British gas industry was nationalised by the Gas Act, 1948, which established a bipartite structure of Area Boards, responsible locally for both production and distribution, and a central Gas

[48] Hrbek, R., "Coal Policy of the Federal German Republic", in Ionescu, G. (ed.), *The European Alternatives* (1979).

Table 8
Coal: Concentration

Country	Organisation	Control	Share of Market
UK	NCB	100% State owned	99% monopoly of production
France	CDF	100% State owned	monopoly of production
	ATIC	100% State owned	monopoly of imports
Holland	–	–	–
Italy	Agip Carbone	Wholly owned subsidiary of ENI	importation of coal
	ENI	100% State owned	monopoly of production
Germany	Ruhrkohle AG	mixed enterprise	77% of production
	Saarbergwerke	Federal/Länder	16% of production
	Rheinische Braunkohle	Wholly owned subsidiary of RWE	85% lignite production

NCB – National Coal Board; CDF – Charbonnages de France; ATIC – Association Technique de l'Importation du Charbon; ENI – Ente Nazionale Idrocarburi

Council. A further Gas Act of 1965 extended the powers of the Gas Council, enabling it to buy gas anywhere in Great Britain, or elsewhere, and to supply gas in bulk to the Area Boards. Reorganisation took place in 1972, under the Gas Act of that year, with the creation of the British Gas Corporation (BGC) which was given all statutory responsibilities for the industry. Until 1982, section 29 of the 1972 Act provided that no person other than the BGC might supply gas through pipes to any premises without the Corporation's consent. A requirement has appeared in various enactments since 1964, and most recently in the Energy Act 1976, sections 8 and 9, that all fuel gas produced in the British sector of the North Sea had to be offered for sale to the BGC at a reasonable price. However, as we shall see in Chapter V, these monopoly supply powers of the BGC have been recently cut down. The present government has also been hostile to BGC's retaining what it regards as ancillary activities. BGC, along with the Gas Council as its predecessor, has been engaged in oil exploration and production, as a natural complement to gas exploration and production, since 1964. These activities have now been transferred to a separate company and sold to the private sector.[49] The nationalised gas industry also

[49] In the exercise of his powers under s. 11 of the Oil and Gas (Enterprise) Act 1982, the Secretary of State for Energy has made a number of statutory instruments for the purpose of transferring to the private sector BGC's offshore interests. These are interests in five producing fields on the UKCS and in twenty offshore blocks in which exploration is currently going on, but no commercial discovery has yet been

inherited in 1948, and has since developed, activities in gas fitting and contracting, and appliance marketing: BGC has up to 95 per cent of the gas cooker market.

France: Along with EDF, Gaz de France (GDF) was also established by the law of April 8, 1946, which attributed to GDF a monopoly of production, transport, distribution and importation of gas. A later law of August 2, 1948, retracted the monopoly on transport, and the right to exploit natural gas was not included in the 1946 law. However Article 197 of the Code Minier confers an exclusive right to search for gas in the Aquitaine basin on the SNPA, and this company, now part of Elf-SNEA, produces 96 per cent of the total domestic production. It should be noted that domestic gas reserves are in steady decline in France and increased reliance is placed on imported gas. Elf-SNEA is engaged in production in the British and Norwegian sector of the North Sea and contracts have been concluded with Algeria and Russia by GDF to secure supplies of natural gas. These will be examined in detail in Chapter V.

Like EDF, GDF has in recent years sought to expand into horizontally and vertically related activities, though its possibilities of diversification have been limited by its weaker financial position. It has, however, several subsidiaries engaged in the distribution of gas, in the construction of related equipment and in research on coal-gas liquefaction and geothermal energy uses. It also has interests, both in its own right and in conjunction with EDF, in several "sociétés immobilières".

In the *Netherlands* today, natural gas plays a greater economic role than in any other country in the world; the Groningen gas field is the largest non-associated gas field in the world and is capable of an annual production of over 80 mtoe.[50]

Shell and Esso originally formed NAM in 1947 as a 50/50 joint venture to explore and develop hydrocarbons within Holland. In 1964, when NAM discovered the Groningen field, the terms of its concession were altered so as to create a partnership between NAM and the Dutch State Mining Company, (DSM), under which DSM obtains a 40 per cent share in production from the field. A formal agreement concluded between NAM and the Staatsbedrijf – the State Gas Board – on July 9, 1948 had obliged the former to sell all surplus gas and in 1954 the Board was accorded a monopoly for wholesale marketing of natural gas throughout the Netherlands. After the discovery of the Groningen field the government decided to end the public monopoly enjoyed by the State Gas Board, but to retain a measure of state participation, via the DSM. In view of the considerable technical problems involved in marketing the gas, the involvement of Shell

made, which have been transferred to a new enterprise, Enterprise Oil, in which the government retains only a "symbolic" shareholding.

[50] N.V. Gasunie; *Natural Gas in Holland* (1979).

and Esso was sought. An agreement of March 27, 1963 formed the basis for the creation of Gasunie which was to act as a single wholesale seller of gas for the Netherlands and which was to acquire the transmission system from the former State Gas Board. Gasunie also sells direct to bulk gas users, such as power stations and industry, but otherwise local sales are in the hands of some 130 provincial and municipal gas utilities and five private companies. These local gas distributors are members of VEGIN (Vereniging van Exploitanten van Gasbedrijven in Nederland), an association which negotiates on prices with Gasunie and the Ministry of Economic Affairs and provides advice on the negotiation of contracts between Gasunie and the distribution companies.

At present domestic gas production in *Italy* accounts for only 8.6 per cent of the country's gas consumption. The Law no. 136 of February, 1953 gave ENI exclusive exploration and production rights throughout the Po Valley, where substantial deposits of gas were found. While ENI thus exercises a monopoly on domestic gas production through its subsidiary AGIP, it has no interests in the production of gas imported into Italy and indeed, ENI has discovered no significant sources of gas outside Italy. Esso was, in 1979, involved in 38 per cent of the expected imports from Libya and the Netherlands.

The distribution of gas in Italy is undertaken by SNAM, a wholly owned subsidiary of the ENI, which supplies directly to industries consuming over 700,000 m^3 p. a. and to gas distributors at the local and regional level. There were approximately 1300 distributing companies, both private and municipal, in 1980. These municipal electricity and gas undertakings are members of the CISPEL (Confederazione Italiana dei Servizi Pubblici degli Enti Locali). In 1976 CISPEL had 109 members – 43 electricity utilities and 66 gas utilities. The Federation represents the interests of its members at regional and national level, on matters concerning tariffs and pricing, siting policies and energy planning. The gas utilities are also members of ANCI-FNAMGAV (Federazione nazionale aziende municipalizzate gas, acqua e varie) which negotiates the terms of the agreements (contratti-tipo) between the municipal utilities and ENI-SNAM as regards pricing and supply.

In 1981 domestic production of natural gas totalled less than 5 per cent of final gas consumption in *Germany*. Domestic production is dominated by four large companies: Gewerkschaft Brigitta (50 per cent Shell/50 per cent Esso) with 44.4 per cent of the market, Mobil Oil AG with 23.7 per cent, Gewerkschaft Elwerath (Shell/Esso 50 per cent each) with 12.8 per cent and Wintershall AG with 10.2 per cent. Texaco AG accounts for a further 2.4 per cent and six smaller German companies make up the remainder.

Market shares for the importation of gas are equally concentrated: the following table gives a breakdown of shares in existing imports contracts:

Table 9
German Gas Imports

Import-unternehmen*	1974		1975		1975		1980		1985	
	a	b	a	b	a	b	a	b	a	b
1. Ruhrgas	11,0	48,2	11,7	42,2	12,0	44,8	27,8	53,9	33,3	57,8
2. Thyssengas	4,2	18,4	4,8	17,3	4,0	14,9	6,5	12,5	6,5	11,3
3. VEW	3,0	13,2	4,0	14,5	(4,0)	(14,9)	5,8	11,1	5,8	10,1
4. BEB	1,7	7,5	3,0	10,8	(3,0)	(11,2)	7,0	13,4	7,0	12,2
5. DETG	1,6	7,0	1,8	6,1	(1,8)	(6,7)	1,8	3,5	1,8	3,1
6. EWE	0,7	3,1	1,0	3,6	(1,0)	(3,7)	1,4	2,7	1,4	2,4
7. RWE	0,3	1,3	0,9	3,3	(0,9)	(3,4)	1,1	2,1	1,1	1,9
8. EVG	–	–	–	–	–	–	0,7	1,3	0,7	1,2
9. Saar FG	0,3	1,3	0,5	2,2	0,2	0,4	–	–	–	–
Insgesamt	22,8	100,0	27,7	100,0	26,8	100,0	52,1	100,0	57,6	100,0

a = absolute quantities in billions m³ b = percentage share of total imports
Source : Monig et al. (See n. 21), p. 590

* VEW = Vereinigte Elektrizitätswerke Westfalen; BEB = Brigitta und Elwerath; DETG = Deutsche Erdgas Transport; EWE = Energievorversorgung Weser-Ems; RWE = Rheinisch-Westfälisches Elektrizitätswerk; EVG = Erdgas-Verkaufs-Gesellschaft mbH.

German companies are also involved in overseas gas exploration and production: Gelsenberg is involved in the Dutch Continental Shell, Wintershall in the Dutch Noordwinning group and Union Kraftstoff in the UK North Sea sector.

The gas distribution market is undoubtedly dominated by Ruhrgas[51] which had a 62.5 per cent share of that market in 1974, followed by Thyssengas GmbH with 9.9 per cent and GV Süddeutschland with 7.7 per cent and Salzgitter AG with 3.9 per cent. These in turn deliver to a large number – 452 in 1974 – of local supply enterprises, most of which are owned by the municipalities. Most of these municipal enterprises are members of the Verband Kommunaler Unternehmen (VKU).

Significant features of national gas markets are summarised in the following table:

[51] The current shareholders in Ruhrgas are: Bergeman KG., Gelsenberg AG, Gewerkschaft Brigitta, Schubert KG, Gelsenberg, now wholly owned by Deutsche BP owns 25 per cent of the shares of Ruhrgas, and Gewerkschaft Brigitta, owned 50 per cent each by Deutsche Shell and Deutsche Esso, owns another 25 per cent. See Jahrbuch für Bergbau, Energie, Mineralöl und Chemie (1981/82).

Table 10

Gas: Concentration

Country	Organisation	Control	Share of Market
UK	BGC	100% State owned	Monopoly of sales until 1982
France	GDF	100% State owned	78% of sales
	SNGSO	Wholly owned subsidiary of GDF	22% of sales
	Elf-Aquitaine (SNEA)	70% State owned	96% of production
Holland	NAM	Shell/Esso – 30% each DSM – 40%	Operates Groningen Concession
	DSM	100% State owned	Can take 40% participation in pre-76 licences and 50% in post-76.
	Gasunie	Shell/Esso – 25% DSM – 40% Dutch State – 10%	Monopoly of sales
Italy	ENI	100% State owned	Monopoly of onshore production
	SNAM Progetti	100% subsidiary of ENI	De facto monopoly of wholesale and industrial distribution
Germany	Ruhrgas	private capital	36.1% overall share in importation and distribution and production**
	Thyssengas	private	5.7% overall share
	BEB	private	18.6% overall share
	Mobil	private	6.4% overall share

** Overall share here means the total share of each company in the different stages of production, importation, transport and distribution.

BGC – British Gas Corporation; GDF – Gaz de France; SNGSO – Société Nationale du Gaz du Sud-Ouest; NAM – Nationale Aardolie Maatschapp; ENI – Ente Nazionale Idrocarburi; BEB – Brigitta und Elwerath; SNEA – Societé Nationale Elf-Aquitaine

E. Crude Oil and Petroleum Products

The original vehicle of the *United Kingdom* government's interests in oil production was the British Petroleum Co. Ltd. (BP). Its shareholding in this company has declined steadily in recent years and now stands at only 32 per cent. Although the government may appoint two directors to the Board of BP, with powers of veto, it was agreed in 1914 that these powers would only be exercised on questions of foreign or military policy or on matters relating to Admiralty contracts.

In 1969 a consortium headed by Phillips Petroleum made the first discovery of large quantities of oil in Norwegian waters and later BP, followed by other oil companies, discovered oil in the British sector. These finds were made within the framework of the system of licensing of exploration and production extended to offshore areas in 1964,[52] which relied heavily on the initiative and investment of major and independent oil companies. The Labour Government which came to power in 1974, however, while not able to abandon this system, was anxious to introduce an element of State enterprise. It considered using BP for this purpose,[53] but anxiety over possible reactions of foreign governments prevented any further development of this kind and instead a State-owned oil corporation – British National Oil Corporation – was created under the Petroleum and Submarine Pipelines Act of 1975, and subsequently obtained – by way of a negotiated right to purchase at market price – secure access to 51 per cent of the crude oil being produced under licences in the UK sector of the North Sea.[54] The 1982 Oil and Gas (Enterprise) Act transferred BNOC's own exploration and production interests, but not its access rights, to a new, separate company Britoil, 51 per cent of whose shares have been sold to private investors.[55]

The larger oil companies, which have operating responsibilities in the United Kingdom sector of the North Sea (as opposed to simply being participants in licence consortia) are represented by the United Kingdom Offshore Operators Association (UKOOA), which was established in order to present a co-ordinated view by the industry to government on matters of operations, safety, technology, commerce and taxation. UKOOA's activities have included the negotiation of an agreement between its members and the government on the use of British goods and services in the North Sea.

The North Sea is now the biggest oil producer outside North America and the Middle East.[56] Of the current production of 2.5 million b. p. d., Britain produces 80 per cent and Norway most of the rest. Britain now ranks fifth among the world's leading oil producers and in 1982 overtook Saudi Arabia as West Germany's biggest single oil supplier. Further, Britain is the richest European country in offshore oil and gas reserves with 60 per cent of Europe's known oil reserves and 32 per cent of its gas. Access to this very significant economic activity is controlled through a licensing regime.

52 Continental Shelf Act 1964.

53 See Cameron, *Property Rights and Sovereign Rights: The Case of North Sea Oil* (1973), pp. 63–67. B.P. was treated as an ordinary British commercial enterprise for the purposes of awards of licences in the first four licensing rounds. Select Committee on Nationalised Industries: Nationalised Industries and the Exploitation of North Sea Oil and Gas, (1974–75) H.C. 345, at p. 251.

54 See Daintith and Willoughby, eds. *Manual of United Kingdom Oil and Gas Law* (2nd ed., 1984), ch. 3.

55 The Government on March 13, 1985 announced its intention to dissolve BNOC and do without access rights to North Sea petroleum.

56 "Western Europe's Oil and Gas: A Survey", The Economist, June 12, 1982.

The Continental Shelf Act of 1964 declared the sovereign rights of the United Kingdom over its Continental Shelf (UKCS), and extended to it the rules for granting licences for the exploration for and production of petroleum in the United Kingdom established by the Petroleum (Production) Act 1934. New licensing regulations and model clauses were introduced, applicable to all offshore activity, whether on the UKCS or beneath the territorial sea.[57] Under the 1964 Regulations all applicants for licences had to be resident citizens of the UK, or companies incorporated in the UK.[58] The application of this requirement was eventually abolished in accordance with the Treaty of Accession to the European Communities,[59] and now any person may apply for a licence. However, sources of possible discrimination do remain, as licences are granted at the discretion of the government,[60] which retains the right to revoke a licence where the company concerned ceases to have its central management and control in the UK.[61]

The first four rounds of licensing were concluded before the creation of BNOC, whereas the award of licences in the fifth round was conditional on acceptance by the applicant of BNOC as a full cost- and profit-sharing co-licensee with at least a 51 per cent share. However all 62 companies licensed in the first four rounds accepted a form of participation by BNOC, under which BNOC became a co-licensee but furnished no capital contribution, and did not participate in production, but had the right to obtain at market price, 51 per cent of oil produced.[62] The fifth round arrangements left BNOC with heavy exploration commitments, and so in the sixth round, in 1978–79, the concept of a carried interest for BNOC was introduced, applicants being invited to offer to carry all or part of BNOC's expenses through the exploration period. In the seventh and eighth rounds state involvement was restricted to BNOC's right, expressed as a condition of the licence, to secure access to 51 per cent of oil at

57 Petroleum Production (Continental Shelf and Territorial Sea) Regulations 1964, S. I. 1964/708.

58 Article 4.

59 Petroleum (Production) Regulations 1976, S. I. 1976/1129, article 4.

60 Petroleum (Production) Act 1934, 2. Thus the government may take into account in exercising its discretion, 'the extent of the contribution which the applicant had made or is planning to make to the economy of the UK, including the strengthening of the UK balance of payments and the growth of industry and employment'. See Department of Energy Press Notice, August 2, 1978.

61 Petroleum (Production) Regulations 1982, (S.I. 1982/1060 Sch. 5, cl. 39(2)g, and Sch. 7, cl. 21(f). The EC Commission contacted the British government about the provision for revocation, but the latter replied that there was no discrimination on grounds of nationality and the provision was necessary for tax purposes and to ensure that staff in the UK company offices would be able to take authoritative decisions. Department of Energy Press Notice, March 14, 1979.

62 Daintith and Willoughby, *supra* note 54, ch. 3.

market prices, on the pattern of the first to fourth round participation agreements.[63]

Seaward licences had been granted only in response to invited applications, in organised licence rounds, with the exception of applications by BNOC or BGC. This preferential right granted in 1976 has now been removed.[64] Although the criteria for award have varied slightly from round to round, the basic factors have, however remained broadly the same since 1964: the financial and technical ability of the applicants, their previous licence performance; relevant exploration work; their contribution to the UK economy.

A production licence is granted for six years. At the end of the term, the licensee has the option to continue the licence for up to half the original licence area for a further term of thirty years. During the second term, the Minister as licensing authority has powers to require further exploration work, together with extensive powers over production and development, first taken in 1975, which are dealt with in Chapter 5 below.

In the petroleum products market, the shares of the four largest majors, Shell, Esso, BP and Texaco declined in the UK from 78 per cent in 1974 to 72 per cent in 1978 while that of the 'new' refiners, Gulf, Fina, Total and Conoco increased from 14 per cent to 16 per cent and that of the remainder from 9 per cent to 13 per cent. The number of companies refining petrol in the UK increased from the mid-sixties on. In 1964 there were eight such companies, but by 1977 there were 12, including all but one of the 12 wholesalers, Elf, which supplied 2.5 per cent of the retail petroleum market in that year. The market share of wholesalers without refining capacity rose from 2.4 per cent in 1970 to 4.3 per cent in 1975, but declined to 3.9 per cent in 1977. The entry of the new majors, Gulf, Fina, Conoco, Burmah and Elf has led to intensive price competition in the wholesale and retail markets.[65]

In *France* the Compagnie Française des Pétroles (CFP) was created in 1924 as a société d'économie mixte, with the State taking a 35 per cent shareholding and exercising 40 per cent of the voting rights, to exploit production rights in the Turkish Petroleum Company ceded by Germany under the 1920 San Remo Treaty.[66] In 1931 the refining subsidiary of CFP, the Compagnie Française de Raffinage (CFR) was created with the right to refine 25 per cent of the nation's needs. In 1955 twenty independent

[63] BNOC and secure access are now to be dispensed with, see note 55 *supra*.

[64] The Petroleum (Production) (Amendment) Regulations 1980, S.I. 1980/721 removed from BNOC and BGC the privilege of making non-invited applications.

[65] Cmnd 7433 (1979), *supra* at note 21.

[66] For an account of the early history of the CFP, see Grayson, L., *The National Oil Companies, supra* note 21. For an account of the company's recent activities see, Chevalier J. M. "L'Energie" in Bellon, B. and Chevalier, J. M. (eds) *L'Industrie en France*. (1982), pp. 55–87.

distributors regrouped under CFP's trademark – Total, thus giving the CFP, via the CFR, its first direct outlet on the products market.

In 1970 ANTAR, hitherto the largest independent, was taken over by Elf-ERAP, the other national oil company. This latter organisation grew out of a series of mergers, beginning in 1965 when ERAP (Etablissement de Recherche et des Activités Pétrolières) was created via the fusion of the Bureau de Recherche de Pétroles (BRP), the state-owned organisation in charge of exploration and development policies, with RAP (Régie Autonome de Pétrole) a company created in 1939 to explore and produce gas in the Aquitaine region. The new organisation ERAP was both a holding company and an operating company of all the activities that had previously been controlled by the BRP, including its holdings in Société Nationale des Pétroles d'Aquitaine (SNPA), the company created in 1941 to explore the Aquitaine region, and its extensive refinery and distribution network. The purpose of this merger was to build up a strong, single coherent enterprise that would limit the influence of the foreign majors. However SNPA, while part of the ERAP group, was a fully integrated company in its own right. The creation of the Union Generale des Pétroles (UGP) in 1960 had given SNPA a refining and market outlet for its oil production in France and Algeria. The financial strength of the Elf-ERAP group was, however, considerably undermined when its Algerian assets were nationalised in 1971. Although the group did diversify its exploratory activities to include Canada, Africa and the North Sea, the SNPA continued to have a healthy cash flow from its non-industrial diversification programme, undertaken to compensate for the depletion of the Lacq gas fields. To direct this flow of funds into prospecting, the two companies were fused to form the Société Nationale Elf-Aquitaine (SNEA) in 1976.[67]

Hence through a combination of mergers and market expansion on the one hand, and until 1978, the judicious allocation of special import licences for crude and for petroleum products on the other, (see below) the two national groups, Elf and Total controlled half the market for finished products by 1976.

Elf-ERAP has numerous subsidiaries engaged in prospecting and production throughout the world, but its recent financial difficulties resulting mainly from losses in the refining and distribution sector have prompted the enterprise to seek greater diversification and to increase its exploratory efforts. These proposals have so far not met with government approval. Elf has also interests in solar energy. The CFP, on the other hand, also adversely affected by the crisis in the refining industry, has diversified into

[67] For an account of the development of state agencies involved in petroleum exploration and production, see Huet, P., "Aspects juridiques de la restructuration du secteur petrolier de l'Etat", Dalloz 1979, Chron. 89.

coal and uranium mining as well as taking shares in Sofrates, with the CEA.

There exists quite an elaborate representational structure for the petroleum industry. The Union des Chambres Syndicales de l'Industrie du Pétrole (UCSIP), a federation of associations representing firms in specific sectors of the oil industry was, until April 1982, responsible for negotiating the base price of petroleum products directly with the Comité du Prix. There are separate "Chambres Syndicales" for exploration and production of gas and oil, refining, products distribution, and petroleum transportation.

Access to oil and gas production rights in France and on the French Continental Shelf is governed, as in Britain, by a regime of concessions. Under the Code Minier,[68] there exist two types of exploration permit: exclusive and non-exclusive. The Decree of May 20, 1955, drew a distinction between 'permis de recherche exclusif' for hydrocarbons (H Permits) and for other minerals (M Permits).[69] The granting of the H Permit is at the discretion of the Conseil d'Etat and is initially for a duration of 5 years, with automatic renewal for two three-year periods if the minimum conditions of operation are fulfilled. A decree of 1980[70] imposes conditions regarding financial and technical capability of the applicants, as well as requiring the submission of a work programme. As for production, this is subject to the grant of a concession by the Conseil d'Etat, if the deposit is estimated to contain more than 300,000 metric tonnes of liquid hydrocarbons, or 3 million m^3 of gaseous hydrocarbons. If the deposits contain less, a production permit may be obtained. A concession is valid for 50 years, subject to surrender provisions, whereas a production permit is valid for five years.

All applicants for concessions must be subject to French law or to the legal system of another Member State of the EEC. If the company is constituted under a legal system other than that of France, it must have its principal offices, central administration or statutory place of business within the EEC.[71]

The authorising decree in the case of a concession, or *arrêté*, in the case of a production permit, is accompanied by a *cahier des charges*. In terms of article 30 of the Code Minier a *cahier* must fix (i) the general conditions of

[68] The various laws regulating mining activities in France were codified by a decree of August 16, 1956.

[69] Originally "permis de recherche exclusif" had only been granted for petroleum exploration under the Law of December 16, 1922, but these permits were extended to other substances by the 1955 Decree. A further Law of January 2, 1970 introduced several reforms for Permis H, including the imposition of a limitation on the extent to which a licensed area could be reduced in each successive renewal of the permit.

[70] Law 77–620 of June 16, 1977, J.O.R.F., June 18, 1977, and Decree 80–204 of March 11, 1980, J.O.R.F. March, 15, 1980.

[71] Decree 69–687 of June 19, 1969 in J.O.R.F. June 21, 1969.

the concession, which must conform to those laid out in the cahiers des charges type for the particular substance, in this case hydrocarbons; (ii) the particular conditions relating to the concession in question, regarding the establishment of consortia, the conditions of sale, transport and distribution, the construction of factories, pipelines and refineries. The *cahier des charges-type* deals principally with the technical and financial obligations of the concessionaire.

Article 107 of the Code Minier reserved the right of search in the Aquitaine region to the State, and as already noted the SNPA has been involved in the production of gas in this region. Although article 64 of the Code envisages that the State may engage directly in the exploitation of reserves, in fact this provision has never been used and the publicly-owned companies, such as Elf-SNEA, have been regulated via the concession and permit system.

The licensing regime relating to the importation of crude oil and refined petroleum products will be examined in the second division of this chapter.

Oil consumption in the *Netherlands* in 1981 accounted for 38 per cent of total demand, second only to gas consumption, and yet Holland only produced 1.5 mtoe of oil and imported for her own use a further 40.4 mtoe. Access to the activities of exploration for and production of natural gas and oil are regulated, in the case of onshore operations, by the Mijnwet of April 21, 1810 and the Mijnwet of 1903, and for offshore operations, by the Mijnwet Continentaal Plat of 1965 and the two Decrees made pursuant to article 12 of that Act of January 27, 1967 – and February 6, 1976.[72]

Licences under the 1965 Act have to be obtained for each stage: prospecting, exploration, and exploitation, although the receipt of the latter implies permission to undertake the former, and receipt of an exploration licence implies permission to prospect. An onshore exploration licence is valid for two years, while an offshore reconaissance licence is valid for six months and the exploration licence itself is valid for 15 years, subject to the relinquishment of half of the area concerned after 10 years if no oil or gas is found. There is no limit to the duration of an onshore production licence, but an offshore licence is limited to 40 years. Onshore concessions are granted by Royal Decree whereas offshore licences are granted by the Minister of Economics. Applications for offshore exploration licences are made pursuant to a notice published by the Minister. The application lists and ranks the blocks desired, technical and financial capability of the applicant, the applicant's prior contribution to Netherlands exploration and production and to the economy of the country generally. All licences granted under the 1967 Royal Decree are governed by that enactment, including production licences issued after the 1976 Royal Decree in connec-

[72] Royal Decree of January 27, 1967 Stb. 75; Royal Decree of February 6, 1976 Stb. 102.

tion with 1967 exploration licences. The work obligation is based on minimum expenditures divided into two periods: the first six-year period and the second third-year period.[73] At the end of the first exploration period, 50 per cent must be relinquished.[74] Much of the area relinquished in 1978 has promptly been relicensed to NAM. Given the preference that companies previously involved in exploration are likely to receive, new companies are best advised to join a group which has had previous success in obtaining a licence.

Production licences, granted only to previous holders of exploration licences, are granted only for discoveries in 'economically producible quantities". This term is not defined by law, and hence the Minister may exercise his discretion. Applications for licences under the 1976 decree must contain a development plan which requires the Minister's approval. In theory, this is not required under the 1967 Decree but it appears to be commonly practised on an informal basis.

The State has a right, upon an application for a production licence, to take a 50 per cent (1967 – 40 per cent) interest in production and facilities under the licence. This interest is held through DSM Aardgas B. V., a subsidiary of the DSM. Except for the first production licence granted, the State has always exercised this right. Licensees enter into an "Agreement of Co-operation" with the DSM and form together a closed company. There are two classes of stock issued in the closed company – one for the licensees and one for DSM, giving each group a 50 per cent (40 per cent) share in the closed company and a like percentage in future costs. The articles of the company provide that no budget or work programme or any substantial operation will take place unless approved by two thirds of the closed company shareholders. Thus the DSM has a veto under the terms of both the 1967 and the 1976 decrees.

The first two Dutch offshore oil fields came on stream at the end of 1982, and are operated by NAM and Nedloyd. NAM, whose constitution we examined when looking at the Dutch natural gas industry, is by far the largest holder of acreage on the Dutch continental shelf.

Through their participation in NAM and in Gasunie, Shell and Esso are heavily involved in the production, distribution and marketing of natural gas as well as oil. It has been argued that given the structure of Gasunie,

[73] These minimum expenditures are specified in the relevant decrees: 1976 Decree: the work obligation is based on minimum expenditures divided into two periods. Licensees must expend $75.00 per km^2 during the first six year period and $20.000 per km^2 during the following three years. 1967 Decree: the sum is $3.000 per km^2 for the first five year period, $6.000 for the second five year period and nothing for the final five year period.

[74] 1967 Decree – at the end of the second period.

that organisation has been limited in its ability to act independently of oil interests.[75]

Production of petroleum and various heating oils is completely in the hands of the large international companies. In 1972 their respective percentages of refining capacity were as follows: Mobil 6.5, Esso 16.2, Chevron 16.1, Shell 30.3, Gulf 4.7, and BP 26.0. Two other companies have petroleum produced for them in Dutch refineries: they are Petrofina and CFP. The smaller, independent distributors usually group together in purchasing consortia, such as the ABG – a central purchasing organisation of 19 members, responsible for some 4 per cent of the petroleum distribution in Holland.[76] The presence of the 'spot market' in Rotterdam exercises an important influence not only on Community oil prices in times of market pressures, but also on the Dutch government's policy towards oil companies.[77]

All oil companies which refine or have refining done for them in the Netherlands are represented in the Olie Contact Commissie (OCC), a discussion group formed in 1966 to facilitate contacts with the government. The OCC has representatives at the Directorate General for Energy Production within the Economics Ministry. The Netherlands Oil and Gas Exploration and Production Association (NOGEPA) represents companies engaged in offshore exploration and production.

Italy is also a country heavily dependent on imported oil. Oil accounted for 71 per cent of total consumption in 1981, but of the total 95.01 mtoe only 1.51 mtoe was domestically produced. A State-owned oil company – AGIP – had been formed in 1926 to explore for oil at home and abroad, and although it had little success in finding oil, it did manage to build up a distribution network: at the onset of the 1973 crisis AGIP accounted for 25 per cent of the market for finished products. Restrictive price controls introduced in mid-1973 lessened the attractions of the Italian market for the big international companies, and in that year, both BP and Shell sold off their distribution networks, the former to the Monti group, and the latter to ENI, the state holding company for the hydrocarbons sector. Hence ENI boosted its market share for all oil products from 25 per cent to 33 per cent. The second largest supplier of petroleum products is Esso with 15 per cent of the market.[78]

ENI has met with little success in its exploration efforts abroad, and increased reliance has been placed on inter-governmental agreements ex-

[75] See also Evans, I. M., "Changing Policy Perspectives for Natural Gas", (1981) 3 Energy Policy.

[76] See *B.P.* v. *E.C. Commission* [1978] C.M.L. Rep. 174.

[77] Arida, T. "Oil Power and Politics" in Speigel, S., *At Issue: Politics in the World Arena* (1977).

[78] Grayson, L., *supra*, note 21, at p. 122.

changing goods and services for oil. Beside its interests in gas and oil exploration, production, transport, refining and marketing, ENI is also involved in nuclear energy (Agip-Nucleare) and in coal (Agip Carbone) as well as mechanical manufacturing (Nuovo Pignone), textiles (TESCON), chemicals (ANIC) and financing (SOFID). Having been allocated the role of state energy corporation by the CIPE, ENI has sought to consolidate its position in coal and nuclear, but whereas in France energy enterprises have diversified to secure greater independence from the State, ENI's extensive interests in chemicals and its refining and distribution activities have led to heavy losses, adversely affecting overall profitability.

The Unione Petrolifera is the professional and trade association for the oil industry. It includes all the leading private sector companies, but the State company, ENI is not a member, in contrast to Britain and France where the State-owned companies are members of such organisations. The Unione represents its members at governmental level on matters relating to the State of the Italian oil market, oil supply and pricing. The Federazione Italiana Gestioni Impianti Stradali Carburanti (FIGISC) is a trade association for retailers of motor fuels, negotiating on contracts and pricing with the major oil companies, State agencies and government departments.

In the field of control of access to national production, the Law nr. 136 of February 10, 1953,[79] conferring on ENI the task of 'promoting and carrying out enterprises of national interest in the field of hydrocarbons and natural gas' was the first specific piece of legislation to distinguish hydrocarbons from other minerals. As we have noted it gave the ENI exclusive rights of exploration and exploitation in the Po Valley. Law nr. 613 of July 21, 1967[80] also gave ENI, for a limited period, exclusive prospecting rights in the territorial waters and on the Italian Continental Shelf. The *permesso di ricerca* is exclusive and if it is for onshore exploration it is issued by the Minister of Industry and is valid for four years with a possible four-year renewal if conditions are fulfilled. An offshore prospecting permit is valid for one year while exploration permits are valid for twelve years, and are issued by Decree of the Minister of Industry.[81] Any applicant company must have its company offices in Italy and be subject to Italian law.[82] Financial and technical capabilities are taken into consideration. The area covered by an exploration permit must not exceed 500,000 hectares, excluding the Continental Shelf. At the end of the first four-year period, the area of the licence is reduced by 25 per cent.

79 In Gazz. Uff. March 27, 1953, no. 72.

80 In Gazz. Uff. August 3, 1967, no. 194.

81 Law no. 6 of January 11, 1957, in Gazz. Uff. January 29, 1957, no. 25.

82 For a discussion of the provisions for reciprocity under the 1967 Law, see Costopoulos, V.T., "Examen de la loi italienne du 21 juillet 1967 relative à la recherche et l'exploitation des hydrocarbures sur la mer territoriale et le plateau continental dans la lumière du droit d'établissement" (1969) Revue du Marché Commun 193.

Concessions for both onshore and offshore production are also granted by Decree of the Minister of Industry, and are initially for a period of 30 years with a possible renewal for a further 10 years. After two-thirds of the initial period has elapsed, the holder is entitled to automatic renewal if he has fully carried out the exploitation programme. The holder of an exploration permit has a priority claim on a production concession, and he must present his claim 120 days before the expiry of the permit. The authorities have powers to determine the viability of the desposits, to approve the work programme and to attach various conditions to the concession. Conditions on the production of natural gas may be imposed without prejudice to the future production of oil. A slightly different system of concessions and permits obtains for the five autonomous regions.[83]

Germany is the largest consumer of oil in Western Europe even though it must import 89 per cent of its oil requirements. While oil produced in Germany had supplied one third, i. e. 3.3 million tons of domestic consumption in 1955, and although local production doubled in the early seventies, consumption had increased fifteen times. As we shall see below, the government had instituted a coal protection policy, and consequently, heavy fuel oils were at a competitive disadvantage vis-à-vis coal, and the less a company produced, the better off it was. However, the government was anxious to ensure that security of the existing small domestic crude base was amplified by having a crude base of some size under the management of German companies. To this end it encouraged the formation of Deminex in 1969 by eight independent German companies, including Veba AG and Gelsenberg AG. Only these two firms had oil refining and marketing operations. The objective of Deminex was to supply crude oil to an independent German oil industry.

The largest producer of domestic oil is Gewerkschaft Elwerath-Brigitta, a company owned by Shell and Esso.

As a result of the merger with Gelsenberg in 1973, Veba, a company which had interests in coal mining and electricity supply as well as an 18.5 per cent holding in Deminex, and in which the State had a 44 per cent holding,[84] now acquired a 54 per cent controlling interest in Deminex and a 56 per cent share in Aral, Germany's largest petroleum distribution network, with a 25 per cent share of the market. In January 1979, after sustaining heavy losses for two consecutive years, Veba decided to join

[83] The regional laws relating to onshore activities are: Sicily — 1. rg. 5 August 1949, no. 45; 1 rg. 20 March, 1950, no. 30; and 1. rg. 1 October 1956, no. 54. Trentino-Alto Adige — 1. rg. 21 November 1958, no. 29. Sardegna — 1. rg. 19 December 1959; 1. rg. 7 May 1957, no. 15.

[84] The State is reducing this holding to 30 per cent, Financial Times, December 31, 1983.

forces with Deutsche BP, a company in a similar financial predicament, both having no access to domestic oil production. In return for DM 800 million and a twenty year contract to supply 3 million tons of crude, per annum, Veba sold to Deutsche BP its original Gelsenberg interests, including its 25 per cent share of Ruhrgas, but retained its shares in Aral and Deminex.

The refining industry is dominated by sixteen companies, twelve of them under foreign control, which account together for about 85 per cent of all product sales, while 'independent' traders account for the remaining 15 per cent.[85] The German subsidiaries of the international companies control a substantial part of the petroleum market: Shell (16 per cent), Esso (15 per cent), and BP (10 per cent), while the small independents account for 21 per cent of this market. As regards other oil products, the importance of the spot market in Rotterdam as a source of a large quantity of Germany's heating oils should not be overlooked, particularly as this is one area where the German private, independent companies have remained dominant. There are over 14,000 independent dealers engaged in the distribution of middle distillates.

Companies engaged in exploration and production of oil and gas are represented by the Wirtschaftsverband Erdöl- und Erdgasgewinnung e. v. (WEG) while companies involved in marketing and refining petroleum products are represented by the Mineralöl-Wirtschaftsverband e. V. which presents the views of the oil industry to the government.

The concern expressed by the German Monopolkommission about vertical and conglomerate forms of concentration in the energy sector, has already been noted in our discussion on electricity.[86] Companies involved in the exploitation of natural gas and oil have extensive interests not only in the respective distribution markets, but also the gas industry has become dependent on the interests of the petroleum industry. Hence the Cartel Office attempted to block the proposed merger of BP and Veba in 1979, on the grounds that the transfer of the Veba holding in Ruhrgas to BP would greatly strengthen the already dominant position of the gas company. Veba still retains considerable interests in coal mining and electricity production.

The supervision of mining operations, including exploration and production of oil and natural gas come within the competence of the individual Länder. At present there is some disagreement between the Federal Government and the Länder concerning jurisdiction over offshore areas. A provisional system was in force until August 1980[87] under which an exploration permit was issued by the regional office of Clausthal-Zellerfeld, which

[85] Petroleum Economist, April 1982.
[86] *Supra* note 17.
[87] The Mining Act, August 1980, BGBI I p. 1310.

covers the Länder of Lower Saxony, Schleswig-Holstein, Bremen and Hamburg. Initial exploration permits are granted for three years and may be renewed for additional periods without limit, although minimum operations conditions are attached. The same is true of onshore exploration permits. Permission to explore for oil on German soil is granted by the Regional Mining Office of the Land in question.[88]

The duration of both onshore and offshore production permits is for an initial period of 30 years and may be renewed automatically for 10 year periods without licence. The size of the area for which onshore permits

Table 11

Concentration in Oil Production

Country	Organisation	Control	Share of Market
UK	BNOC	100% State owned	can acquire 51% of oil produced
France	Elf-Aquitaine (SNEA)	70% State owned	
Holland	N/a		
Italy	ENI	100% State owned	exclusive production rights
Germany	Gewerkschaft Deutsche Texaco	Shell/Esso – 50% private	40% domestic production 35% domestic production

Table 12

Oil Distribution: Concentration

Country	Organisation	Control	Share of Market
UK	BP Shell Esso	Private	22% retail petroleum market 25% retail petroleum market 22% retail petroleum market
France	Total Elf	Subsidiary of CFP Subsidiary of Elf-Aquitaine	50% finished products
Holland	Shell BP	Private	30.3% refining 26% refining
Italy	Agip	Subsidiary of ENI	34% finished products
Germany	ARAL	VEBA 54% Mobil 28%	25% petroleum products

[88] The Mining Act of 12 May, 1934.

may be granted differs according to the Land in question. Unless otherwise specified, the area must lie within the area covered by the grant of exploration rights.

III. Permanent Controls on the Operation of Energy Markets: Imports and Exports

In this section we will examine two aspects of regulatory activity which are important to the management of strategic energy resources: regulation of imports and exports of energy supplies, and price regulation of and subsidies to the energy industries. In discussing the latter aspect it is important to distinguish between general price régimes and arrangements adopted for particular energy industries.

A. Coal

Although the volume of sales of Community coal has stabilised in the last few years, Community coal production has been under competitive pressure from imported coal, and the coal industry has been repeatedly forced to align its own prices on the low prices for imported steam coal. Intra-Community trade in coal, however, remains low, with the UK only delivering 2 per cent of its production to other EC countries in 1979 and Germany delivering 14.6 per cent of its production, mainly coking coal, to other Member States. France delivers a further 2 per cent of its production to other members.[89]

In the *United Kingdom* there are at present no administrative controls on the importation or exportation of coal, and the low percentage of exports is a result of the lack of competitiveness of British coal.[90]

In *France* Article 6 of the 1946 law nationalising the coal industry provided that a *règlement d'administration publique* (R. A. P.)[91] would establish conditions on which coal imports and exports would be regulated by the State. A décret of January 24, 1948, enacting the R. A. P. set up the Association technique de l'importation charbonniere (ATIC) to act as an 'intermédiaire obligatoire' in the importation of coal. The obligations and responsibilities of the ATIC are laid down in a Convention of April 7, 1948 and Article 19 of the Convention reserves the right to the State to appoint a Commissaire du Gouvernement who can exercise a veto on all decisions of the Association. Representatives from CDF, SNCF, EDF, GDF and the steel

[89] Memorandum from the Commission on the Financial Aid awarded by the Member States to the Coal Industry in 1980, COM(81) 96 Final.

[90] I.E.A.; Energy Policies and Programmes of IEC Countries (1980) at p. 29.

[91] De Laubadère, *supra* note 31, at para 827.

industries sit on the ATIC Conseil d'administration. The Convention gave the ATIC a monopoly on coal imports over the next 45 years, but it is doubtful whether this monopoly will be renewed at the end of the period. The VIIIth Plan stresses[92] the role that imported coal will play in future energy supplies, and stresses the need for French companies to gain direct access to foreign coal reserves. This could be achieved either by long-term contracts negotiated between French companies and foreign producers, or by French coal companies directly undertaking production abroad. At present four French companies are engaged in production abroad – CFP (via Total), COGEMA, CDF International and Elf.

A recent Rapport Préparatoire by the Ministry of Industry suggested that French coal imports policy should be revised within the next three years and that ATIC's monopoly be withdrawn and replaced with a system of licences, similar to those in force for petroleum products.[93]

Neither *Italy* nor the *Netherlands* operate a specific regime pertaining to coal imports and exports.

In *Germany* tariff quotas on coal imports have been imposed since 1958. In September of that year the High Authority, acting under article 74 (3) of the ECSC Treaty, sent a recommendation to the Federal Government inviting it to impose a provisional customs duty on all imports from third countries and to fix a minimum free quota of 5 million tonnes for 1959. That quota remains in force today.[94]

B. Oil and Gas

Given the strategic importance of these two products it is more than likely that we will find some sort of permanent regulation of the movement across borders.

In the *United Kingdom*, the primary obligation on licence holders is that all petroleum won and saved must be delivered on shore in the United Kingdom, unless the licensing authority gives written consent to deliver elsewhere once delivered onshore. The rules for oil and gas differ, and so each product will be treated separately. The United Kingdom has no formal export restrictions on oil at the present time,[95] and the only official

92 The VIIIth Plan, Section II, *supra* note 89.

93 Le Ministre Délégué auprès du Ministre de l'Industrie Chargé de l'Energie, Document Préparatoire au Débat sur l'Energie (1981), at p. 118.

94 The validity of this recommendation was sustained by the European Court of Justice in case 36/83, *Mabanaft GmbH* v. *Hauptzollamt Emmerich* (June 28, 1984, not yet reported).

95 Orders can be made under the Import, Export and Customs (Defence) Act 1939, s. 1. Several orders were made under this Act during the 1973 oil crisis, e.g. Export of Goods (Control) (Amendment No. 4), Order S.I. 1973/1779. There still exist informal restrictions: see 967 H.C. Deb., col. 185 (May 24, 1979) and *Bulk Oil (Zug)* v. *Sun International Trading Co.* [1984]; W.L.R. 147.

formulation of a policy restriction on freedom of disposal of oil was the so-called refining policy of the Labour Government 1974–1979, which required that two-thirds of UK production should be refined in the United Kingdom.[96]

At present there are no direct prohibitions on the export of gas from the United Kingdom. However there are three indirect barriers to its export: the requirement that all petroleum won and saved be, with minor exceptions, landed onshore in the United Kingdom, unless permission to land it elsewhere has been given:[97] the necessity for the Secretary of State's consent to the liquefaction of natural gas[98] and the necessity for permission for the construction of an export pipeline through controlled waters.[99] Together these requirements give the Secretary of State the means, by the selective withholding of this consent, to ensure that virtually all gas is consumed in the United Kingdom. Of these controls, the landing requirement is the most significant, and although taken alone it is of strictly temporary significance, over the long term is has meant, when taken in conjunction with the other controls, that virtually all the gas from those offshore fields currently in production is now contracted to be sold in the domestic market, mainly via the BGC.

In *France*, control over imports of crude oil, its derivatives and residues, was introduced into France by Article 53 of the Law of April 4, 1926, and the Law of March 30, 1928 introduced a system of quotas based on import licences as the means by which the State would exercise control. Two types of licence were introduced: A20's (later to become A13's and then A10's as the duration was shortened) for refining of crude oil and A3's for the importation of finished products.[100] Article 2 of the 1928 Law specified that authorisations for the importation of crude were discretionary and granted exclusively to refining companies, permitting them to process a specified quantity annually. Authorisations were granted to the individual companies by Décret in the Conseil d'Etat, whereas A3 authorisations were granted by a 'décret commun', to all companies, fixing an annual quota for internal consumption.

Hence the 1928 law set out to fulfill two objectives: to guarantee security of supplies and to develop a national oil industry, particularly in refining, and this was achieved primarily through the regulation of imports. Licences were however used to impose further obligations on the oil companies,

96 Speech by R. Morell, reported in the Financial Times, March 30, 1976.

97 Petroleum (Production) Regulations 1982, Sched. 5, cl. 27.

98 Energy Act 1976, s. 9, as revised by Sched. 3, para 37 of the Oil and Gas (Enterprise) Act 1982.

99 Petroleum and Submarine Pipelines Act 1975, s. 20.

100 A 20's were shortened in validity from 20 years to 13 years (A13's) by decrees 50–1319 to 50–1326 of October 18, 1950 and to ten years (A10's) by decrees 63–198 to 63–207 of February 27, 1963.

with regard to the maintenance of stocks, and requirements that two-thirds of all imports would be carried on French flag ships, and that companies would be under French management, and finally that on request from the government they conclude contracts of 'national interest'.[101] In 1964 the Conseil d'Etat ruled that the 1928 law was intended to allow the State to exercise a 'contrôle étroit' over the entirety of the activities of the oil industry.[102]

The French government regarded the system as being in the nature of a 'delegated monopoly', and offered considerable resistance to Commission efforts to secure its modification, under article 37 of the EEC treaty, in the interests of free movement of oil products within the Community. While minor modifications were made to allow for the inclusion of Franc Zone oil in 1961[103] and in 1968[104] to allow for the provisions of the EEC Treaty on the right of establishment, even in 1968 the then Minister of Industry, Bettencourt, issued a statement in the National Assembly, in effect reaffirming the original objectives of the 1928 law: i.e., that security of supply was to be sought, that the national companies were to retain at least 50 per cent of the domestic market and that the refining industry was to be strengthened.[105] Only in 1978, as we shall see[106], were major modifications agreed with the Commission.[107]

In the *Netherlands* article 24 of the 1976[108] Decree and article 24 of the 1967 Decree stipulate that a licence holder must not sell natural gas produced on the Dutch Continental Shelf if the approval of the Minister of Economic Affairs has not been obtained. If the natural gas is intended

101 See the decree of February 27, 1963, *supra*, note 100, and Decree No. 58–249 of March 10, 1958.

102 See the Conseil d'Etat decision in the *Société Shell-Bèrre* case, RDP. 1964. 1019.

103 A decree of June 1956 assimilated national oil production to crude oil originating from within the Franc Zone, with both types being exempted from the quota system provided for under the 1928 Law. A further Decree No. 70–839 of August 28, 1970 subjected all persons processing crude oil, or its derivatives or residues for the supply of the domestic market to the obligations set out in the 1928 Law.

104 Following two recommendations from the Commission of April 13, 1962 and July 24, 1968, the quotas for the importation of petroleum products originating in member states were augmented. The Decree of February 27, 1968 gave increased market shares to AGIP and SIPEC and the earlier Decree of 1965 granted A3's to ARAL and Zeller. As noted in note 100 supra, the Decree of 1970 subjected all persons, physical or moral, processing crude, its derivatives or residues for domestic consumption as petroleum products, whatever their origin, to the law of 1928. For a review of the EC Commission's attitude to the French system of import licences, see Touret, D. *Le régime français d'import du pétrole et la CEE* (1968).

105 J.O.R.F. Ass. Nat. November 5, 1968, p. 3909.

106 See Chapter V, p. 124 *infra*.

107 See Chapter VI for the implications for this regime of Articles 34 and 37 of the EEC Treaty.

108 See note 72, *supra*.

for consumption in the Netherlands, the licensee is required to supply that gas to the N.V. Gasunie (Article 25(1)), and furthermore he is required to supply natural gas to Gasunie insofar as the Minister determines that such natural gas is needed for the gas supply in the Netherlands. Such a determination is valid for two years, but if the Minister has already approved alternative destinations on the part of the licensee, in accordance with article 24, then this requirement cannot apply (Article 25 (5)).

Following the discovery of the large Groningen field, NAM/Export pursued an elevated price policy for Dutch gas, giving Soviet gas a competitive edge in Western European markets in the late sixties. However, fearing that she might be left with an unmarketable reserve of gas, once cheap North African gas flooded the market, the company's policy was re-adjusted to give a cost advantage to European markets. Long-term contracts of between 20 and 25 years were negotiated and by 1972 export markets were absorbing 42 per cent of Dutch gas production. From 1973 to 1983 the Netherlands committed itself to a policy of reducing export obligations. This meant that exports, which peaked in 1977 at 50 billion m^3, would as existing contracts terminated have declined to 30 billion m^3 by 1990 and to almost zero by 1998.[109] The relaxation in 1983 of the ban on new export contracts will mean higher export levels at these dates.

In Italy the law no. 613 of 1967 regulating exploration and production on the Italian Continental Shelf imposes an obligation on all concessionaires to deliver any oil or gas found to a place on the mainland, as indicated by the Minister of Industry. The concessionaire has the right to be refunded the costs of transportation. Import levels are indirectly regulated through controls on refinery construction.[110]

It should be noted that in *Germany* there are no legal controls on the importation or exportation of oil or gas.[111]

IV. Permanent Controls on the Operation of Energy Markets: Price Control in the Energy Sector

In this section we examine existing price controls in each energy sector in the context of the general system of price regulation in each country under study, and focus on particular price controls adopted with respect to each energy industry. We will also examine whether the operation of general, counter-inflation measures, has resulted in the implementation of a compensa-

[109] I.E.A., *Energy Policies and Programmes of I.E.A. Countries 1980 Review*, p. 203.
[110] R.d. July 20, 1934, no. 1303.
[111] EC Commission, Report on the Behaviour of the Oil Companies (1975).

tory scheme of subsidies. Such financial adjustments may give governments a potential control over the activities of their energy industries, without the need to resort to individual or specially designed legal measures.

A. Electricity, Oil, Gas and Petroleum Products

1. The United Kingdom

General statutory price controls have from time to time been established in the United Kingdom as part of a response to inflationary pressures, most recently in the periods 1966–70, under the Prices and Incomes Act 1966, and 1972–80, under the Counter-Inflation (Temporary Provisions) Act 1972 and the Counter-Inflation Act 1973. Each of these regimes began by imposing a standstill on all price increases, followed by a period of control by reference to quantitative limits and procedures for notification and scrutiny of proposed price increases. The 1973 Act was repealed by the Competition Act 1980, so that no general scheme of price control presently exists. The application of the 1973 scheme to energy prices is described in Chapter V.

1.1. Electricity and Gas

The nationalised industries, including the nationalised gas and electricity industries, are required by their respective statutes to break even, taking one year with another. Hence final product pricing will be linked to investment levels. Three White Papers[112] have been published in an attempt to clarify the economic and financial objectives of nationalised industries and to compensate for the lack of operational guidance contained in the nationalisation statutes themselves. Whereas the 1967 White Paper gave an explicit though not unambiguous, instruction to adopt long run marginal cost pricing, the 1978 White Paper emphasises the role of the various Boards in pricing decisions "to ensure that the main elements of the price structure are sensibly related to the costs of supply and the market situation"[113] and to avoid arbitrary cross-subsidisation. However the directives of the various White Papers have seldom been adhered to, as the nationalised industries have consistently been primary targets in the anti-inflation policies of successive governments, and their tariffs and prices frozen.

The government may also exercise substantial control over the pricing policies of the nationalised industries through the power to set cash limits for them. These are known as External Financing Limits (EFLs). An EFL sets a ceiling on the total of government grants, issues of Public Dividend Capital, net borrowing and leasing. A "negative" ceiling may be set, requiring

[112] The Financial and Economic Obligations of the Nationalised Industries, Cmnd.1337 (1961); Nationalised Industries: A Review of Economic and Financial Objectives, Cmnd.3437 (1967); the Nationalised Industries, Cmnd.7131 (1978).

[113] Cmnd.7131, *supra* note 112, para 68.

the industry to make a surplus. They will have less impact on the more profitable nationalised industries which are self-financing, such as BGC, but can be harmful to the more vulnerable industries such as the NCB which has fragile current finances and a heavy investment commitment. If there is no source of price monitoring, EFLs can be met through price increases.[114]

Direct, but non-statutory, intervention in the tariff structures of any of the nationalised industries is also possible. As part of the British government's counter-inflation policy, gas and electricity prices were frozen between 1972 and 1973, and as a result, the government was obliged to grant financial aid to both the CEGB and the BGC following a period of price restraint on the part of the two nationalised industries.[115]

1.2. Oil

Through BNOC, which handles more than half of UK North Sea oil production, the government sought, until March 1985,[116] to ensure that term prices of North Sea oil remained broadly in line with levels set by OPEC; the price of petroleum products on the domestic market is not currently regulated.

2. France

Control of prices on all products is exercised on the basis of the powers attributed to the administration by Ordonnance 45—1853 of June 30, 1945, which enabled the government to determine prices and margins at all stages of the production of a product. In practice four types of price control evolved: ***liberté controlée, liberté contractuelle, liberté conventionelle*** and ***programmation des prix industriels,*** each being applied to different products at various times.[117]

2.1. Electricity

Following the publication of the Nora Report in 1967[118] which recommended that the public enterprises be given more freedom in the management of their affairs a 'contrat du programme' was concluded between EDF and the State on the December 23, 1970. In exchange for this liberty of management, EDF was to observe certain objectives over the next five-year period, relating to productivity, profitability, and self-finance. EDF was also to be free to set its own tariffs, subject to the limitation that the

[114] See Heald, D. "UK Energy Policy: Economic and Financial Control of the Nationalised Energy Industries", in (1981) 6 Energy Policy 99 at p. 109.

[115] Prices and Charges (Notification of Increases) Order 1978, S.I. 1978/1083.

[116] See note 55, *supra*.

[117] See Chapter V, p. 101.

[118] Rapport sur les entreprises publiques, 4th April 1967, Ed. Documentation Française, 1967.

annual increase in average tariffs would not exceed 1.85 per cent. In fact the contract was revised each year between 1971 and 1975 to allow for greater increases in tariffs, and in 1976 the contract was finally abandoned. The overall financial position of EDF suffered as a result of the delay in permission to raise tariffs to compensate for the rise in fuel prices following the 1973 crisis.

As a result a large proportion of EDF's investment programme, particularly the development of nuclear power generation, has had to be financed from outside the company, and because of its heavy indebtedness, the possibilities on the financial market were restricted, leading to a heavy reliance on State finance. Initially the State contributions were made exclusively in the form of loans from the Fonds de Developpement Economique et Sociale (FDES), but in order to help the company break out of the vicious circle of increasing indebtedness the State several times converted old loans from the FDES into allocations of capital.[119] With the signing of the *'contrat du programme'* in 1968 EDF was given greater freedom in pricing policy and its financial situation improved. However the rise in fuel oil prices checked this period of recovery, and EDF once more was forced to rely on allocations of capital and loans from the FDES, especially to finance its heavy investment programme of nuclear generators. The FDES is an important source of finance for the whole energy sector.[120]

2.2. Gas

Gas prices are still subject to a system of *liberté surveillée*. Any change in the price must be authorised by an *arrêté* of the Minister of Industry or of Finance. These orders lay down the permissible price variations, for domestic and trade tariffs. Industrial contract tariffs and certain two-part tariffs for high levels of consumption are linked to an index which is fixed in the *cahier des charges* of the concessionaires, and in the contracts between GDF and its customers. However limited use is made of this index as contract tariffs were made subject to the prior approval system by an *arrêté* of April 28, 1971. All new price schedules must be approved by either the Minister of Industry or Finance. GDF has also suffered from cash flow problems, as a result of prices being held down between 1970 and 1976, and has also had to rely on external finance, notably from the FDES, to finance its extensive investment programme.

119 For an explanation of the role of the FDES in the funding of public enterprise, see Fromont, M., "Le Contrôle des aides financières publiques aux entreprises", Actualité Juridique Droit Administratif, 1979.3.

120 See Hau, E., "Le Fonds de Développement Economique et Social (FDES) et les Investissements des Entreprises Publiques", (1977) 4 Revue Française d'Administration Publique 761.

2.3. Petroleum

Powers to regulate the price of petroleum have existed since 1925 when a law of that year gave the local Prefet powers to fix prices. In 1937 a Comité Nationale de Surveillance des Prix was given responsibility for petroleum prices. After the enactment of the 1945 Ordonnance the prices of gasoline and diesel were subject to a so-called system of *liberté controlée*, but in fact the *barèmes* were set by the DICA and the Direction du Prix and could not be negotiated.

3. The Netherlands

General powers to set prices in the Netherlands exist under the Prijzenwet of 1961.[121] However this law was never applied to gas prices. Only maximum prices can be imposed under the Prijzenwet, but part of the policy of the government has been to secure minimum prices for natural gas.

Following the increase in oil prices after October 1973, the Dutch government sought a basis on which to renegotiate prices for natural gas in long term contracts, finding it in the Wet Aardgasprijzen of 1974, which gives the Minister of Economic Affairs powers to fix minimum prices for the sale of both domestic gas and gas for export.[122] Moreover, we should note that prior to the issue of the 1976 Decree based on the 1965 Mijnwet Continentaal Plat, the pricing policy of NAM and Gasunie was based on a 'convention' concluded between these bodies and the government in 1963,[123] whose comprehensiveness limited the utility of other controls.

[121] The aims of the Prijzenwet 1961 are as follows:
(i) maintenance of short-term equilibrium in face of threats to excess supply or demand which could lead to undesirable concentration in a sector;
(ii) to take action against asymmetrical price formation via price fixing in a sector;
(iii) to assure transparency in conditions of sale.
Article 1(2) applies the provisions of the Act to the entire economy, or to specific sectors, and to all goods and services. Measures may be taken under the law when the general socio-economic situation so demands. The Minister of Economic Affairs has complete discretion in deciding whether or not measures are necessary. Prices are regulated by a "ministeriele beschikkingen" issued by the Minister of Economic Affairs and any other Minister involved. Article 4 provides for prior consultation with the enterprises which will be affected. There is no time limit on duration of a ministerial decision.

[122] See further, Chapter V.

[123] The Agreement of Cooperation signed on March 27, 1963 gave the Minister of Economic Affairs certain powers regarding prices of natural gas:
- the right to approve transfer prices between NAM and Gasunie;
- the right to approve the gas sales plan;
- the right to approve conditions and tariffs for the delivery of gas to the public distribution companies in the Netherlands as well as the right to approve price levels to other consumer categories supplied by Gasunie:
- the right to approve construction of transmission lines and other equipment for the storage of gas;

4. *Italy*

In Italy all gas, electricity and petroleum product prices are fixed by the CIP (Comitato Interministeriale dei Prezzi). This body was set up by the Decree Law no. 347 of October 19, 1944 and its operations are governed by Decree Law no. 363 of April 23, 1946. Article 4 of the former decree gives the CIP extensive powers to determine prices at each stage of the production and commercialisation of a product. With the reform of the CIPE in 1967, the CIP was given major responsibility for price formation. Article 2 of the Decree of June 30, 1968 states that the CIP would be subject to the directives of the CIPE as regards the determination of sectors and the categories of goods and service to be regulated. In the case of electricity and gas, the CIPE issues general guidelines on pricing and tariff policy and these are implemented by the CIP, which also fixes conditions of sale. At the time of the oil crisis of 1973, a general price freeze was in force.[124] The freeze was imposed in two phases: in the first prices were completely frozen from July 16, 1973 to October 31, 1973 but from December 1, 1973 until July 31, 1974 a *blocco elastico* applied. Under the latter system the CIP had to approve price increases at every stage of production and distribution.[125]

The State electricity utility, ENEL, has been subject to the constraints of a pricing policy based on political exigencies: domestic tariffs have always been held down, resulting in the under-capitalisation of the company. The financial difficulties of the ENEL have been heightened by increased investment demands necessary to convert oil-fired stations to coal and to construct nuclear plant. It has been estimated that a 48.5 per cent increase in investment levels for the period 1981–84 as compared to the period 1970–80 will be needed to meet the requirements of the 1980 National Energy Programme.[126] Heavy reliance is placed on the "fondo dotazione" from the State, but increasingly this must go to service long-term debts rather than to improve productive capacity. These funds were provided for under the Law no. 253 of May 7, 1973, but numerous additional grants have been made since that date.[127]

– the right to approve Dutch border prices for export sales;
– the right to have a limited quantity of gas supplied by Gasunie at prices and on conditions, after consultation with that company, to customers designated by the Minister, should he consider this desirable for the economic development of certain parts of the country.

124 See decreto-legge July 24, 1973, no. 473, converted by the law of August 4, 1973.

125 See Quadri, G., *Diritto Pubblico dell'Economia* (1980), at p. 364.

126 Mondo Economico, November 11th 1981, p. 57.

127 For example Law no. 309 of July 15, 1981 in Gazz. Uff., July 18, 1981, no. 166 makes provision for an extra grant of 3.000m. Lire.

5. *Germany*

In Germany the law of April 10, 1948, as extended by the law of March 29, 1951, gives the Federal Minister of Economics powers to set prices for goods and services of whatever nature when the orders are to apply to more than one Land, or when the formation of a price will have repercussions on more than one Land. Otherwise the Minister of Economics of the individual Länder have competence to set prices.[128] The Federal Constitutional Court has ruled that Article 2 of the law only authorises a 'defensive' pricing policy, rather than an 'active' one, designed to overcome certain market anomalies.[129] However special regulations exist for gas and electricity tariffs. The 1935 Law on the Energy Industry, article 7 provides that the tariffs of gas and electricity distribution companies must be approved by the Minister of Economics of the Länder. Although non-tariff customers are also in theory covered by state regulation, in practice it would seem that this control has proved ineffective.[130] Municipally owned companies are required to pursue socio-economic objectives, services being provided as a public utility.[131] However most municipal companies have interests in other areas and electricity and gas tariffs are usually used

[128] Zacher, H.F., *Rapport sur le droit économique en République Fédérale d'Allemagne* (1973) at p. 107.

[129] Decision of the Federal Constitutional Court, vol. 8, pp. 274 and 311, 313, quoted in Zacher, *supra* note 128 at p. 108.

[130] Zacher, *op. cit. supra* note 128, at p. 169.

[131] The enactment in December 1976 of the Law Governing Standard Business Conditions (Gesetz zur Regelung des Rechts der Allgemeinen Geschäftsbedingungen – AGBG) (BGBL I, 3317) is of relevance to standard contracts for the supply of electricity and gas. Tariff customers (i.e. private customers) are not covered by the law, as these contracts are not based on private contractual agreement, but have been publicly regulated since 1942 by the Anordnung of 1942 (Reichs Anzeiger no. 39), made under para. 9 of the Energy Law of 1935. It seemed that special customer contracts, made under private agreement would be covered by the AGBG but following pressure from the utilities a derogation from para. 23,2 n. 2 of the AGBG was made, exempting special customer contracts in the electricity and gas sector from the operation of paras. 10 and 11 of the same law. However, para. 9 is applicable to these contracts, and states the general principle that standard conditions which "unreasonably disadvantage" one party will be invalid. In addition para. 23 states that the terms of these special customer contracts should not "deviate to the disadvantage of the customer" from the AVB applying to tariff customers. The AVB will therefore act as a kind of minimum standard for the special customers. Furthermore para. 26 of the AGBG amends para. 7 of the 1935 Energy Law, confirming the authority of the Minister of Economic Affairs to regulate the general conditions of supply, but introducing the notion of "balanced supply conditions". New general conditions of supply were introduced by executive order in 1979: the Verordnung über Allgemeine Bedingungen für die Elektrizitätsversorgung von Tarifkunden – ABGEltV, BGBl I, 684, and Verordnung über Allgemeine Bedingungen für die Gasversorgung von Tarifkunden – AVBGasV, BGBl I, 676 both of which improve the position of customers vis-à-vis the supplying companies.

to subsidise less profitable activities, for example in the public transport sector.[132]

Hence the five countries considered here divide broadly into those favourable to an administered system – France and Italy, with detailed controls on pricing and supply, and those who use controls to achieve more limited, energy policy goals, e.g. Holland and the United Kingdom. Germany relies heavily on legislation relating to competition and the control of the abuse of the market, although it should be pointed out that these regulations are often used in such a way as to ensure the continued presence of German companies in their relevant markets.[133]

B. Coal

The coal industry is perhaps a special case in France, Germany and the United Kingdom in that subsidies and capital grants have been an almost permanent feature of coal policy since the 1950's. The nationalised coal industries of the United Kingdom and France have been kept under-capitalised for the last two decades, but are now expected to sustain increased production of an uncompetitive energy source, and hence they rely heavily on subsidies. It should be pointed out that in this sector we find a mixture of economic and social aids, coal mines being concentrated in particular regions in France, Germany and Britain and hence generating problems of structural adjustment. The following tables show the production costs and returns of Community coal mines in 1979 and the level of subsidies granted in that year. It should be pointed out that the sum of 10.98 EUA per tonne for *Germany* does not include the effects of the Third Electricity from Coal Law of 1974 which lays down that German power stations must buy steam coal from the coal industry at break-even prices. The additional cost incurred by the electricity utilities using coal is offset by increased electricity prices, via the imposition of the 'Kohlepfenning'.[134] This off-set levy amounted to some 2.1

132 An attempt to define the objectives of the municipal utilities was made by the Verband kommunaler Unternehmen in 1975: "10 Thesen zur Stellung der kommunalen Versorgungsunternehmen" in Wirtschaft und Gesellschaft, Köln, p. 8 et seq. These objectives include the statement that municipal public utilities fulfil the public tasks of providing electricity and gas according to social economic principles. Prices are fixed by social economic principles. Any surplus is exclusively used for the pursuit of public objectives.

133 Levy, G., "The Relations between Oil Companies and Oil Consuming Countries" (1984) 2 Journal of Energy and Natural Resources Law 9.

134 The "Kohlepfennig" introduced by the 1974 electricity-from-coal law, was originally levied at 2.7% of the invoiced price of electricity consumed by both domestic and industrial customers. In 1976 the rate was raised to 4.5% but as from January 1, 1978 different rates applied according to region, although the federal average remained at 4.5%. On January 1, 1979, this federal average rose to 6.2% with the regional difference being maintained. This supplementary charge (Ausgleichsabgabe) is transferred to the Federal authorities in full. See further, Chapter V, note 141, *infra*.

Table 13

Production Costs and Returns of Community Coal Mines in 1979

	Production Costs	Returns	Difference(EUA/t)
Germany	66	59	– 7
France	68	43	–25
UK	48	41	– 7

(EUA/t) (= European Unit of Account/per ton)

Table 14

Coal Subsidies (1979)

	Total (millions EUA)	Amounts per tonne (EUA)
Germany	1,023.5	10.98
France	296.8	48.65
Britain	279.2	2.31

Source: COM (81) 96 final[135]

thousand million DM in 1980 (8.90 EUA per tonne of coal output). It is not included in the EC tables because it is not considered a State aid. Moreover a substantial portion of the subsidies in all three countries are not related to current production, as Table 15 shows:

Subsidies to the *United Kingdom* coal industry have existed since 1965 when the sum of £ 415 million of capital debt was written off under the terms of the Coal Industry Act 1965. Substantial relief payments were made available under that Act and the later Coal Industry Act 1967 to mitigate the social costs arising from rapid contraction.[136]

[135] Memorandum from the Commission on the Financial Aid awarded by the Member States to the coal industry in 1980, COM (81) 96 final.

[136] The Treasury met one half of the costs arising from the redundancy payments and travel and transfer costs payable under the Act of 1965, subsequently raised to two-thirds under the 1967 Act. The total contribution on these counts rose from £1.3 million in 1966/7 to almost £10.8 million in 1967/9. In addition the 1967 Act stipulated that the State would meet the cost of supplementing the income of miners over 55 years of age who became redundant. These measures, due to expire in 1971, were extended subject to certain amendments. For example discretion could be exercised in setting the age limit for the early retirement scheme and instead of meeting a rigid two-thirds of social costs identified in the 1967 Act, grants were operated on a tapering basis over a number of years. For further details, see Select Committee on Nationalised Industries, The National Coal Board (1969) HC 471-I.

Table 15

Non-production Related Subsidies

Country	Social Security Measures		Aid to Cover Inherited Liabilities		
	1979	1980	1979	1980	
Germany	2,507.7	2,650.8	203.2	186.6	(million EUA)
France	1,202.0	1,340.9	78.7	97.5	
UK	52.1	67.4 (1)	26.6	28.4	

(1) The UK case is somewhat different as it has an integrated social security system and the figure here only covers the special miners' pension fund.

Source: COM (81) 96 final

In *France* where numerous plans dating from 1959 until 1974 planned for the gradual run-down of the coal industry,[137] government financial aid grew as rapidly as the CDF's commerical viability declined. Total aid had increased from FF 50 million in 1960 to FF 1,958 million in 1973. The Conseil de Planification of 1974 set new targets for coal for 1980[138], although the target was to be met by both imported and national coal. The 1978 'contrat du programme' set a lmit of 2.5 centimes per thermie on the level of state subsidisation. As in Germany a substantial portion of aid goes to non-productive charges.[139]

The use of coal has been encouraged in *Germany* since 1965, with the passing of the first electricity from coal law, which provided tax relief for firms using ECSC coal. In 1966 a second Electricity from Coal law granted a subsidy towards the extra cost of using Community coal.[140] From 1960 onwards a tax of DM 10 per tonne was placed on light fuel oil and DM 15 per tonne on heavy fuel oil.[141] The Coal Adaptation Law (Kohleanpassungsgesetz) of 1968 greatly increased the scope of State intervention in the coal industry with the appointment of a 'Coal Commissioner' who was empowered to make recommendations for the rationalisation of the industry. His recommendations resulted in the formation of the Ruhrkohle AG and under the "Verordnung über die Maßstäbe für die Ermittlung der optimalen Un-

[137] The Jeanneney Plan of 1959; the Plan de la Table Ronde of 1963; The Plan Bettencourt of 1967.

[138] See Chapter III, p. 41.

[139] "Le Renouveau du Charbon", Les Annales des Mines, mai-juin 1981, at p. 89.

[140] Second Electricity-from-coal law ("Zweites Verstromungsgesetz") BGBl I 1966, p. 545. See also the Third electricity-from-coal ("Drittes Verstromungsgesetz") December 13, 1974, BGBl I 1974, p. 3973.

[141] See coordinated text of the Petroleum Taxation Law "Mineralölsteuergesetz" or "MinöStG," BGBl I 1978, p. 1669.

ternehmensgröße im Steinkohlenbergbau"[142] the Commissioner could withdraw financial privileges and subsidies – i.e. interest subsidies on guaranteed loans and subsidies for inherited charges – if companies did not implement his recommendations. With the new league table position accorded to coal in the first Revision of the Energy Programme,[143] the decline in coal production was to be halted and further measures to assist the coal industry including aid to cover the costs of establishing coal stocks of up to 10 million tonnes were introduced. The Federal government was to bear two-thirds of the cost of establishing the stocks, and the Länder would bear the other one-third. Aid for capital investment and research was also increased.

V. Conclusion

These institutional structures and the legislative frameworks which shape the markets in which they function offer two possible approaches from which to assess national energy policies.

Firstly we have noted that, for a variety of reasons, energy markets are highly concentrated, and often dominated by monopolistic or oligopolistic structures. There is a strong vertical integration of the operational functions of the three principal energy sectors in each country: electricity, gas and oil. The oil industry has always been the vertically integrated industry par excellence, but many of the gas and electricity utilities control all the functions in the chain from production to distribution.

While it would be impossible in the context of this work to enter into a discussion of the complexities of organisational theory, the importance of institutional and market structures cannot be overlooked. Powerful institutions can intervene in decision-making by influencing the flow and interpretation of information, especially as many such institutions often possess a monopoly on the control of technical information. Large, publicly owned firms may be in a position to impose their own decisions with respect to long-range investment on governments. Governments seeking to formulate policies with respect to oil supplies sought to establish national companies which would compete with the existing 'majors' and hence operate as a source of information about the workings of the market. However, governments quickly found themselves presented with a dilemma: in order to compete on the international scene, these companies had themselves to become fully independent, integrated organisations, hence restricting the potential for government access and influence.

[142] January 7, 1969, BGBl I 1969, p. 16.

[143] See Chapter 3, p. 40.

Secondly, we have explored some of the existing patterns of state intervention in the functioning of energy markets, either through ownership or by regulation. At the beginning of the chapter we suggested that in most cases governments will tend to use powers stemming from existing relationships or will use existing sets of instruments to achieve their objectives. In the following chapter we will examine the extent to which this has been the case, and in Chapter 6 and 7 we will examine the implications for Community policy.

Chapter V

National Energy Policies

In this chapter we will present a brief overview of the main instruments deployed in each State to achieve the three objectives outlined in Chapter III:

- management of short-term disturbances in energy supplies
- alterations in the structure and level of energy demand
- alterations in the pattern of energy supply.

At the beginning of each of these sections we briefly recall the Community energy policy constraints, if any, on national policies in these fields. The background material provided in Chapter IV should provide a basis on which to assess the extent to which choice of instruments was influenced or constrained by existing institutional and regulatory frameworks.

I. Management of Short Term Disturbances in Energy Supplies

It is in the area of crisis management that there exist the most precise Community constraints on national policy, comprising the obligation to maintain stocks of petroleum sufficient for a given period of consumption,[1] and to possess (though not necessarily to use) powers to require the deployment of stocks, to restrict consumption, allocate supply, and control prices.[2]

A. General Measures

The immediate response of the governments of most of the States under study to the oil embargo of late October 1973 was to regulate the supply and utilisation of fuel by invoking powers in general emergency legislation: the Emergency Powers Act 1920 in the United Kingdom, the defence Ordonnance of 1959[3] in the case of France, and the Distributiewet 1939[4] in the

[1] Above, Chapter II, pp. 20–22.
[2] Above, Chapter II, p. 22.
[3] Ordonnance no. 59–147 of January 7, 1959, on the Organisation Générale de Defence, in J.O.R.F. January 10, 1959, p. 691.
[4] See Mok, M. R., "Distributiewet Rediviva", S.E.W. 1974, p. 23.

Netherlands. Various orders made under these laws gave the respective governments powers to introduce measures such as driving restrictions[5], petroleum rationing[6], and restrictions on the heating of public and private buildings.[7]

In *Italy*, the constitutional device of the *decreto-legge* was available for this as for other emergency situations, enabling the government to issue binding *decreti*, with the effect of laws, with a validity limited to 60 days. Thereafter a *decreto-legge* ceases to be effective, if not confirmed by Parliament in legislative form. In fact the only *decreto-legge* immediately issued was that restricting the circulation of vehicles during holiday periods.[8] Otherwise, the Italian government initially relied on powers under ordinary legislation, on road traffic or on exports,[9] to achieve energy saving effects.

The *German* government, by contrast, did not rely on general powers, but began immediately to prepare specialised legislation for the energy emergency. It soon became apparent to other Member States, too, that reliance on emergency and general legislative powers would not suffice to meet the crisis nor, more concretely, their Community commitments. With varying degrees of rapidity, governments set about securing specialised powers to deal with the current, and future, energy emergencies. Two kinds of approach may be distinguished: on one hand, that of the United Kingdom, France and Germany, each of which designed a comprehensive system of domestic control powers; on the other, the Netherlands and Italy, which relied more directly on adoption of the relevant international arrangements under the International Energy Programme.

In the *United Kingdom*, the Fuel and Electricity (Control) Act received Royal Assent on December 6, 1973. The Act provided, on a temporary

5 *E. g.* Dutch restrictions on the use of motor vehicles at the weekends, Staatscourant, October 31, 1973, no. 211.

6 In Holland a National Office for Petroleum Products was set up to prepare a rationing system for petroleum. (Staatscourant, November 13, 1973, no. 220). A Car Petroleum Rationing System Order was introduced in December 1973, based on a coupon system. (December 27, 1973, Staatscourant, no. 238).

7 In the United Kingdom, for example the Electricity (Heating) (Restriction) Order 1973, S.I. 1973 (no. 1900) made under section 2 of the Emergency Powers Act 1920, prohibited the consumption of electricity for space heating, except under licence, in certain premises used for certain purposes. In several countries, speed limits were also introduced, on the basis of general traffic regulation laws: see e. g. the Dutch Royal Decree amending road traffic rules, 31 January 1974, Stbl. 40, based on the Wegenverkeerswet.

8 Decreto Legge no. 741, November 23, 1973, in Gazz. Uff. November 26, 1973, no. 304, and converted into the law of December 22, 1973, no. 842 in Gazz. Uff. December 31, 1973, no. 334.

9 On exports, see Ministerial Decree of October 6, 1973, in Gazz. Uff. October 8, 1973, no. 260 for gas oil and middle weight oils, and Ministerial Decree of December 1, 1973, in Gazz. Uff. December 7, 1973, no. 316 for petroleum products and other derivatives.

basis, for sweeping controls on energy production and use. It required annual confirmation by Parliament if orders made under it were to remain in force. In addition, the provisions of the Act were overtaken by the conclusion of the Agreement on an International Energy Programme in November 1974[10] and by the obligations to be borne by participating states in the information and sharing schemes thereby established. Parliament therefore passed the Energy Act 1976 to place its framework of response to an energy supply emergency on a permanent footing and also to provide for legislative compliance with EEC and IEA obligations. For the most part the provisions of the Act contemplate an obligation on the United Kingdom, by virtue of its membership of one or other of these two organisations, to adopt emergency measures in the face of an interruption or reduction in fuel supplies, or, at the very least, presuppose that the United Kingdom, (if no other country) is facing an actual or imminent emergency as to fuel supply which necessitates a temporary accession to the government of "exceptional powers for controlling the sources and availability of energy".[11]

Where such circumstances exist, an Order in Council may be promulgated by the government implementing the principal provisions of the Act.[12] When an Order is in force, the Secretary of State for Energy is given power to issue regulations, controlling or prohibiting the supply, production, acquisition or use of all the principal energy sources (crude oil, petroleum products, coal, gas and electrcity). He may also issue specific directives to consumers of primary energy sources or of electricity limiting or even, in extreme cases, forbidding the use of that energy, either for a particular purpose or during a particular period of time.[13] At any time, moreover, even when no order is in force, the Secretary of State may make regulations limiting or prohibiting the *use* of fuels and electricity, if he considers that such controls are desirable for the conservation of energy[14]. In such a case the Secretary of State is under a duty to consult organisations which seem to him to be representative of both suppliers of energy and their customers. Such consultation is not required if an Order is in force. These provisions therefore confer on the Secretary of State extensive powers of a general nature to restrict consumption.

Similarly in *France*, existing general emergency legislation was found to be an unsatisfactory basis upon which to found permanent measures to deal with disruptions to energy supply. The initial decree of December 21,

[10] Cmnd 5826, (1975) 14 International Legal Materials.

[11] Section 3(1)(b).

[12] An Order in Council made on the occasion of a purely national emergency lapses if each House does not ratify it within 28 days but if so approved it continues in force for 12 months.

[13] Energy Act 1976, s. 2.

[14] *Ibid.*, s. 1(1).

1973[15] was passed under the auspices of the Ordonnance of January 7, 1959, which by virtue of article 6, gave the government certain powers "en cas de menace portant notamment sur une partie du territoire sur un secteur de la vie nationale ou sur une fraction de la population".[16] Hence this legislation was inappropriate as it referred to 'substantial threats' rather than to potential disruption of the economic well-being of the country.

The Law of October 29, 1974 specified that powers were to be made available to the government in the event of shortages or threats to external trade balances.[17] The law gave the government powers to control production, importation, exportation, circulation, transportation and stockage of all forms of primary energy, energy based products and petroleum products destined for non-energy related usage. If in the opinion of the government circumstances warrant action on its part, it may issue a decree in the Council of Ministers. The 1974 Law specifies that the duration of such a decree must be limited in time, whereas the 1973 Decree had not envisaged such a limitation. The validity of the decrees made under the law has been extended on several occasions.[18] The provisions of the 1974 law were amended by the Law of July 19, 1977[19], which gives the government greater powers in respect of potential threats to energy security[20], and also conferred wider powers in respect of pricing and the financial aspects of energy supply. A further law of July 15, 1980[21] gives the government power to deal with crises resulting from economic disturbances on the energy market, whereas the former legislation had limited its powers to situations of physical shortage, or threat of such a shortage.

In *Germany*, the Federal Government drew up a draft energy protection bill, which was approved by the Cabinet on November 7, 1973 and adopted as the "Law to secure the Energy Supply in the Case of Actual or Potential disruption of Imports of Crude Oil or Natural Gas" on November 10, 1973.[22]

This law gave the government extensive powers to control the production, transport, distribution, storage, sale, supply and use of all types of energy, as well as powers to prescribe maximum prices and to impose

15 Decree no. 73–1136 of December 21, 1973, in J.O.R.F. December 23, p. 13761.

16 Ordonnance 59–147, note 3, *supra*.

17 Article 1 – "En cas de pénurie ou de menace sur l'équilibre des échanges extérieurs".

18 The initial Decree no. 74–940 of November 12, 1974, in J.O.R.F. November 13, 1974, p. 11407, limited the application of the 1974 powers until December 31, 1976, and a further Decree no. 76–755 of August 15, 1976 in J.O.R.F. August 14, 1976 extended the validity of the Decree no. 74–790 until December 31, 1980.

19 Law no. 77–804, in J.O.R.F. July 20, p. 3831.

20 The words 'en cas de' are replaced by 'en vue de'.

21 Art. 31, Law no. 80–531 of July 15, 1980, in J.O.R.F. July 16, 1980, p. 1786.

22 See Volkmar, S. "Das Energiesicherungsgesetz vom 9.11.73" in Neue Juristische Wochenschrift 1974, p. 113.

obligations to supply information on the state of the market. Originally the law was to expire on December 31, 1974, but an amendment of December 20, 1974 removed this limitation and the law is now in permanent operation.[23] Section 1 of the law authorises the Federal Government to issue statutory orders to deal with crises should the level of oil imports or natural gas imports be endangered or disrupted. The law is also designed to meet the obligations contained in the International Energy Programme and in the various EEC directives applying to crisis measures. The measures which can be implemented in the event of an energy supply crisis vary in scope and content, depending on the level of shortfall in energy supplies. Several orders have so far been made under this law, including an authorisation of individual orders as to the production, distribution and consumption of electrical energy by both industry and private consumers,[24] and similar authorisation orders relating to gas distribution and consumption;[25] to rationing systems for petrol;[26] and for deliveries of heating oil.[27]

As already noted, the pattern in the other two countries was rather different. In the *Netherlands*, attempts to reactivate the old Distributiewet of 1939 were in practice partly unsuccessful due to legal objections based on the interference involved with the principle of free movement of goods, and to the absence of any real shortage of oil and petroleum products. Eventually IEA obligations in respect of crisis mechanisms were enacted by the Wet uitovoering internationaal energieprogramma 1979 (Act to implement the IEP) conferring powers on the Minister of Economics Affairs to cope with emergency situations envisaged by the IEP.[28]

In *Italy*, a law giving the IEP legal effect in Italy was promulgated in 1977[29], but no domestic measures of application were developed. The government has largely relied on the device of the *decreto-legge* to take quick-acting measures in areas[30] which in other countries might be covered by the specialised emergency powers above referred to. Considerable inconvenience has re-

[23] Orders made under it – see BGBl I 1974, p. 3681, as amended by the Law of December 14th, 1976, BGBl I 3373, and by the Law of December 19th, 1979, BGBl I p. 2305.

[24] Verordnung zur Sicherung der Elektrizitätsversorgung in einer Versorgungskrise (Elektrizitätssicherungsverordnung – EltSV, April 26, 1982 (BGBl I 1514).

[25] Verordnung zur Sicherung der Gasversorgung in einer Versorgungskrise. (Gassicherungsverordnung – GAS SV April 26, 1982. BGBl I 517.

[26] Verordnung über Lieferbeschränkungen für Kraftstoff in einer Versorgungskrise (Kraftstoff-Lieferbeschränkungs-Verordnung – Kraftstoff LBV (April 26, 1982, BGBl I 520).

[27] Verordnung über Lieferbeschränkungen für Leicht-Heizöl in einer Versorgungskrise. (Heizöl-Lieferbeschränkungs-Verordnung Heizöl LBV, (April 26, 1982 BGBl I 536).

[28] April 4, 1979 Staatsblad no. 187.

[29] Law no. 883, November 7, 1977 in Gazz. Uff. December 7, 1977 no. 883.

[30] For example Decreto-legge no. 5 of January 11, 1980, in Gazz. Uff. January 14, 1980 no. 12, which limited the periods when heating could be used in buildings.

sulted from the fact that *decreti-leggi* have often not been converted to law by the date of their expiry. An exception was the law no. 178 of May 16, 1980,[31] on heating controls and other matters, converting *decreto-legge* no. 5, but this law was operative only for one year, after which the same problems have recurred.

We can see, therefore, that while general emergency legislation normally provided an initial legal basis for the implementation of measures to deal with the supply shortages that resulted from the 1973 crisis, it has been necessary in all countries to enact some sort of legislation which gives governments more specific and better defined powers to cope with crisis management. This could in part be attributed to obligations under the International Energy Programme and to Community commitments, but it should be remembered that France, which is not a member of the IEA, has furnished its government with an extensive set of powers, whereas Italy, which is a member, has relied on a somewhat precarious legislative basis for its crisis measures.

B. Stocks

As regards the stocks obligations of the EEC and IEA agreements, we find that most countries have introduced legislation carrying these obligations into domestic law[32], though sometimes only after the threat of article 169 enforcement proceedings had been issued by the Commission.[33]

In certain cases, provisions on stocks could be incorporated into existing legislation as in France[34], but in most cases new legislation was enacted, either as part of the general package of anti-crisis powers, as in the United Kingdom[35], or as quite separate legislation, as in Germany, where the institution of stock requirements raised constitutional difficulties[36], and Italy,

[31] In Gazz. Uff. May 17, 1980, no. 12.

[32] For the United Kingdom, see section 6 of the Energy Act 1976; for Italy, Law no. 22 of February 10, 1981, note 37 infra; for Germany, the Gesetz über die Bevorratung mit Erdöl und Erdölerzeugnissen (Erdöl Bev G) June 25, 1978 BGBl I 1073; and for Holland, the Petroleum Products Stockpiling Act, October 21, 1976, Staatsblad, no. 569.

[33] Evans, A. C. "The Development of a Community Policy on Oil", (1980) 17 C.M.L.Rev. 373.

[34] For France, the Decree of October 18, 1950, on import licences for crude oil products gave the Minister in charge of hydrocarbons powers to impose certain technical requirements on the oil companies, and the Decree 58—249 of March 10, 1958 provided that companies in receipt of import authorisations for both crude oil and refined products had to maintain stocks equivalent to 25 per cent of the level of deliveries in the previous year. This decree was amended by Decree 79—504 of June 26, 1979, which provides that stock levels must be seasonally adjusted.

[35] Energy Act, s. 6.

[36] The 1978 Law, see note 32, *supra*, was a result of a challenge in the Constitutional Court (B Verfg E vol. 30, p. 292) to the 1965 Law Governing Oil Reserves (BGBl I 1965 p. 1217).

where the usual difficulties of Parliamentary immobility delayed action until 1981.[37]

Furthermore, in order to ensure that the electricity supply industry is able to continue power generation during periods of uncertainty as to the supply of primary fuels there is legislative provision in most countries for the implementation of Community Directives on stocks of fuel to be held at power stations.[38]

While in all the Member States under study, stocks obligations fall primarily on importers, refiners and distributors, there is also provision in certain countries for small, State-owned strategic reserves.[39]

C. Prices

Powers to regulate prices at which certain fuels might be sold have been likewise based, in most cases, on the general legislation described in Chapter IV.[40]

In the *United Kingdom*, the Counter-Inflation Act 1973 was already in force when the energy crisis developed, and energy prices fell within the comprehensive regime of the Act. Proposed increases in gas, electricity and petroleum product prices all had to be notified to the Price Commission, which carried out a number of investigations. In 1979 it set limits on wholesale and retail price increases for petroleum products which, however, met in full the requests of the companies.[41] Paraffin prices, on the other hand, politically sensitive because of the use of the fuel by the old and the poor, were for several years directly regulated by the government by orders made under the Fuel and Electricity (Control) Act 1973 and continued by the Energy Act 1976. The regime of general price control was brought to an end by the Competition Act 1980 and there are no present plans to reintroduce it.

[37] Law no. 22, of February 10, 1981, in Gazz. Uff. February 17, 1981, no. 47, articles 2, 3 and 4.

[38] For the United Kingdom, section 7 of the Energy Act 1976; for Italy, article 1 of Law no. 22 of February 10, 1981, *supra* note 37; for Holland, the maintenance of minimum stocks of fossil fuels at thermal power stations is assured by a private law agreement between the Minister for Economic Affairs and the Electricity Companies (Agreement of August 17, 1981, Staatscourant no. 158); and for Germany, the Verordnung über die Brennstoffbevorratung von Kraftwerken of February 11, 1981 (BGBl I 164).

[39] In Germany a reserve of 10 million tonnes of crude oil is maintained by the "Industrieverwaltungsgesellschaft" on behalf of the Federal Government (Haushaltsplan 1982). The British government also maintains a strategic reserve of some 12 million tonnes of crude oil.

[40] Above, Chapter IV, pp. 82–89.

[41] See its reports on BP Oil Ltd, the Esso Petroleum Company Ltd, and Shell UK Oil, (1979) H.C. 87, 88 and 178.

In *France*, we saw that powers to regulate prices were based on an Ordonnance of 1945.[42] The Barre Government favoured a policy of *liberté contrôlée* after 1975, but in September 1976 a general freeze was imposed on fuel prices. Certain petroleum products such as naphta and heavy oils and lubricants which had been liberalised in the spring of 1976 were made subject to the September price freeze, and were only reliberalised subject to the conclusion of *engagements de modération* in July 1978. This latter system was based on agreements negotiated between the administration and the professional organisations without the individual commitment of any one firm or company. These agreements would specify the way in which prices were to evolve over a particular period and, should targets be exceeded, a price control could be imposed by Ministerial Decree. The engagements were abolished in 1978 to make way for a progressive liberalisation of prices.[43] However, the prices of motor and heating fuels remained the subject of direct government control, until April 1982 when a new system was introduced for these products.[44] Under the new formula, prices vary monthly according to European market prices comprising, on a 50/50 basis Rotterdam spot prices and the EEC weekly oil index. A differential per tonne is added to compensate for the specific constraints on the French market, i. e. the obligation to build up stocks and to carry two-thirds of all imported crude on French ships. Price fluctuations will be held within a 'tunnel' which is made up of the cost of refined products in France plus or minus 8 per cent.[45] These arrangements were successfully challenged before the European Court of Justice and, in consequence motor fuels are now subject to the *liberté surveillée* regime.[46]

Additional, specialised energy price control powers are now available to the government under the Law of 1974 as amended in 1977 and 1980.[47]

The general powers to set prices in *The Netherlands* have been described in Chapter IV.[48] Orders made under the 1961 Act operated in relations to petroleum products from 1973: the order made in December 1981 was withdrawn six months later when, due to the surplus of oil supplies, the maximum price order had the effect of pushing prices up,[49] and no subsequent orders have been made. Additional energy price control powers are now available under the IEP Act of 1979.

[42] See Chapter IV, p. 84.
[43] Arrêté 78–67/p in B.O.S.P. of May 31, 1978.
[44] "Le gouvernement ne fixera plus les prix." Le Monde, April 19, 1982.
[45] See B.I.P. no. 4582, April 1982 for a review of the new system.
[46] See case 231/83, *H. Cullet and Chambre Syndicale des Réparateurs Automobiles v Centre Le clerc.* January, 1985 (not yet reported).
[47] Above, p. 97.
[48] See Chapter IV, p. 86.
[49] Beschikking houdende intrekking Prijsbeschikking aarolieproducten, 1982, July 29, 1982, Staatscourant, no. 144.

Italy has relied heavily on the price-fixing powers of the CIP (Comitato Interministeriale dei Prezzi). We have already described the pricing regime which was in place in 1973.[50] Since the suspension of the so-called *blocco elastico* in July 1974, a system of price control based on production costs was implemented by the CIP for petroleum products until 1977. This system was the subject of much complaint by the oil companies who criticised the delay which arose between changed circumstances and the appearance of decrees updating prices.

In 1977 a new system was introduced[51] which provided for two categories of price control: administered prices and supervised prices, the former being set by the administration and imposed on the companies, and the second being set by the companies and notified to the administration. Initially supervised prices were applied for naphta, jet fuel and other minor products, but shortly afterwards heavy fuel oil was added to the list. The Secretariat of the CIP calculated the overall costs of the oil industry in accordance with a specified formula and the industry then notified the CIP of its prices for supervised products. The CIP on the basis of this calculated the revenue from administered and supervised prices — if the revenue fell below costs, then the prices of the administered products were adjusted. This system collapsed in 1980 when the Italian crude oil supply was jeopardised by the loss of a contract between ENI and Saudi Arabia. The Italian market had to be made more attractive to the international majors and hence a new system was introduced in the spring of 1980, based on a comparison of ex-refinery revenues with ex-refinery revenues in other European countries. Comparison is made every six months and discrepancies accommodated in the administered prices at the discretion of the CIP.[52]

In *Germany*, general price control powers have not been used for the purpose of restricting energy prices in the post-crisis period, but additional powers have nonetheless been taken in the 1974 Law to Secure the Energy Supply.[53]

II. Alterations in the Structure and Level of Energy Demand

In this section we will examine measures adopted by national governments to influence levels and patterns of demand for energy in general, and for particular fuels such as oil. We saw in Chapter II that the Community had

50 See Chapter IV, p. 87.

51 Provvedimento C.I.P. 43/77, in Gazz. Uff. November 7, 1977, no. 303.

52 It was announced in 1982 that petroleum products and diesel fuel would not be subject to the system of supervised prices, but would be transferred to the administered price regime. La Repubblica, June 18, 1982.

53 Above, pp. 97—98.

been active in this area since 1973, and in relating national policies to Community policy three types of Community commitment should be borne in mind:

- Council Resolutions committing Member States in general terms, to energy saving policies and in some cases setting import reduction targets;[54]
- highly detailed, but non-binding, Council Recommendations on energy-saving methods;[55]
- a fairly small number of specific Council Directives imposing binding obligations in relation to such matters as power station fuelling, insulation standards, and energy consumption labelling.[56]

In addition, of course, important direct Community actions, such as funding for energy research and development or for boiler conversion schemes, have been aimed at the same objective. These fall beyond the ambit of our concern with the interaction between national and Community legal instruments.

A. Promotion of Economy in Energy Use

Broadly the approach of the *United Kingdom* government, especially after 1979, to the promotion of energy conservation has been permissive rather than coercive and there are relatively few examples of statutory powers having been taken or used to compel the adoption of energy saving techniques. The present government has adopted a policy which places responsibility for the success of energy conservation with the consumers themselves. Hence there are few major governmental programmes devoted to the promotion of energy saving and the several, small-scale schemes which do exist, e. g. the "save-it" campaign introduced in 1974, are intended only as pump-priming operations. The government has, however, recently announced the creation of an 'umbrella' body to further the United Kingdom energy conservation industry and to co-ordinate "save-it" campaigns.[57]

This emphasis on advice and co-ordination is perhaps illustrative of the shift in energy policy away from direct government expenditure, for instance through grants to encourage energy conservation in industry,[58] to the provision of the right framework in which energy decisions can be made by consumers. The government has, however, continued with some regulatory and subsidy activity. The Energy Conservation Act 1981, implementing an EEC Directive, provides for official testing of certain types of heating apparatus, and the subsequent control of their sale, together with

[54] Above, Chapter II, pp. 27–29.
[55] *Ibid.*, p. 30.
[56] *Ibid.*, pp. 29–30.
[57] Financial Times, April 7, 1983.
[58] Industry Act 1975, s. 8.

financial provisions for advisory and audit schemes approved by the Secretary of State for Energy. The Homes Insulation Act 1978, introduced by the previous Labour administration, has continued in force and provides for grants by local authorities towards the costs of insulating dwelling houses. Other measures relating to fuel consumption tests for vehicles introduced by the previous government remain in force.[59]

The present government's commitment to rational consumer choice in energy conservation implies an undistorted price structure. While crude oil and petroleum product prices have remained largely unregulated, government policies towards pricing by the nationalised gas and electricity industries have tended in the past to depress prices artificially.[60] The present government, which in 1979 adopted a policy of gas and electricity price increases, partly in response to EEC and IEA pressure, has retreated in the face of protest from industry about consequent competitive disadvantage,[61] and has called for moderation of gas price increases and a review of CEGB tariffs.[62] At the same time it continues to seek certain minimum levels of nationalised industry surplus ("negative external financing limits"),[63] though the reduction of the public sector deficit, rather than energy conservation, seems to be its main preoccupation.

The government also exercises control in the field of conservation of resources *in situ*. The 1976 Energy Act[64] provides for the imposition of controls over the flaring of natural gas as an incident of petroleum operations. A similar control has been contained, since 1975, in the petroleum production licence.[65]

In *France* we saw above that the first Energy Plan of 1974 stressed two elements to reduce dependence on imported oil: the development of nuclear power and energy conservation.[66] The primary importance that was accorded to the implementation of the new energy policy is reflected in the number of administrative changes that have occurred, beginning with the creation of *Délégué général à l'énergie*, in 1973[67] and after several reorganisa-

[59] See S.I. 1973, No. 1486, revoking and re-enacting with amendments the Passenger Car Fuel Consumption Order 1977, S.I. 1977 No. 1603.

[60] See Heald, "UK Energy Policy: Economic and Financial Control of the Nationalised Energy Industries." (1981) 6 Energy Policy 99, at p. 109.

[61] See National Economic Development Office, Industrial Energy Pricing (December, 1980).

[62] See Select Committee on Energy, Industrial Energy Pricing Policy (1980–81) H.C. 422, at p. xiii.

[63] See Treasury Minute on the Fifteenth to Thirty-Fifth Reports of the Committee of Public Accounts, Session 1979-80, Cmnd. 8125 (1981), paras. 45–47.

[64] Energy Act 1976, s. 12.

[65] Petroleum and Submarine Pipelines Act 1975, Part II, and see now, Petroleum (Production) Regulations 1982, S.I. 1982 No. 1000, Sch. 5 cl.20 (3)–(7).

[66] See Chapter III, at pp. 38–43.

[67] Decree 73–1136 of December 21, 1973, *supra*, note 15.

tions within the Ministry of Industry[68] the creation of a *Ministre délégué auprès du Ministre de l'Industrie, chargé de l'énergie*, with responsibility for all aspects of energy policy.[69] As far as energy conservation is concerned the most important administrative innovation was the creation in 1974 of the *Agence pour les économies d'énergie* (AEE)[70] as the sole organisation with responsibility for the problems of energy conservation. Hence it was given both an innovative and a co-ordinating role, with a wide range of functions, including the overall direction of energy conservation policy, the dissemination of information on energy saving, the promotion of new research techniques and materials, through the granting of financial assistance. The Agency, which has enjoyed considerable financial resources (FF 751.7m in 1980), and also received the proceeds of a para-fiscal tax on petrol, was in 1982 merged, along with the *Commissariat de l'énergie solaire* (COMES), into an even more broadly based body, the *Agence Française pour la Maîtrise de l'Energie*, alongside which a *Fonds Spécial Grands Travaux* has also been set up.[71]

There exists a vast body of legislation in France aimed at energy conservation techniques resulting from a policy approach which has been described as a *dirigisme incitatif.*[72] This legislation could be divided into four distinct categories: measures aimed at reducing waste in energy use;[73] measures aimed at encouraging energy saving techniques;[74] the co-ordination of energy conservation and pollution control[75] and measures designed to encourage an economical use of heat.[76] In addition a number of decree laws have been passed designed to promote energy savings in specific sectors (e. g. electrical energy, lighting, heating and the regulation of advertising).[77]

68 For a chronological account of the various changes which have taken place within the Ministry of Industry, see Massenet, V., and Maurice, P. Y.: "L'Adaptation de l'Administration Française à la Situation Nouvelle de l'Energie", presented at the I.I.A.S. Colloquium on the Adjustment of Administration to the Energy Crisis, Brussels 1982.

69 Decree no. 81–731, July 30, 1981.

70 Decree 74–1003 of November 29, 1974, in J.O.R.F. December 1, 1974, p. 12014, as amended by Law no. 77–804 of July 19, 1977, in J.O.R.F. July 20, 1977, p. 3831, article 3.

71 Decree no. 82–404 of May 13, 1982, in J.O.R.F. May 14, 1982.

72 Quoted from an interview with M. Guy Braibant, November 15, 1977.

73 Law no. 74–908, of October 29, 1974 and Law no. 77–804 of July 19, 1977.

74 *Ibid.*

75 Law no. 75–633 of July 15, 1975 in J.O.R.F. July 16, 1975.

76 Law no. 80–531 of July 15, 1980 in J.O.R.F., July 16, 1980.

77 For example Decree no. 74–1039 of December 6, 1974 in J.O.R.F. December 7, 1974, regulating publicity and Arrêté of April 29, 1977, on heating apparatus controls. Two Arrêtés of July 12, 1979 and November 16, 1979 deal with electricity and gas consumption. See J.O.R.F. July 20, 1979 and J.O.R.F. November 23, 1979.

In *The Netherlands*, as in the United Kingdom, pricing is an element of conservation policy. The Minister of Economic Affairs has taken powers under the Wet Aardgasprijzen to ensure that natural gas prices reflect market values.[78] In addition, a number of grants are available to encourage energy conservation in both domestic and industrial consumption. Subsidies to provide for thermal insulation in existing private housing were introduced in 1974,[79] for public buildings in 1975,[80] and for new private housing, in October of that year.[81]

Energy advisory programmes for industrial energy conservation are also available[82] and within the context of the Investment Account Act 1978 and 1980, specific subsidies are available to companies making energy saving investments. More recently, special allowances for such investment have been given to Dutch bulb-growers[83] and further incentives for energy saving measures were provided specifically for this sector by an earlier order of July, 1982, issued by the Minister of Agriculture.[84] It should be recalled that the Commission recently ruled that the special reduced tariffs which had been accorded to Dutch horticulturalists in respect of natural gas, constituted as a State aid in the sense of article 92 of the Treaty, and these special tariffs were subsequently amended.[85]

In *Italy*, the 1975 Energy Plan recommended the setting up of a single institution to co-ordinate efforts in the field of energy conservation. This, however, has never materialised, and instead we find a number of scattered measures dealing with various aspects of energy conservation, such as insulation, building standards, advisory campaigns.[86] It is hoped that the new Law No. 308, of 1982, which gives the regions a more active role in energy policy, will result in a more co-ordinated and more positive approach to energy conservation.[87]

In *Germany* we find an array of measures designed to promote energy conservation in both the private and industrial sector, which may at first

[78] See Chapter IV; and also see Akyurek-Kievits, in Ars Aequi, 1980, p. 634.

[79] Financial Subsidies for the Thermal Insulation of Existing Houses Order, June 13, 1974, Staatscourant, no. 114, 1974.

[80] Financial Subsidies for Restriction of Energy Use in New Buildings, June 16, 1975, Staatscourant, no. 112.

[81] October 9, 1975, Staatscourant, no. 199, 1975.

[82] Order concerning Information on Subsidies on Restriction of Energy Use in Companies, September 2, 1977, Staatscourant, no. 173.

[83] Order of December 29, 1982 Staatscourant, no. 253.

[84] Staatscourant, no. 136.

[85] See Chapter VII, note 2, for details.

[86] Law no. 373 of April 30, 1976, in Gazz. Uff. June 7, 1976, no. 148 regulates the design, installation, operation, and maintenance of heating systems and insulation of residential buildings, and Law no. 675 of August 12, 1977, in Gazz. Uff. September 7, 1977, no. 243 applies to industrial buildings.

[87] Law no. 308, of May 29, 1982 in Gazz. Uff. June 7, 1982.

seem surprising, given the traditional stress on the price mechanism in this country. Hence we find laws setting standards for thermal insulation[88], and laws relating to the performance of hot water heaters and heating apparatus.[89] An Order of 1981 requires that consumers be billed the full price of heating and hot water consumption.[90]

There are also subsidies available to the construction sector to improve insulation standards, and to encourage the installation of new technologies. The total programme provides for tax deductions and grants up to a total of DM 4,350 million over four years.[91] Special tariffs have also been introduced to encourage the use of heat pumps.[92] Deductions from income tax for investment in improved heating installations and heat pumps were provided for in the Income Tax Acts, and the Second Budget Structure Act of 1981[93] provides that tenants may use their building society savings for the purposes of improved insulation or other energy conservation purposes without loss of either premiums or tax allowances.

The Investment Allowance Act, introduced in 1975, but amended on several occasions, provides for a 7.5 per cent allowance from Federal funds for investment in a wide range of energy saving projects.[94] In addition, there are several advisory schemes on energy saving, sponsored by the Federal Government.[95]

B. Alteration of Energy Consumption Patterns

In all countries we find an expressed desire to retreat from the use of oil as a fuel in electricity generation, although in *The Netherlands* the immediate emphasis has been more on the substitution of oil for natural gas.[96]

Italy, has recently passed legislation to encourage the development of the use of energies other than combustible hydrocarbons for the fuelling of power stations.[97] In the *United Kingdom*, *France* and *Germany* we find

88 Law on the Conservation of Energy in Buildings, July 22, 1976, BGBl – I – 1873, as revised by an amendment dated June 20, 1980.

89 Heating Equipment Order BGBl – I, p. 158.

90 Statutory Order on the Billing of Heating Costs, BGBl – I, p. 261.

91 Law to Amend the Housing Modernisation Act, 1978.

92 Energiewirtschaftsgesetz – Zweite Verordnung, January 30, 1980, s. 7.

93 BGBl – I – p. 1523.

94 BGBl – I – 1975, p. 24.

95 Allgemeine Aufklärung über die Möglichkeiten einer rationellen und sparsamen Energieverwendung von 1982 und Forderung der Beratung privater Verbraucher sowie kleiner und mittlerer Unternehmen über Möglichkeiten der Energieeinsparung 1982 – both measures being based on the Bundeshaushaltsplan, 1982.

96 A private law agreement between the Ministers of Economic Affairs, Public Health and the Environment, the municipal authorities and the energy utilities was signed in 1980 (White paper no. 15891, Brandstoffeninzetplan centrales).

97 Law no. 308, *supra* note 87.

measures aimed at encouraging the use of coal in electricity generation[98] and there are various programmes in each of these countries to encourage the use of coal in industry,[99] and to encourage research and development in coal conversion techniques.[100]

In addition we find that taxation, and pricing and tariff policy are often used as a means of making the use of one fuel more attractive than another. For instance, in *Germany*, the tax on light-heating oils has been doubled in 1978[101] and differential taxes are imposed on fuels, higher on petroleum and lower on diesel and on cars using such fuels. Again in *The Netherlands* lower taxes are levied on diesel fuel.

Preferential tariffs are often given for consumers willing to take interruptible gas supplies, or for the installation of heat pumps in buildings.[102] In *France*, the consumption of domestic heating oil has been restricted through a series of regulations limiting amounts supplied to distributors and consumers.[103]

III. Alterations in the Pattern of Energy Supply

Under this heading we will consider measures taken in the five countries under study to reduce dependence on imported oil, by the better management of their energy *supply* situation. Such measures may be organised into two groups: those involving the development of domestic energy supplies, and those involving the diversification of sources of supply of imported energy. Here Community policy imposes little constraint. The Council Resolution of 1974 did no more than commit Member States to work towards these objectives, and was in any event subject to the Dutch reservation on nuclear energy.[104] The Commission's campaign for rational and transparent energy pricing has so far produced only Council Recommendations on gas and electricity tariffs[105] together with acknowledgment, by way of Resolution, that energy pricing *should* be rational and

98 See below, pp. 114–115.

99 E. g., in the United Kingdom, a 2-year programme for the conversion of industrial boilers from oil to coal: see Select Committee on Energy, Industrial Energy Pricing Policy, *supra* note 62.

100 See p. 114.

101 Neuntes Gesetz zur Änderung des Mineralsteuergesetzes 1964, BGBl I 1105.

102 See note 92, *supra*.

103 For a full account of the various decrees and arrêtés see Faberon, Y., *Les Economies d'énergie en France*, pp. 163–166.

104 Above, Chapter II, p. 28.

105 Council Recommendation 81/924 on electricity tariff structures, O.J. 1981, L 337/12; Council Recommendation 83/230 on the methods of setting natural gas prices and tariffs in the Community, O.J. 1983 L 123/40.

transparent.[106] Otherwise the main thrust of Community policy has been supportive, particularly through aids for exploration and production investment.

A. Domestic Energy Supplies

Sources of supply may be grouped here under headings which correspond broadly with those used for the analysis of energy markets in Chapter IV. We omit electricity, however, dealing with power station fuelling under the heading of the relevant primary energy source; and we include an additional heading, that of renewable energies, for which the institutional and legal structures in the States under study are still in course of development.

1. Nuclear Energy

In December 1979 the *United Kingdom* government announced a new programme of development in the field of nuclear power generation. In view of the decline of the British nuclear industry during the preceding decade it had formed the conclusion that the future of the industry and the security of long-term supplies of nuclear-generated electricity could only be assured if the Government embarked on a continuing programme of construction of nuclear installations.[107] In practice, the realisation of this programme requires a number of legal hurdles to be surmounted, and progress on the current proposal by the CEGB to construct a pressurised water reactor at Sizewell in Suffolk is slow: a negative design assessment has been made by the Nuclear Installations Inspectorate,[108] and a lengthy public inquiry under the Town and Country Planning Acts has only recently been concluded.

As we noted in Chapter III, *France* is not well endowed with primary energy resources. She does, however, have uranium reserves which are significant by West European standards, at 2.2 per cent of the world's known reserves. Between 1973 and 1981 the share of nuclear energy in total final consumption has increased from 1.7 per cent to 11.8 per cent. Nuclear capacity at the end of 1981 comprised 30 operational reactors, with an installed capacity of 21.2 GWe, and 25 PWR reactors with an installed capacity of 28.6 GWe were under construction together with the experimental 1,200 MEe breeder Superphénix. The overall capacity on comple-

106 E. g. Council Resolutions of December 3, 1981, and March 16, 1982, in Bull. EC 12–81, pt. 2.1.159, and 3–82, pt. 2.1.110.

107 See Select Committee on Energy, The Government's statement on the new nuclear power programme (1979–80) H.C. 397.

108 The Inspectorate is part of the Health and Safety Executive, which must grant a nuclear site licence if construction is to proceed: see Nuclear Installations Act 1965 (Repeals and Modifications) Regulations 1974, S.I. 1974 No. 2056.

tion of the programme adopted in 1974[109] was to stand at around 51 GWe. As we shall see, these projections have been slightly modified by the Socialist government, elected in 1981. However, up to that date France had the largest nuclear capacity among the five countries under study.[110] Most commentators attribute the success of nuclear policy in France to the highly centralised decision-making process, which ensured co-ordination and the necessary levels of investment. Central to this process was Electricité de France (EDF) which, it will be recalled, is a public enterprise with an effective monopoly of electricity generation and supply.

EDF's position as the sole reactor constructor is reinforced by the highly centralised procedure for the siting of nuclear plants in France. EDF draws up a list of possible sites, and submits this list to an interministerial committee at which regional representatives may put their views. The OECD Report on the Siting Procedures for Major Energy Facilities notes that over a third of the possible sites were selected by this committee and then submitted for regional consultation.[111] The results of the ensuing discussions at regional and local level are only of an advisory nature, and once a site has been deemed feasible by the interministerial committee and local and regional viewpoints have been taken into consideration, the central authorities can then go on to authorise the EDF to file for a *Declaration d'Utilité Publique* (DUP) before the Minister of Industry. A law of July 10, 1976[112] introduced a compulsory environmental impact assessment study, to be undertaken before a DUP could be granted.

The new Socialist government was elected partly on a promise to improve public participation in nuclear power plant siting decisions and to introduce more democratic procedures. Construction at six plants was halted immediately after the election, pending the consultation of local and regional authorities. A report adopted by the party in 1981, the Quilès report,[113] called for a curtailment of the nuclear programme. After a debate on nuclear energy in the National Assembly in October 1981 the government reduced to six its predecessor's plans for 9 PWR orders in 1982 and 1983, partly because of the slower rate of electricity growth; but further reductions were not made because of the risk of underutilising Framatome's construction capacity. Critics of the government's decision argued that in case of excess electricity production over domestic demand,

109 See Appendix 3.

110 Compare a capacity of 8.6 GWe in the United Kingdom and 10.4 GWe in West Germany.

111 O.E.C.D., The Siting of Major Energy Facilities, Paris 1980.

112 Law no. 76–629, of July 10, 1976, in J.O.R.F. July 12, 1976.

113 Quilès, P., *Energie, une autre politique*, January 1981.

EDF might have sold its surplus production at a profit to neighbouring countries.[114]

In *The Netherlands*, in contrast, there has been considerable opposition to nuclear power. A very limited amount of nuclear power is generated by the private or provincially owned electricity companies via the Gemeenschappelijke Kernenergiecentrale Nederland NV, set up in 1964. As noted in Chapter IV, the only direct state influence on nuclear power development is by means of registration and licensing on the basis of the Kernenergiewet of 1964. This Act makes inadequate provision for procedures controlling the disposal of nuclear waste, an issue which was to become politically important following the 1973 crisis. As we noted in Chapter III, two separate energy plans, one in 1974 and another in 1979, have advocated the building of more nuclear reactors, but following the advice of the Algemene Energie Raad (General Energy Council), a body created in 1975, it was decided that endorsement of the nuclear power programme should be based on the outcome of the so-called Brede Maatschappelijke Diskussie (Broad Societal Discussion), whose recommendations of a cautious approach to nuclear power are not seen by government as preventing consideration of construction of new nuclear plants.

In *Italy*, despite the fact that the country was dependent on imported energy to cover 83.3 per cent of its total energy requirements in 1979, with oil imports dominating (70.1 per cent of total final consumption), the development of the nuclear power programme has been extremely slow. Of the twelve nuclear power plants approved in 1977 only two are under construction. Nuclear power contributed only 0.9 per cent to electricity generation in 1973 and this had only increased to 1.1 per cent by 1981.

It should be noted while Italy, like France, possesses a public monopoly in nuclear energy production and electricity generation, responsibility for the various aspects of the nuclear fuel cycle was divided between three public institutions. The CNEN (Comitato Nazionale per l'Energia Nucleare) created in 1960[115] was responsible for research and development, for research and development; ENEL, the electricity authority, was given responsibility for the production of nuclear power for use in electricity generation [116] while ENI, the national hydrocarbons board, was given the function of 'taking initiatives in the national interest in the sectors of chemicals and the exploration for and production of and the sale of nuclear fuels'.[117]

[114] Gihel, J., "La Tunique de Nessus" in Revue de l'énergie no. 339, November 1981, p. 557.

[115] Law no. 933 of August 11, 1960, in Gazz. Uff. September 6, 1960, no. 218.

[116] Law no. 1860 of December 31, 1962 in Gazz. Uff. January 30, 1963, no. 27 and Pres. Decree no. 185 of February 13, 1964, in Gazz. Uff. May 3, 1964 no. 112.

[117] Law no. 1153 of November 14, 1967 in Gazz. Uff. December 13, 1967 no. 340.

Although all three boards are subject to the supervision of the Ministry of Industry and to directives emanating from the CIPE, it appears that there was little co-ordination of their respective aspirations. While the National Energy Plan of 1975 recognised this defect, and called for urgent measures to ensure the effective co-ordination of the three public entities operating in the sector, it was only in March 1982 that the organisational structure of the CNEN was reformed and its functions and powers increased.[118] It is envisaged that the new organisation, the ENEA,[119] will be responsible for all aspects of the research and development of nuclear power and alternative energy sources, and it will also be able to offer consultation services and undertake technical inquiries on behalf of local authorities.

It would seem, however that the 1981 Energy Plan does not envisage a great increase in the contribution of nuclear power to total final consumption, with projections for 1985 and 1990 accounting for 1.2 per cent and 4.3 per cent respectively.

The second factor contributing to the slow development of nuclear power in Italy has been local opposition to proposed sites, and the lack of a suitable administrative machinery to deal with that opposition. A law of 1975[120] introduced a new licensing system in an attempt to surmount local opposition by providing for consultation with regional and local governments at the various stages of the siting procedures. This act regulates the national nuclear programme as a whole and provides for a special, two tier siting procedure involving the regional authorities as well as the CIPE, ENEL and the CNEN, and it lays down the basic administrative procedure for determining the location of nuclear plant in a regional and national context. Final say in granting site authorisation rests with the Ministry of Industry. The nuclear power programme continues, however, to suffer from severe delays, and in 1979 an emergency plan, drawn up by ENEL, and approved by the CIPE, introduced selective black-outs at off-peak hours. In an effort to speed up construction a decree-law was promulgated at the end of 1980[121] with the aim of halving the time taken for consultations between the CIPE and the Regions on siting. A government bill of 1979 (which never became law) proposed the granting of financial aid to those regions accepting sites, and on the basis of this new policy a number of conventions between central government and the regions and local authorities were drawn up, providing for financial aid in

118 Law no. 84 of March 5, 1982, in Gazz. Uff. March 22, 1982 no. 79.

119 The full title is: Comitato nazionale per la ricerca e per lo sviluppo dell'energia nucleare e dell'energia alternativa.

120 Law no. 393 of August 2, 1975, in Gazz. Uff. August 23, 1975 no. 224. For the pre-1975 position see above, Chapter IV, p. 57.

121 Decreto-Legge no. 684, of December 30th, 1979 in Gazz. Uff. January 8, 1980 no. 6.

exchange for positive decisions on proposed sites. A new law of January 1983[122] has however made provision for the allocation of grants to Communes and Regions operating electrical power stations fuelled by combustibles other than hydrocarbons. This law obliges ENEL to give grants to the Communes and to the Regions in whose territory plants for the production of electricity are located.

In *Germany*, we find that government forecasts on the contribution of nuclear power to energy supply have also been over-optimistic, mainly due to intense local opposition, channelled through the administrative courts.

Licensing procedure is now regulated by a Decree of 1977.[123] A recent report issued by the Minister of the Interior[124] aimed at speeding up the commissioning of nuclear installations by side-stepping the delaying tactics of anti-nuclear groups. It aimed to give courts and nuclear plant constructors much clearer guidelines on safeguards required, and in addition recommends that constructors standardise their designs. In 1982 a new amendment to section 7 of the 1959 Law was introduced, accelerating the procedure for awarding nuclear plant licences.[125]

Conclusion: We can see, then, that in the last decade, most of the states have tried to reconcile the aims of their nuclear programmes with demands for public participation and representation, with varying degrees of success. It should be added that in the United Kingdom,[126] Italy,[127] France[128] and Germany there has been considerable State support for various aspects of the nuclear industry, although in Germany where the generation and supply of nuclear power is undertaken by the EVU's[129], Federal State support has been limited to research and development activities.[130] It should perhaps be added that it has often been suggested that the motivation for this support lies not so much in a desire to keep the costs of electricity generation low, as to ensure the continued survival of national nuclear industries.[131]

122 Law no. 8 of January 10, 1983, in Gazz. Uff. January 14, 1983, no. 13.

123 Decree on Licensing Procedure for Nuclear Installations, issued pursuant to Article 7 of the 1959 Atomgesetz, February 12, 1977, BGBl I 1280.

124 See Financial Times, September 10, 1981.

125 Erste Verordnung zur Änderung der Atomrechtlichen Verfahrensverordnung, March 31, 1982. BGBl I 409.

126 Nuclear Finance Act 1977.

127 There have been various additions to ENEL's finances. Law no. 253 of May 7, 1973 in Gazz. Uff. June 1, 1973, no. 141 established a 'fondo di dotazione'. This was augmented by Law no. 309 of June 15, 1981, in Gazz. Uff. June 18, 1981 no. 166.

128 EDF receives capital from the Fonds du développement économique et social — see Chapter IV, pp. 54–55.

129 See Chapter IV, pp. 51; 57.

130 See Chapter III, pp. 39–43.

131 For the United Kingdom see Surrey *et al*: "The A.G.R. A Case Study in Reactor Choice" in [1977] Energy Policy 97.

2. Coal

Domestic coal production is encouraged in the three Member States still possessing a coal industry. State subsidies are available to encourage the use of coal, especially in electricity generation and for industrial purposes.

In the *United Kingdom*, the oil crisis of 1973 encouraged the NCB (National Coal Board) to revise its production level forecasts. The most recent document, entitled Coal for the Future, published in 1977 as a result of the studies of a Tripartite Group, consisting of the NCB, the unions involved in the coal industry and the Ministry concerned, recommended a 37 per cent increase in production by 2000.[132] Financial assistance to the coal industry was provided under the Coal Industry Act 1973 which reduced the book value of NCB assets, wrote off accumulated deficits and provided a new borrowing structure for the NCB. In addition, grants were made available to meet the social costs of colliery closure, the cost of 'extra-burn' of coal at power stations and the costs of stocking coal at power stations. In aggregate these measures conferred grants on the industry of up to £720 million for the following five year period.[133] Further grants were made available under the Coal Industry Act 1977 towards pit closures, redundancy payments, stocking coal and coke and regional aid. Originally these grants were to run until the end of 1981, but the Coal Industry Act 1980 provided for their extension, together with a raising of various financial limits, until the end of 1983.[134]

In *France*, we have noted in Chapter III that the VIIIth Plan envisaged an increasing role for coal, particularly imported coal.[135] Following the signing of a 'contrat du programme' in 1978, CDF (Charbonnages de France) was given complete liberty in fixing domestic selling prices, with the provision that the state would guarantee coverage of non-operating costs and a fixed subsidies on every therme of coal produced. CDF would be allowed complete freedom in managing its financial affairs so long as it observed the limits imposed by the levels of subsidisation.[136]

In *Germany*, the First Revision to the Energy Programme, in 1974[137] gave coal a new 'league position' in energy production projections. To ensure that the new targets would be reached, the Federal Government stepped up its aid for capital investments, for research and development into conversion techniques and deep drilling techniques. In view of the cost disadvantages resulting from unfavourable geological conditions and in consideration of the appreciable capital investments which will continue

132 Coal for the Future, Tripartite Group, 1977.
133 Coal Industry Act 1973, s. 1.
134 Coal Industry Act 1980, s. 1.
135 Chapter 3, p. [14].
136 L'Avenir du Charbon, in Annales des Mines, mai—juin 1981.
137 Erstes Verstromungsgesetz: See Appendix 3.

to be required to maintain production capacity, the German coal industry continues to receive considerable government support. For the year 1979–1980 Ruhrkohle[138] spent DM 430 million on R and D, of which state subsidies accounted for DM 170 million. The company received a further DM 723 million in state aid, of which DM 470 million was in the form of investment subsidies and a further DM 253 million went towards the rationalisation programme. At the beginning of 1980, Saarbergwerke AG, the subsidiary of the state steel firm Salzgitter, received DM 100 million in state subsidies towards research over the next five years.[139]

The 1974 Energy Programme Revision prescribed that 33 million tonnes of coal should be consumed annually by the electricity industry, until 1980. An 'equalisation fund' was set up from which the following measures were to be financed:

- compensation to meet the additional costs incurred in using coal of Community origin in the production of electricity as against using heavy fuel oil;
- grants towards investments costs;
- grants towards electricity transport costs.

To finance the increased aids to the coal industry, the Kohlepfenning, a levy raised on the consumers of electricity, was introduced by the Third Electricity from Coal law in December 1974.[140] The rate of this off-set levy was increased in 1976 from 3.75 per cent to 4.5 per cent of the invoiced price of electricity consumed by both domestic and industrial users. As of January 1, 1978 different rates applied according to region, but the Federal average was still 4.5 per cent. On January 1, 1979 this Federal average rose to 6.2 per cent, with regional differences being maintained.[141]

3. Gas

By the Oil and Gas (Enterprise) Act 1982 the *United Kingdom* government has attempted, inter alia, to introduce more competition into the gas industry. BGC has a monopoly over important areas of the industry, owning the on-shore pipeline system and having a virtual monopoly of supply in the United Kingdom. BGC was also entitled to first refusal of gas landed in the UK from the continental shelf. In the view of the present government, these factors resulted in an unsatisfactory development of United Kingdom gas reserves, too few operators being prepared to engage in production to

138 The structure of Ruhrkohle is explained in Chapter IV, at p. 60.

139 Handelsblatt, February 8, 1977.

140 On the general development of the Electricity from Coal Laws see Chapter IV, pp. 91–92.

141 Drittes Verstromungsgesetz. BGBl I 1974, p. 3973. The constitutionality of the Kohlepfennig has been sustained by the Federal Administrative Court: see judgment of June 6, 1984 (J C140.81, Betriebs-Berater 1985, p. 229 et seq.).

be offered a monopolistic price by BGC. The 1982 Act limits the monopoly of supply to customers buying less than 25 thousand therms per annum who are situated within 25 yards of an existing main. Other customers may be supplied by persons other than the BGC although consents from the Secretary of State will be required for supplies of less than one million therms per annum. Private suppliers will also be given access to the BGC's pipeline systems , subject to the BGC's own operations and the right of other persons already permitted to use the system. These changes are seen as being likely to increase United Kingdom gas production. Under other powers conferred by the Act the Government has also compelled BGC to sell off its oil production and exploration interests,[142] but this should be seen rather as an element of the Government's general "privatisation" policy than an energy policy measure.

In *France*, where the domestic gas field of Lacq covered 30 per cent of consumption in 1981, but will yield only half of its present output by 1990, tax incentives have been introduced to encourage exploration for gas and oil on the national territory,[143] and procedures for the application for exploration and production licences have been simplified.[144]

The second largest producer of hydrocarbons, *The Netherlands* has also introduced some changes into the legislative regime governing the disposition of domestically produced gas. The position of the Minister of Economic Affairs with respect to the setting of prices for natural gas destined for both domestic and foreign markets was strengthened by the adoption of the Wet Aardgasprijzen in 1974. This Act empowered the Minister of Economic Affairs to fix minimum prices for the sale of gas, in the event that prices for domestic gas, agreed between Gasunie and the provincial distribution companies did not reflect market values. This Act was one of the main instruments of the government's then operative policy of conserving natural gas for premium uses. Renegotiation of the prices for export contracts was however secured on the basis of agreements reached between companies involved in exportation and a special high commissioner appointed by the government for that purpose in 1978.[145] The 1976 Decree[146] now requires notification of prices and destination to the Minister of Economic Affairs.

The State participation level in companies engaged in natural gas exploration and production was originally 40 per cent, but this was raised to 50 per cent for new fields in 1976. The licensee must sell natural gas to the NV Gasunie, if this gas is intended for consumption within the Netherlands,

142 Ss. 9–11: see generally Page, "Competition and Monopoly in United Kingdom Energy Supply: The Case of Gas", (1984) 2 Jl. of Energy and Natural Resources Law 30 for details.

143 The 'provision pour la reconstitution des gisements' Code Minier, article 39.

144 Law no. 77–620 of June 16, 1977 in J.O.R.F. June 18, 1977.

145 Royal Decree May 23, 1980, Staatscourant, no. 192.

146 See Chapter IV, p. 86.

and the Minister may also determine that other gas must be supplied to the Gasunie, if he deems it necessary. With the enactment of the 1974 Law, the State now exercises complete control over Gasunie, and hence is in a position to influence that company's sales policy. Another feature of the regulation of the natural gas market which deserves mention is the recently concluded agreement between the State and the major oil companies, Shell and Esso, which participate in the production company NAM. The profits derived from the sales of natural gas have risen considerably, following the 1979 oil crisis, and pressures were exerted by trade unions and political groups for a closer control on the destination of these profits. The government chose to influence the investment decisions of the two companies, not by legislation, but by means of an unpublished gentlemen's agreement.[147]

In *Italy*, domestically produced gas covers some 45 per cent of gas needs at present, but this will decline to 20 per cent by 1990. The government has made available over one billion lire to Snam Progetti, a subsidiary of the state hydrocarbons company, ENI, under the Programma Energetica of 1975 for exploration for natural gas in the Po Valley.

In *Germany*, natural gas production covered some 32 per cent of domestic requirements in 1981, while domestic oil production covered less than 5 per cent of total energy demand. However, the various Revisions to the Energy Programme have provided for funds for exploration and deep drilling in the territory of the Federal Republic, and additional subsidies have been made available to Deminex, to encourage its overseas exploration activities. The present system of subsidisation takes the form of a loan of 75 per cent of the amount paid for exploration, and this loan needs only be repaid if oil or gas is found. The two Federal Research programmes, referred to in Chapter III, have also made provision in the form of grants for various projects on prospecting and recovery technology.

4. Oil

Here the only country whose policies need special mention is the *United Kingdom*, where the most striking development in energy matters in the last decade has been the meteoric growth of the domestic oil industry. Policy developments relating to oil production in the remaining countries are covered in the preceding section or in Chapter IV.

The United Kingdom government's goal in the early licensing rounds was to secure that hydrocarbons were explored for and produced as early as possible and the licensing regime, as adapted in 1964 for offshore operations, has always been strongly stamped by this objective.[148] While

[147] Barents, R., "Legal Aspects of Dutch Energy Policy" (1983), Jl of Energy and Natural Resources Law 160, at p. 166.

[148] See Dam, K. W., "Oil and Gas Licensing in the North Sea" (1965) 8 Jl. of Law and Econ. 51.

the scheme today retains its encouragements to rapid *exploration* – regular allocations of territory in small parcels, competitive work programmes, stringent surrender provisions – since 1974 the government's attitude to speed of *production* has become more nuanced. Along with the idea of greater State control over operations and, in particular, disposal of production, expressed through the creation of BNOC and the negotiation of participartion agreements with existing licensees, came a concern about depletion policy. Government took powers, in both new and existing licences, to delay the start of commercial production, to set rates of production and, within strict limits, subsequently to vary those rates.[149] Governments have, however, been extremely cautious in the use of these powers, partly in order to avoid accusations of depriving existing licensees of vested rights[150], partly because of major uncertainties about production and market profiles for North Sea oil. On only one commercial field, discovered and operated by BNOC (now Britoil), has the start-up of production been explicitly delayed under these powers.

Financial returns to companies – and hence the level of taxes and royalties – have been a much more important factor in determining speed of development and production than have direct government controls. In addition to royalties, which have remained fixed at 12.5 per cent, Governments have since 1975 taken a major share of oilfield revenue through the imposition of a special Petroleum Revenue Tax (PRT).[151] This tax has been levied at steadily increasing rates since its introduction – from 40 per cent to 70 per cent on the value of production, less certain deductions as to costs of exploration and development and a 'tax free' allowance on

[149] See Petroleum (Production) Regulations 1982, S.I. 1982 No. 1000, Sch.5, c11. 14, 15.

[150] In 1974 the then Secretary of State for Industry, Mr. Eric Varley, in response to pressure from the oil companies for some reassurance about the way depletion controls would be exercised, issued a set of guidelines covering five points (882 H.C. Deb., cols. 648–50 (written answers) December 6, 1974):

(i) that no delays would be imposed on the development of finds already made or on any new finds made up to the end of 1975 under existing licences, and if it proved necessary to delay the development of finds made in 1976 or later, there would be full consultation with the companies;

(ii) that no cuts would be made in production from any finds made before the end of 1975 under existing licences until 1982 at the earliest, or until four years after the start of production, whichever was later;

(iii) that no cuts would be made in production from any field found after 1975 under an existing licence until 150 per cent of the capital investment had been recovered;

(iv) that full regard would be paid to the technical and commercial aspects of fields;

(v) that the needs of the offshore supply industry for a continuing and stable market would be taken into account.

The present Government's approach to depletion policy has remained in line with the above: for the latest statement see North Sea Oil Depletion Policy (1982–83) H.C. 134.

[151] Oil Taxation Act 1975, Part I.

each field. In 1981 the government decided to increase its take further by adding a Supplementary Petroleum Duty (SPD)[152], at the rate of 20 per cent gross returns from oil field operations in 1981 and 1982. Intense industry criticism described this tax structure as damaging to the prospects for the United Kingdom oil industry, but until 1983, the government retained confidence that the United Kingdom remained an attractive and politically stable base for oil operations and continued to describe the regime as 'fair and economically justifiable'. The Finance Act 1983, however, acknowledged the case for financial encouragement of exploration and production by offering major tax reductions for new and marginal fields. Accompanying legislation, the Petroleum Royalties (Relief) Act 1983, provides for the exemption of such fields from royalties.

The Government's other recent preoccupation, with the privatisation of activities of BNOC, and its subsequent abolition, has been discussed in Chapter IV.

5. Renewables

In April 1974, the *United Kingdom* Department of Energy established the Energy Support Unit, under powers granted by the Science and Technology Act 1965. The purpose of the unit was seen to be the assessment of the various energy options open to the United Kingdom and the formulation of research and development programmes in appropriate fields outside the nuclear power industry. Initially, the Unit concentrated on technical aspects of alternative energy sources, especially solar and geothermal, and on the possibilities for conservation of energy in industrial processes. Practical demonstration projects have also been undertaken, on solar space-heating and the use of organic waste products. Current expenditure runs at about £12 million per annum. Some efforts have been made to develop the combined heat and power industry, with grants being provided to local government with the aim of introducing schemes in their areas.[153] The Energy Act 1983, recently passed by Parliament, divests the CEGB of some of its monopoly powers, and encourages private generation based on combined heat and power production (CHP), and the use of waste heat from industrial processes. While a thriving, but small-scale solar industry exists in the United Kingdom, that industry complains of discriminatory planning laws, unsympathetic planning authorities, and of the disincentives arising out of property taxation.[154]

The role of renewables has perhaps achieved more recognition in *France*, where the development of alternative energies was made a programme of

[152] Finance Act 1981, Parts VII and VIII.

[153] See Financial Times, April 25, 1983.

[154] See Assessment Report on the Community Demonstration Projects in the field of energy saving and alternative energy sources, COM (82) 324 final, June 1982.

priority action under the VIIth Plan. France ranks second in the world, after the United States, in respect of the levels of subsidies accorded for research in this field. A *Commissariat à l'énergie solaire* (COMES) was created in 1978[155] to liase with institutions and with public and private enterprise, and to develop their awareness of solar energy and the research and development which would permit its economic utilisation. This organisation succeeded the *Délégation aux énergies nouvelles* created by a decree of April 9, 1975[156] which had been charged with the promotion and development of all new sources of energy, not yet exploited at a commercial level. COMES has now been merged into the *Agence pour la Maîtrise d'Energie* endowed with a budget of some 1.2 billion FF, which it may dispense in the form of grants to encourage energy saving investments and research and development in the utilisation of renewables.

In addition we find new regulations on the use of thermal electricity, designed to encourage the use of waste heat from industrial processes[157] and new tariff structures for self-generators, again aimed at encouraging the level of co-generation in France.[158]

In *The Netherlands* we find several public institutions engaged in research and development of renewable energy forms and combined heat and power production — the Beleidsgrope Stadsverwarming, set up in 1975 and the Voorlopige Raad voor het Energie Onderzoek, set up in 1980. In addition subsidies are available to encourage the use of new energy forms in industry.[159]

The 1978 Investment Account Act, as modified by a further Act of 1980[160] introduced special allowances for energy saving investments which include the production of combined heat and power, the use of waste heat, wind energy and solar power.

In *Italy*, there have been a number of organisational initiatives aimed at promoting research and development and exploitation of renewable energy resources. We have already mentioned the creation of the ENEA.[161] An earlier law of 1981 authorised the state-owned electricity monopoly, ENEL, to further initiatives taken by local and regional authorities to bring about the more rational use of energy and the utilisation of renewable energy sources.[162] These reforms are important in that they pave the way for municipalities engaged in electrical power generation to operate what are

155 Decree no. 78–268, of March 9, 1978, in J.O.R.F. March 10, 1978, p. 1019.

156 Decree 75–231, April 9, 1975 in J.O.R.F., p. 3798.

157 Law no. 80–531, of July 15, 1980 *supra*, note 76.

158 Arrêté no. 77–37/P of March 31, 1977 in B.O.S.P. no. 10 of April 1, 1977.

159 Order Concerning the Investment Subsidies for the Restriction of Energy Use for Companies, September 6, 1977, no. 175.

160 June 29, 1978 Staatsblad no. 368 and June 25, 1980, Staatsblad no. 389.

161 By Law no. 84 of March 5, 1982, *supra* note 118.

162 Law no. 309 of June 15, 1981 in Gazz. Uff. June 18, 1981 no. 166.

known as "total energy plants" which combine several energy sources in the production of electricity.

The new law no. 308 of May 29, 1982[163] makes a number of important innovations in respect of renewable energy and also seeks to involve the Regions both in consultations on the formation of national energy policy objectives and in the provision of grants for investment in renewable energies and energy conservation.[164] Article 4 of this law allows for the production of electrical energy by local authorities, thus derogating further from the ENEL monopoly, in cases where new plant is fuelled by renewable energy sources – solar, hydro, geothermal or waste heat. Prior to the passing of Law no. 308 in 1982, several regions had already passed laws providing incentives for the development of renewables, and in particular solar and hydro-electric energies.[165]

In *Germany*, measures to promote district heating and combined heat and power production include Federal grants, and administrative conventions (concluded between the Federal and Länder governments on the granting of financial assistance in accordance with article 104 of the Grundgesetz) providing for a programme of assistance to district heating projects with an expenditure of DM 1.2 billion over a period of four years. In addition the Anregung von Verträgen zwischen der industriellen Kraftwirtschaft und den Energieversorgungsunternehmen[166] of August 1979 provides for government-backed agreements between the electricity supply industry and industry in general with the aim of encouraging the use of industrial waste heat.

B. Diversification of Imported Energy Supplies

The need to diversify supplies of imported energy is particularly pressing in countries such as Germany, France and Italy which are heavily dependent on imported oil and gas and whose own domestic production levels are declining. Government efforts have tended to be directed towards diversification and hence security of imports of each separate energy resource. In relation to natural gas the large investments required, whether for pipeline or LNG transport, have meant the negotiation of new supplies on a 'State-to-State' basis.

163 *Supra* at note 87.

164 Articles 1–3 of Law no. 308 provide that the C.I.P.E. may issue directives co-ordinating public activity in relation to conservation of energy and the development of renewables, after consultation with the regions. See Spaziante, V. (a cura di), *Le regioni nella politica dell'energia* (Milano 1982).

165 For example Regional Law no. 57 of December 4, 1978 in Boll. Uff. Reg. 1978 n. 52 on the use of Solar Energy in Sicily and Provincial Law no. 14 of May 29, 1980 in Boll. Uff. Reg. June 10, 1980 on measures for saving energy and for the utilisation of alternative energy sources in the autonomous province of Trento.

166 3 Energieprogramm TZ78, 91 of August 1979.

1. Coal

In the *United Kingdom*, coal importers require a licence under the Import, Export and Customs Powers (Defence) Act 1939, section 1. While there are no official restrictions on the grant of licences, various agreements between the CEGB and the NCB promote the purchase of domestically produced coal by the former organisation with subsidisation by the government to cover the extra cost over the price of foreign coal. There are however signs that the CEGB might increase its purchases of foreign coal.[167]

The VIIIth Plan envisaged an increased role for coal, and especially imported coal, in *French* energy consumption. To this end, the Plan exhorted the CDF to extend its coal mining interests abroad, and a recent report from the Ministry of Industry recommended the withdrawal of ATIC's coal import monopoly[168] and the introduction of a system of licences similar to those presently issued for petroleum products.

The Netherlands' government has as yet made no special arrangements for increasing or diversifying coal imports.

In *Italy* ENI entered in October 1981 into a joint venture with the American energy company Occidental to manage a collection of ENI's chemical plants in Italy and Occidental's coal mines in the USA.[169] While the joint-venture agreement quickly broke down, the transfer of the US coal mines has gone through. Despite the high operating costs of the mines, the deal has been justified on the grounds that Italy's energy strategy provides for a doubling of coal consumption from a low base in the course of the next decade.[170]

In *Germany* coal import quotas have been raised by virtue of the Dritte Verordnung zur Durchführung des Gesetzes über das Zollkontingent für feste Brennstoffe.[171] Quotas have been extended until 1995, but are set at an average of 4 million tons of coal equivalent (mtce) for 1981–85, increasing to an average of 8 mtce for 1986–1990 and to 12 mtce for the period 1991–1995. Quotas on coking coal have also been adjusted, and a further 5 mtce is to be made available for the coal conversion industry. Hence, under the new quota schedule, imported coal could rise from 8 per cent of total final demand for coal in 1979 to 18 per cent by 1990 and 24 per cent by 1995.[172]

167 See Financial Times, December 12, 1982.
168 See Chapter IV, p. 79.
169 See Financial Times, November 12, 1981.
170 The Pandolfi Plan of 1981 recommended a large increase in the use of coal.
171 December 12, 1980, BGBl I 2261. As to the validity of the empowering ECSC Recommendation, see Chapter IV above, note 94.
172 As the legality of these quota arrangements, see European Court of Justice Case 36/83 *Mabanaft GmbH* v. *Hauptzollamt Emmerich* (June 28, 1984, not yet reported).

2. Gas

The political controversies and legal vicissitudes attached to the conclusion and execution of the contracts for the supply of natural gas from the Soviet Union to France, Germany and Italy – which it is not necessary to discuss here – should not distract attention from an important contrast in this sector of policy between the United Kingdom, Germany and the Netherlands on the one hand, and France and Italy on the other. Both groups of countries have sought to enlarge and diversify their imports of natural gas. In the former group, negotiations have been carried on, and contracts concluded, as a matter of commercial arrangement between gas wholesalers – BGC, Ruhrgas, Gasunie – and external suppliers (albeit sometimes in a highly political atmosphere). French and Italian practice is well illustrated by their respective recent contracts for the supply of Algerian gas.

In January 1982, the French government signed a dual contract with Algeria. On the one hand, the Algerian oil and gas company, Sonatrach will sell GDF 9.15 billion m^3 of gas at a basic price, indexed wholly to that of a basket of eight crude oils. On the other hand, the French government will make available to Algeria 'a bonus for the valorisation of the commodity'. To these two factors must be added the cost of transportation and regassification, bringing the final price to a level which far exceeds current prices for Dutch and Soviet gas.[173] The reason for this extra price is that "the Franco-Algerian agreement is not a simple commercial deal, it is a fundamental co-development achievement".[174]

Similar controversies have been aroused by the Italian contract with Sonatrach, a contract concluded only in early 1983 after several years of discussion and disagreement.

In April 1983, the Italian Parliament finally approved a law which allows the State to pay the 'political premium' being charged by Algeria on the market price.[175] Hence the way was clear for SNAM, the gas subsidiary of ENI, to sign a technical agreement with Sonatrach, at an agreed price which is up to 50 cents per therm higher than the price which SNAM considered as economic. The government then agreed to pay SNAM the difference between what the latter considered the economic price and the agreed price, but SNAM refused to sign the agreement with Sonatrach until Parliament had actually passed the Bill authorising the provision of Lit. 540 billion over the three years, the cost of the 'political' premium.

3. Oil

A similar contrast may be observed in the way in which States have sought to secure diversified supplies of crude oil.

173 De Thomas, B. and Junqua, D., "L'Algérie livrera à la France ...", Le Monde, February 4, 1982.

174 Delarue, M., "Deux Logiques", Le Monde February 4, 1982.

175 Law no. 151 of May, 2, 1983, Gazz. Uff. May 6, 1983 no. 123.

French policy has been to assure supply through government-to-government contracts. Since 1974 such contracts have been signed with Saudi Arabia, Mexico, Venezuela and Iraq. The largest contract, with Saudi Arabia, signed in 1974, provides for yearly supplies of 12 million tonnes of crude over twenty years, to be lifted in equal shares by Elf and CFP, and under the terms of the contract, they must process the crude in France. In the initial eight years this proved to be a highly satisfactory arrangement for both companies which even in tight market conditions had access to relatively cheap and steady supplies of Saudi crude. Following the oil glut in late 1981, the companies complained that they were locked into lifting too much crude which, because of destination restrictions, they could not resell. Eventually the government allowed the companies to ease their liftings and President Mitterand, in an official statement, suggested that an effort would be made to introduce more flexibility into long-term oil contracts.[176]

Saudi Arabia has once again increased its dominant share of *Italy*'s crude oil imports. In 1979 Saudi Arabia had abruptly terminated a long-term supply contract when it became the centre of bribery allegations, and the new contract, concluded in late 1982, between Petromin and Agip, the ENI oil subsidiary, was concluded only after a year of diplomatic exchanges, culminating in an agreement between the foreign ministers of the two countries in January 1982.[177]

Germany and *The Netherlands*, in contrast, have remained committed to their belief in the validity of limited intervention in the oil market, though the activity of the German government in promoting the formation of Deminex as an overseas exploration and production vehicle, and in subsidising these activities, is worthy of note.

In the field of petroleum product imports we need mention only the recent changes in the French regime under the 1928 law. In 1979 the government introduced a new system of A3 licences, substituting for the former quota system a new system of supply programmes which all applicants must submit to a special commission for approval.[178] All licence holders must satisfy the obligations relating to security, defence and the national economy imposed by article 2 of the 1928 Law; in addition companies must guarantee that at least 80 per cent of their supplies are supplied on three year contracts concluded with refineries situated within the European Community, and in any event the part covered by any other form of contract must not exceed 20 per cent annually of the total supply of each operator. Two-thirds of total supply must be carried under the French Flag.

176 See Petroleum Economist, September 1982, p. 382.
177 See Financial Times, November 30, 1982.
178 Decree 79—1139.

IV. Conclusions

Over the last ten years, each of the States with which we are concerned has consecrated a considerable legislative effort to the achievement of energy policy objectives, an effort to which we can hardly do justice in the few foregoing pages. Yet despite its brevity and incompleteness, this survey can help us to assess the significance of legal diversity to the progress of energy policy and to the likely progress of its successor, the Community energy strategy.

A first observation that might be made is that there is a good deal of common ground between the States in relation to the instruments they employ for the achievement of certain objectives. Subsidies and information are widely encountered as means of promoting the development of domestic resources, encouraging import diversification, and promoting energy conservation and fuel substitution. Forms of subsidy may vary, for example as between grants, cheap loans, and tax concessions, and the legal incidents of a subsidy may differ from one legal order to another, but these seem likely to be factors of only marginal importance. Again, regulation appears to have a role to play in all States in promoting conservation and substitution (for example in the form of thermal insulation standards). Some States, notably France, appear to employ regulation for a wider range of conservation goals than do others such as the United Kingdom and the Netherlands, and such differences, though apparently marginal, may reflect quite deeply-rooted ideas about the proper scope of regulation, which could be hard to harmonise. By contrast, in the field of response to short-term disturbance, reliance on regulation has been quite general, and differences in forms of regulation or responsible authorities should cause no greater problem in the energy sector than in any field of Community activity.

These similarities can be quite briefly described, but in terms of a common legal background to energy policy they in fact carry us quite far. They mean that, over most of the field of energy policy (and it will be noted that we have not yet referred to nuclear development) Member States are apt to have in mind a similar *range* of instrumental possibilities for the promotion of a given objective, whether by direct Community action or by Member States in pursuance of a Community obligation. When, however, we come to consider which possibilities Member States, left to themselves, might actually choose, and what difficulties they might experience in implementing given choices, the problems of the diversity that surrounds this common core of instruments begin to emerge.

Many of these problems are, of course, strictly non-legal. The difficulty, for Italy, in accepting the Commission's proposals for subsidies for intra-Community coal trade and for Community aid for the financing of cyclical coal stocks lies not in any legal obstacle to the employment of subsidies in such circumstances in Italy, but in the fact that Italy is, in effect, a non-producer of coal whose economic interest lies in maintaining access to cheap and, if possible, secure third country imports rather than in supporting higher-cost British and German production. Similarly, political divergences may far outweigh legal ones in impeding the formulation of a Community policy on the diversification of third-country natural gas supplies.

The areas of legal diversity within the Community are, however, still big enough to matter. The obligation to maintain stocks of petroleum offers a simple example. It might be thought that a simple obligation on the State to ensure that the country maintained a given number of days' stock of products would cause no problems: it was imposed by directive and did not limit, even de facto, the choice of means open to Member States. Yet no less than five Member States, including Germany, Italy and the Netherlands, were so slow to implement the 1972 Directive raising the stock requirement to 90 days' consumption that the Commission had to institute article 169 procedure against them, in September 1975, in order to secure compliance. The problems were essentially of a legal and instrumental nature. In Germany, the 1976 law requiring companies to hold larger stocks was the subject of constitutional challenge with the result that while the Federal Constitutional Court did not find the requirement for private persons to carry out public duties (in this case the duty to build up strategic stocks) in itself unconstitutional, the Federal government was led to accept a joint proposal submitted by the majors and independents to create a 'corporation at public law' for the purpose of petroleum stockpiling in the context of more equitable financing arrangements.[179]

In the *Netherlands*, even without the benefit of such constitutional protection (but fortified by a tradition of government policy-making towards industry through consensus and gentlemen's agreements, rather than arm's length regulation), the interim Central Petroleum Storage Organisation was set up in response to the need to ensure the availability of stocks that *could* be utilised in an emergency, on the initiative of the companies themselves. The particular problem for the Dutch was that while Dutch refiners held stocks in excess of the requirements imposed by the 1976 Law, these stocks could not be separated from commercial inventories. It should be remembered that about 50 per cent of the output of Dutch refineries is destined for export and another 15 per cent is sold as bunkers for international trade.

In *Italy* the unusual slowness of the legislative procedure meant that it was not until 1981 that a law was passed giving all the necessary powers to require the creation and maintenance of clear-cut emergency stocks by both refiners, importers and retailers. Previously, the practice of including

[179] BVerfg.E vol 30, p. 292.

part of the non-oil industry stocks in the national storage target (90 days) meant that emergency reserves were often amalgamated with commercial inventories.

We may contrast the difficulties encountered in these countries with the fortunate situation of the French government which has for many years imposed a stock maintenance obligation as an element of licences for the importation both of crude oil and of products.[180]

Difficulties experienced in relation to stocks are suggestive of the major problems which might arise in attempting to impose or implement concrete Community obligations in other areas where there is wide variation in legal circumstances as between Member States. Two examples will suffice. The first can be found in Member States' approaches to energy pricing, which has obvious uses as a tool of energy policy (restraint of windfall profits, conservation, fuel substitution) and of other policies also (such as competitive advantage for national industry and agriculture through low energy prices). Almost the least of the problems here is the professed difference of attitude between States as to the extent to which they should interfere in "natural" processes of energy price formation. The real difficulties arise from the existence and use of legal mechanisms of intervention which vary not only from country to country but also from fuel to fuel. Straightforward price regulation of a general kind is used only in Italy and in France; in these countries it conditions the whole operation of the oil market. Elsewhere such prices are free, though crude oil prices are heavily influenced by the United Kingdom government through BNOC and the complex series of agreements it maintains with producers. In some countries gas or electricity tariffs, or both, are subject to statutory regulation, as for Dutch gas; in other cases, governments may rely on agreements with producers, or on the wide range of influence they can exert on State enterprises with ostensible legal autonomy in tariff-setting. Harmonising substantive price policies across this range of legal intervention mechanisms can hardly be easy; even if it were achieved, faithfulness of performance would be hard to check. "Quality" standards in price intervention, such as transparency, may be the best that can be achieved without a harmonisation of intervention methods which would involve basic changes in domestic legal practice and would therefore be sure to meet the strongest resistance.

A second example can be drawn from the field of nuclear energy. What is remarkable about this area is that despite a commitment by all States except (currently) the Netherlands, performance in the achievement of nuclear goals should be so varied. Doubtless there is no single reason for such variation which, it should be noted, cuts right across the ownership

180 The Decree of October 18, 1950 on import licences for crude oil required that all licence holders must conform to technical requirements specified by the Minister in charge of hydrocarbons.

structures adopted for the nuclear and electricity industries: France and Italy alike rely on State monopolies in nuclear research and development, and in electricity generation, but with quite different results in terms of rate of installation of nuclear generating capacity, while German performance, with nuclear plant construction in the hands of private or mixed enterprise electricity utilities, falls somewhere between the two. Legal circumstances, however, almost certainly contribute to national variations in this field. Procedures for the siting of nuclear power plants encapsulate really significant differences in national approaches to the taking of major individual decisions of this kind. The French approach, even after the changes of 1976, is highly centralised; the Italian approach involves a diffusion of power among a number of centres at national, regional and local levels; the United Kingdom relies heavily on elaborate pre-decision procedures at local level; the German approach is the most legalistic, in terms of offering opportunities for judicial challenge of the various administrative decisions in the procedure. Again, any harmonisation of procedures in the interests of a more uniform rate of nuclear development would involve departures from strongly rooted ways of thinking about the legal organisation of decision-making; though without such harmonisation, one may question whether the current disparities are ever likely to be lessened.

The examples here cited are major ones which involve most or all of the Member States under examination. The reader should not find it difficult, in reviewing the contents of this and the preceding chapters, to identify other, more particular cases in which it is legal and institutional factors, rather than differences in the economic interests of Member States, which have constituted, or would constitute, impediments to a more uniform, or centralised, Community energy policy. Such factors, along with economic interests, can of course also be the occasion of breaches of basic Community rules regarding free movement of goods. The operation of these rules in the energy sector is the subject of our next chapter. Our final chapter considers, *inter alia*, how the new energy strategy may cope with the kinds of diversity we have here identified.

Chapter VI

The Operation of Basic Common Market Principles in the Energy Sector

I. Introduction

The subsidiary question posed by this study is whether an energy strategy flexible enough to accomodate the range of national divergences we have discussed can be faithful to the general and basic principles of the European Community treaties, in particular to the commitment to a free and uncompartmented energy market. This is not a question directly addressed by the Commission's strategy document: indeed, its references to free trade within the Community are at best glancing. In stating that "differences of effort and achievement [in energy policy] between Member States will ... adversely affect the level of economic activity in the Community as a whole"[1] the Commission doubtless has in mind a chain of causation one of whose links is the maintenance of barriers to trade between Member States and the economic disadvantages flowing therefrom. In the context of pricing and taxation policy, it stresses the need for the avoidance of distortions in intra-Community competition and for the presence, within the Community, of a common market in primary energy to secure this end.[2] These remarks are not, of course, directed to the operation of the basic treaty rules on trade barriers designed to secure a single market, like those prohibiting quantitative restrictions and measures of equivalent effect. Arguably, however, they imply a view of these rules, as of price and tax harmonisation, as being in the nature of a means to the end of effective energy policy within the Community, rather than as representing an end in themselves. From this it would follow that under the new strategy such rules might, with the connivance of the Commission, be ignored or sidestepped, if such action seemed likely to promote the achievement of energy policy goals.

If this is a correct interpretation of the approach of the Commission, within the framework of the strategy, to the enforcement of free trade

[1] COM (81) 540 final, para 6.

[2] Ibid., paras 16, 17.

principles, it becomes important to know whether it signals a new flexibility of approach, or simply the continuation of enforcement trends or practices already present in the energy sector. This involves looking at the way in which the Commission has carried out its enforcement function in the energy sector hitherto. In so doing we confine ourselves to a quite narrow segment of the history recounted in broad terms in Chapter II, considering only those Treaty rules and principles which may be implemented or enforced by the Commission — whether through article 169, EEC Treaty, or more specific procedures — without the intervention of the Council. Even this segment is too rich for comprehensive analysis here, and we limit our examples to the field of the EEC Treaty in which, as already noted,[3] free trade rules were seen as forming the most important element of policy for the energy sector as for other sectors. It will be easiest if we follow the order in which the Treaty itself deals with barriers to intra-Community Trade.

II. Customs Duties

It does not appear that customs duties have been imposed by Member States either upon the intra-Community import or export of energy products or resources. Such imposition would, of course, be clearly contrary to the Treaty. This does not mean that energy taxation has been an unproblematical field: energy taxation, along with pricing, is indeed picked out by the Commission, in the strategy document, as a topic for priority Community action. The Treaty, however, seeks to maintain a clear distinction between customs and equivalent duties on one hand, and internal taxation on the other. All customs duties are proscribed, but only *discriminatory* internal taxation is prohibited. Energy taxation falls exclusively into the internal category, and we shall look at it in more detail under that heading.

III. Quantitative Restrictions on Imports and Exports

Each Treaty provides for the abolition of any existing quantitative restriction on trade between the Member States and the prohibition of any new ones.[4] A clear prohibition is therefore placed on the use of traditional mechanisms such as export licensing, through which Member States might seek to restrict the volume of their exports of their natural resources to other parts of the Community in order to ensure the security of their own

[3] See Chapter II, pp. 15–16.
[4] ECSC Treaty, art. 4(a), EEC Treaty arts 30–34, Euratom Treaty, art. 93.

supplies, or to sell to more attractive markets. There is a possible exception, however, in the shape of article 36 of the EEC Treaty, which allows Member States to prohibit or restrict imports or exports on grounds which include that of "public security",[5] as long as this is not a means of arbitrary discrimination or a disguised restriction on trade between Member States. Up to 1984, the European Court of Justice had never been called upon to pronounce upon the meaning of "public security" in article 36, but the possible relevance of the phrase to situations of energy shortage is clear. Secure energy supplies are surely a key element in the economic life of any nation[6]; moreover a drastic reduction in supply levels might jeopardise other grounds referred to in article 36 — public order, and human life and health. But with the installation of machinery at Community level for taking decisions on export restrictions in times of supply difficulties the case for unilateral restrictions is gravely weakened. The Court has now however decided, in the *Campus Oil Case*, that a Member State can use the public security ground to justify intra-Community trade restrictions relating to oil *imports* in times of shortage.[7] Restrictions on *exports* were imposed by several States in 1973—74, but were of brief duration and led to no Commission action. The essential fragility of the energy common market was, however, exposed. The Commission's response, already briefly noted,[8] was to secure the promulgation by the Council of emergency arrangements for periods of energy supply difficulties in one or more States, under which export licensing may be reintroduced (either for surveillance or prohibition purposes) under the supervision of Commission and Council.[9] In one sense these arrangements are a signal of failure: had a real common market in crude oil and petroleum products been created by 1977 they would not have been necessary. In another sense they are a practical step towards integration, in that the installation at Community level of machinery for taking decisions on supply problems should, following the rules on pre-emption developed by the European Court, make it more difficult for Member States to rely on article 36 to justify unilateral trade restrictions

5 Article 36 provides that "the provisions of Arts. 30—34 shall not preclude prohibitions or restrictions on imports, exports or goods in transit, justified on grounds of public morality, public policy or public security".

6 Hence in the United Kingdom, a Royal Proclamation of December 12, 1973 issued under the Emergency Powers Act 1920 (as amended by the Emergency Powers Act 1964) stated that "the reduction of oil supplies reaching Great Britain [was] among factors which do, in our opinion, constitute a state of emergency within the meaning of the said Act of 1920". (S. I. 1973, Vol. III, p. 8035).

7 Case 72/83, *Campus Oil Ltd.* v. *Minister for Industry and Energy* [1984] 3 C. M. LR. 544.

8 See Chapter II, p. 27.

9 Council Decision 77/186, O.J. 1975, L61/23, as amended by Decision 79/879, O.J. 1979, L270/58, and applied by Commission Decision 78/890, O.J. 1978, L311/13.

outside the framework on this machinery.[10] It should be noted, however that the Court adopted a restrictive view of the pre-emption doctrine in the *Campus Oil* case.[11]

Quantitative trade restrictions need not take the form of straightforward prohibitions or quotas. A wide variety of measures, ranging from government purchasing preferences to labelling requirements, may be taken by governments with the object or effect, or both, of reducing the flow of cross-frontier trade in a given product, either generally or in particular trade channels. The EEC Treaty recognises this in its prohibition of measures having equivalent effect to quantitative restrictions. The Court's interpretation of this phrase has been as follows: whereas the Commission in its Directive 70/50[12] (which was concerned only with imports) indicated that the prohibition would only apply in cases where imports were subjected to some rule different from that applied to domestic products, the Court of Justice has made it clear that a measure applying in identical terms to domestic products and to imports may likewise be prohibited, if its effect is to disadvantage imported products by reference to domestic ones. Thus a maximum price measure, albeit quite general in its application, might infringe article 30, if 'fixed at a level such that the sale of imported products becomes, if not impossible, more difficult than that of domestic products".[13] From this quotation it will appear also that the Court has adopted a very broad concept of "effect". As it said in the case of *Procureur du Roi* v. *Dassonville*, the Treaty prohibition covers

> all trading rules enacted by Member States which are capable of hindering, directly or indirectly, actually or *potentially* intra-Community trade.[14]

Subsequently, the Court has somewhat reduced the impact of these holdings by indicating, in a case involving national marketing laws which, while identical for domestic and imported products, nonetheless produced a restrictive effect on imports, that such effects might be legitimate if the laws were

> necessary in order to satisfy mandatory requirements relating in particular to the effectiveness of fiscal supervision, the protection of public health, the fairness of commercial transactions and the defence of the consumer.[15]

[10] For a review of recent Court decisions, see Waelbroeck, M., "The Emergent Doctrine of Community Pre-emption" in Sandalow and Stein (eds.), *Courts and Free Markets*, pp. 548–583.

[11] See note 7, *supra*.

[12] J.O.C.E. 1970, L13, p. 29.

[13] Case 65/75, *Tasca* [1976] E.C.R. 291 at 305.

[14] Case 8/74, *Procureur du Roi* v. *Dassonville*, [1974] E.C.R. 837 (emphasis supplied).

[15] Case 120/78, *Rewe Zentral AG* v. *Bundesmonopolverwaltung für Branntwein* [1979] E.C.R. 649 (*Cassis de Dijon*].

Thus it appears that for the future measures apparently applying indifferently to imports and domestic production will be tested against such broad categories of purpose, rather than the narrower ones listed in article 36.

In the energy sector it is restrictions on exports, rather than imports, which are likely to be problematical in view of the concern of Member States with the security of their own supplies. It is not clear that the Court will apply the same tests to export as to import restrictions. In two recent cases, in which production restrictions were alleged to have an effect equivalent to quantitative restrictions on exports, and therefore to be contrary to article 34 of the Treaty, the Court held that article 34 covers only measures

> which have as their specific object or effect the restriction of patterns of exports and thereby the establishment of a difference in treatment between the domestic trade of a Member State and its export trade in such a way as to provide a particular advantage for national production or for the domestic market of the State in question at the expense of the production or trade of other Member States. This is not so in the case of a prohibition like that in question which is applied objectively to the production of goods of a certain kind without drawing a distinction whether such goods are intended for the national market or for export.[16]

The significance of these different dicta can be appreciated if one considers the compatibility with Community law of measures by resource-rich States like the United Kingdom and the Netherlands restricting the rate of depletion of resources like oil and gas. If depletion rates were matched to national consumption, would this constitute an indirect restriction on exports? While some earlier cases indicated this as a possibility, the Court's recent decisions[17] suggest the contrary. In these circumstances, and bearing in mind also the highly sensitive nature of such decisions in political terms, and the hitherto generous depletion policy of the United Kingdom, it is not surprising that the Commission has never apparently raised the question of depletion rates.[18]

More difficult issues are raised by the attitude of the Commission towards Dutch and British policies regarding the disposition of the oil and gas produced onshore and in their continental shelf areas. The Dutch government's revised policy on exports of gas from the Continental Shelf was the subject in 1973 of article 169 proceedings, instigated by the Commission.

[16] Case 15/79, *Groenveld* v. *Produktschap voor Vee en Vlees* [1979] E.C.R. 3409 at 3415; Case 155/80, *Oebel* [1981] E.C.R. 19.

[17] For instance, Cases 3, 4 and 6/76, *Kramer* [1976] ECR 1279 indicates the former approach taken by the Court, while *Groenveld, supra* at note 16, gives an indication of the new approach.

[18] Evans, A., "United Kingdom North Sea Oil Policy and EEC Law" (1982) 7 European Law Review 335.

In this case the Commission sought and obtained a lifting of the restriction and a withdrawal of the policy.[19] Nonetheless when the Dutch government revised its concession terms for offshore production in 1976[20], it provided for the inclusion in future licences of quite explicit provisions which could be used in just the way condemned in 1973. These new terms, combined with the powers reserved to the Minister of Economic Affairs under the 1974 Wet Aardgasprijzen,[21] which apply to domestic and export sales alike, have been the subject of a number of questions asked in the European Parliament,[22] but no action has been taken in this regard by the Commission, which has taken the view that the Act itself does not contravene Community law though its application could be contrary to article 34, and has not commented on the 1976 licence provisions.

More complex restrictions are to be found in the United Kingdom's offshore oil and gas regime The framework of the licensing regime – the principal vehicle of regulation – has been set out in Chapter IV.[23] Notwithstanding the fact that the resources being produced are, at least up to the time of production, subject to the proprietary rights of the Crown, and the licences are in the nature of a contract transferring property, it seems clear that licence controls are capable of falling within articles 30–36, either directly or via article 90(1) which applies the rules of the Treaty to measures enacted by Member States "in cases of ... undertakings to which Member States grant special or exclusive rights". We will return to the question of State undertakings below. Under the licence, the licensee must not produce oil or gas otherwise than in accordance with a development programme approved by the Secretary of State for Energy for a production consent given by him.[24] In addition he is required to land any oil or gas he produces in the United Kingdom unless the Secretary of State consents to an alternative landing place.[25]

On the United Kingdom's accession in 1973, this latter provision attracted the immediate attention of the Commission, as a possible restriction on exports. Though the Commission has never initiated any complaint on this score nor published its views, its reasoning is not hard to reconstruct.

[19] See The Times, January 5, 1973 and May 4, 1973; EC Commission, Seventh General Report (1973) para. 109; Eighth General Report (1974), para 105.

[20] Chapter IV, above, pp. 71–73.

[21] Chapter V, above, pp. 66–68.

[22] *E.g.* Written Question No. 703/74 of Mr. Gerlach, J.O. 1975, C 108/13.

[23] Above, p. 116.

[24] Licences are granted under the Petroleum (Production) Act 1934, as applied to the Continental Shelf by the Continental Shelf Act 1964 and contain standard terms set out from time to time in regulations made under the former Act; currently the Petroleum (Production) Regulations 1982, S.I. 1982 No. 1000, Schs. 4–8. See clause 15(1) of the model clauses for petroleum production licences in seaward areas, Sch. 5.

[25] Clause 27.

Where the offshore producer would otherwise have the choice between direct shipment to a foreign port and direct shipment to the United Kingdom, the requirement that he land his production in the United Kingdom adds extra transport and trans-shipment costs to the export of oil and gas in its crude state. It is calculated, in fact, to render such an option less attractive than the refining of the crude in the United Kingdom and its export as higher-value petroleum products. Direct export requires the special permission of the Minister, to which onerous conditions (for example, as to sale price) may be attached. By reason of its explicit references to exports, it is hard to see how this provision, any more than the Dutch licence terms, can escape the prohibition of article 34.

The United Kingdom is understood to have sought to justify the provision on landing by reference to the need to ensure the effective assessment and collection of taxes due from holders of production licences, but this objective is not among those mentioned in article 36 as providing grounds for derogating from the ordinary prohibition on quantitative restrictions. Moreover, we have seen that while article 36 makes provision for derogations on grounds of public security, the Community's own provision for situations of supply difficulty might pre-empt unilateral recourse to this part of the article.

One possible explanation for Commission acquiescence in the continuation of these restrictions is the political cost involved in their enforcement, given the generally nationalistic attitudes of the Member States to their natural resource supplies. To this political calculation may be added a strategic one. In the absence of a common policy on oil – and it should be noted that oil and petroleum have remained 'for the present' outside the general Community regime of liberalisation of exports[26] – the British and the Dutch controls represent the only instrument available within the Community to secure that exports of the major oil and gas resources existing within the Community are directed primarily to the Community rather than to third countries.[27] There being no appropriate Community regime, these powers are better than nothing, and the Commission may monitor their exercise to ensure that (as largely appears to have been the case up to the present time) their use in fact is not incompatible with the objectives of Community energy policy. The case offers a good example of the kind of instrumental approach to basic free trade obligations implicit in the new strategy.

26 Council Regulation no. 1934/82 of 12 July 1982, in J.O. 1982 L211/1, amending Regulation no. 2603/69, O.J. 1969 L324/25.

27 Council Decision 79/879, O.J. 1979, L270/58, amending Decision 77/186, O.J. 1977 O.J. L61/23, only applies to the exporting of crude oil and petroleum from one Member State to another.

IV. State Undertakings and Competition

We have already seen that in the European Community, State enterprises are heavily involved in the production, transformation and distribution of energy.[28] The economic importance of State enterprises clearly poses a problem in relation to the construction of a common market involving the free movement of natural resources among Member States. They are capable of being used as an instrument of policy whose workings are far from transparent. In the EEC Treaty specific rules on State enterprises appear in articles 37 and 90, while the ECSC Treaty and the Euratom Treaty make no express provision for State enterprises.

Article 37 makes provision for the adjustment of the structure and operation of State monopolies of a commercial nature so that no discrimination exists between nationals of Member States regarding the conditions under which goods are procured and marketed. The French system of import quotas on crude oil and refined products[29] was challenged by the Commission as a State trading monopoly. Arguably the Commission could have relied on article 34, insofar as the system might be regarded as restricting the movement of oil between Member States, but the system constituted an important means by which France sought to promote domestic refining, and the Commission was reluctant to take action, once again, when there was no common oil policy to replace the national system.[30]

There was, moreover, evidence that the framers of the Treaty had the French import system in mind when drafting article 37(1);[31] and the French Conseil d'Etat had already ruled, in the *Shell-Berre* case in 1964[32] that the import arrangements constituted a monopoly in terms of article 37. Though the European Court had been prevented from ruling on the matter by reason of the Conseil's refusal to make an article 177 reference, the Commission may still have felt some reluctance to ignore the *travaux préparatoires* or to proceed on the footing that the Conseil's ruling was incorrect. By relying on article 37 rather than 34, the Commission was able to take account of the French position and accept a certain delay in the process whereby the French system was brought into conformity with Community law.

Changes to the monopoly regime were achieved in 1979 after nearly twenty years of negotiation between the Commission and the French

[28] See Chapter IV, Part I.

[29] See Chapter IV, p. 81.

[30] Sixth Report on Competition Policy, para. 268.

[31] See Colliard, "Régime de l'Article 37: aspects juridiques" in Semaine de Bruges, *L'Entreprise Public et la Concurrence* (1969), at pp. 147, 150.

[32] *Shell-Berre*, R.D.P. 1964, 1019.

government.[33] The Commission's final report on the matter shows clearly its desire to balance respect for basic free trade principles with respect for energy policy objectives, in this case the security of French oil supplies, and with the preservation of each Member State's freedom to pursue such objectives through the use of the instruments it prefers. The Commission notes that the French arrangements are compatible with the Treaty in that they are based on the legitimate objective of securing oil supplies, go no further than is necessary to attain this objective, and subject all oil products marketed in France to the same conditions, regardless of whether they were refined in France or in other Member States. The fact that the French measures remain highly dirigiste, requiring import authorisation holders to adhere to submitted three-year plans and determining the contractual arrangements for their purchasing,[34] while other Member States appear satisfied with the security they achieve through private market arrangements, was not seen by the Commission as a barrier to approval.[35]

In relation to State production enterprises such as BNOC, BGC, or Gasunie, the significant question for the Commission is not whether they qualify as monopolies in terms of article 37, the time for 'adjustment' being now over, but whether, as State enterprises, they are subject to the general competition provisions of the Treaty, and whether they are capable of being used by States as instruments to secure results which, if sought through regulatory mechanisms, would be contrary to articles 34 or 16. These issues are directly addressed by article 90. It comprehensively recognises the special position and potentialities of public enterprises (and, indeed, private enterprises in a special relationship with the State). Article 90(1) regulates the behaviour of the State towards public undertakings and undertakings to which it grants special or exclusive rights, providing that the State shall not, in their case, enact or maintain in force any measure contrary to the rules contained in the Treaty, especially its general prohibition against discrimination, and its rules on restrictive agreements, abuse of dominant position and State aids. The aim of this provision is to prevent the State from using its *de facto* or *de jure* powers over such undertakings to secure behaviour by them which, if engaged in by the State itself, would be contrary to the Treaty. Article 90(3) gives the Commission a particularly powerful weapon of intervention for the enforcement of the obligation created by article 90(1), enabling it to address directives or decisions to States

[33] See EEC Fifth General Report, 1962, p. 131; Bull. of E.C. 1979 no. 6, 1237.
[34] For details see Chapter V, p. 124.
[35] Ninth Report on Competition Policy, point 205.

without the formalities normally requisite under article 169 where States are alleged to have failed in their obligations under the Treaty.[36]

The Commission's first use of this power was the promulgation of a general Directive on the transparency of financial relationships between the State and public enterprises, which was unsuccessfully challenged by several States before the Court as being *ultra vires*.[37] The significant point, in terms of the argument in this chapter, is that the Directive does not yet extend to energy undertakings. This, we shall see, raises a question-mark over an important element of the new energy strategy.[38]

Article 90(2) has quite a different purpose. In relation to a narrower category of undertakings than is covered by article 90(1), that is, "undertakings entrusted with the operation of services of a general economic interest or having the character of a revenue-producing monopoly", it provides for the application of Treaty rules in so far as this "does not obstruct the performance, in law or in fact, of the particular tasks assigned to them". Even this limited exception is restricted by the requirement that "the development of trade must not be affected to such an extent as would be contrary to the interests of the Community". The Court has moreover held that since this provision derogates from general Community law, the class of undertakings which can benefit from it must be strictly defined.[39]

The arrangements whereby BNOC, BGC and Gasunie enjoy, respectively, access to at least 51 per cent of United Kingdom-produced petroleum, and domestic monopolies of natural gas supply, have been described in Chapter IV. These arrangements, and the use made of this privileged position by these enterprises, clearly raise questions of compatibility with the Treaty as applied by article 90 and of the significance of the lack of any enforcement activity by the Commission. The situation of each of these bodies is somewhat different and the complexity of the issues precludes full treatment here, but some comments can be offered on the position of BNOC, which in terms of Community interest is certainly the most important of the three enterprises.[40]

[36] The first such Directive, Commission Directive 80/723 J.O.C.E. 1980 L195, was designed to secure transparency in financial relationships between States and certain classes of State enterprises.

[37] Cases 188–190/80, *France, Italy and United Kingdom* v. *Commission* [1982] E.C.R. 2545.

[38] Chapter VII, below, at pp. 149–150.

[39] Case 127/73 *BRT* v. *SABAM* [1974] E.C.R. 313.

[40] Since the following paragraphs were written, the UK government has announced its intention to wind up BNOC and abandon its participation arrangements. (Financial Times, March 14, 1985). The precise nature of the new arrangements for protecting the public interest in North Sea oil supplies, to be introduced by new legislation remains unclear, and the arguments in the text may continue to be relevant.

To understand the problem we need to recall the legal machinery under which BNOC came into possession of 51 per cent of United Kingdom-produced petroleum. Under the ordinary forms of consortium agreement used in the North Sea the licensees, who hold the whole petroleum production licence from the Minister jointly, agree on the apportionment among themselves of the oil produced, ordinarily in proportion to their respective contributions to the costs of exploration and production. The participation agreements concluded in 1976–79, and licence conditions applicable since then, secure that on the making of a commercial find of petroleum BNOC becomes a joint holder of the licence and a signatory of the consortium agreement. In these capacities, however, BNOC does not make any contribution to the consortium's costs or receive any of the economic benefits of the licence. Rather, it acquires the right to take up to 51 per cent of the oil that would otherwise have enured to each consortium participant, on paying the market price therefor. At first sight this looks like an option to purchase. BNOC and the United Kingdom government maintain, however, that it is not. When, they say, BNOC exercises its right of election, it does no more than claim for itself oil which, by reason of its being a holder of the licence, already belongs to it jointly along with the other licensees.

The way in which BNOC comes into possession of at least 51 per cent of crude oil produced in the United Kingdom continental shelf calls for two comments from the standpoint of Community law.

First, the argument that BNOC gets the oil as producer rather than as purchaser, while not developed within the context of a consideration of Community law, seems relevant to it, in the sense that it may be easier under the Community legal regime to accept BNOC as the holder of production rights to 51 per cent of United Kingdom oil production than as the imposed purchaser of that percentage from the producers. A straightforward legislative measure compelling the sale of 51 per cent of produced oil to BNOC would, it is suggested, be treated as a measure equivalent to a quantitative restriction on exports, in that it deprives the producers of all possibility of themselves exporting any of that 51 per cent.[41]

Second, conditions for the award of licences, which effectively ensure that BNOC will become the owner of at least 51 per cent of oil to be produced under new production licences, while denying it any of the

[41] In *Pigs' Marketing Board v. Redmond* a sale obligation of this kind, operating in relation to an agricultural product covered by a common organisation of the market was held incompatible with Articles 30 and 34 and with market regulations. It is not clear that the Court would have reached the same decision in the absence of a common market organisation, but clearly the Advocate-General would have done so. Case 83/78 [1978] E.C.R. 2517.

economic rent from the field, clearly give BNOC a different position from that of other prospective licences. Such a discrimination is not, however, based on nationality so as to be contrary to article 7, and it is in any event implicit in the wording of article 90(1) itself that States retain the power to grant 'special or exclusive rights' to undertakings.[42] *A fortiori* it must be open to the State to devise arrangements whereby a public enterprise obtains rights to only a majority share of production of a particular good, particularly, perhaps, where the State is the owner of the good in its 'unproduced' form, that is oil *in situ*. If that majority share causes BNOC to possess a dominant position on the relevant market, of course, then behaviour which would, under article 86, constitute an abuse of that position must be avoided, a point that we look at in a moment.

If the mode of endowing BNOC with oil steers clear of Treaty obstacles, its use of that oil is still fully subject to applicable rules of the Treaty. Article 90(2) can hardly apply to relieve BNOC of any of its obligations.[43] Oil supplies are certainly of general economic interest, but it is not easy to see either how BNOC, in performing oil trading activities is performing a service, nor how any of the tasks assigned to BNOC by its constitutive statute[44] could be obstructed by any of the Treaty rules. BNOC is presently able to dispose of over half of North Sea oil production. This suggests the possibility of a dominant position within the meaning of the Treaty, a possibility which is reinforced by the fact that it is BNOC that sets the market price of North Sea crude: its prices are followed by other licensees in the sale of their remaining production. BNOC is, indeed, now by far the world's biggest trader of light, low-sulphur crude, and may thus be dominant even in a market including other such crudes from Nigeria, Libya and Algeria.[45] BNOC must therefore avoid any discrimination in its sales policy which might constitute an abuse under article 86, for example, by refusing supply to the European market or making sales on more onerous terms. The former kind of behaviour, and perhaps the latter also, would seem at the same time to entail a breach by the United Kingdom government of articles 34 and 90(1), as being an indirect mode of maintaining a measure equivalent to a quantitative restriction on export.[46]

42 Thus the existence of the Italian State television monopoly was approved by the European Court in *Sacchi*, Case 155/73 [1974] E.C.R. 403.

43 For the relevant wording of Art. 90(2) see text at p. 138 *supra*.

44 Petroleum and Submarine Pipelines Act 1975, s. 2(1), (2).

45 Financial Times, December 15, 1982.

46 The existence of such a breach would not depend upon BNOC's holding a dominant position in terms of Art. 86.

To date, there is no evidence that BNOC has discriminated, at least in regard to nationals of other Member States, in its supply policies.[47] Following the disruption of supplies in 1979, the Secretary of State announced that the Government expected companies exporting North Sea oil to sell it to countries belonging to the Community or to the IEA.[48] Moreover, in a supply crisis, satisfactory criteria on which to demonstrate the existence of discrimination might be difficult to find, as the case of *BP* v. *Commission*[49], arising out of the 1973–74 oil crisis, demonstrated.

In these circumstances it is hardly surprising that the Commission should have refrained from any enforcement action. The case of the Wet Aardgasprijzen shows that the Commission is prepared to tolerate potentially trade-restricting national powers so long as they are not exercised with this purpose and effect. Again, the Commission's readiness to tolerate BNOC's capacities for discrimination and abuse of dominant position is doubtless reinforced by awareness of how BNOC's right of secure access, like the landing requirement, can (and has) been used to steer United Kingdom oil exports to the EEC rather than to other destinations.

V. State Aids

The framers of the Treaties foresaw that one of the ways in which competition might be distorted was by the granting of State aids to industrial and commercial activities. Under the ECSC Treaty, national aids to the coal and steel industries were forbidden save in closely-defined cases[50]; we have already seen that the pressures created by the decline of the coal industry in the late nineteen-fifties and thereafter proved stronger than that prohibition and the Commission's capacity to enforce it, with the result that the Treaty was amended in 1960 (by the addition of Article 56(2)), so that a large part of Member States' policies towards their coal industries — where these survive — now consists of a variety of aid programmes administered with the approval of the Commission.

In contrast, the EEC Treaty accepts that aids may in certain circumstances be acceptable, especially where they are regional or sectoral in nature, but requires the approval of new aids by the Commission. In considering the compatibility of such aids with the Treaty, obviously the Commission may

[47] 30.3 per cent of UKCS production was exported to other Member States in 1982 — see Department of Energy: Development of Oil and Gas Resources of the UK (London) 1983.

[48] 961 HC Deb. Col. 461 (January 31, 1979). This policy is being challenged in Case 174/84, *Bulk Oil (Zug)* v. *Sun International Trading Co. Ltd.* (to be heard by the ECJ).

[49] Case 77/77 [1978] E.C.R. 1511.

[50] ECSC Treaty, Arts. 4 and 67.

take into account not only the need to preserve, so far as possible, undistorted competition, but also other Community policy objectives, such as those it has frequently articulated in the energy policy sphere. This approach is exemplified in its practice in the assessment of State aids in the energy sector.

One of the aims pursued with some persistence by Member States in recent years has been the preservation of their oil refining industries. Since crude oil producing States conquered the world market in the nineteen-seventies, they have considerably accelerated the process of refinery construction, seeking to obtain for themselves the added value of the refining process. The consequence is that an increasing proportion of European oil imports are in product form, and that the capacities of European refineries are substantially under-utilised. The Commission has never been sympathetic to the efforts of Member States to buy refinery utilisation away from their neighbours or, more recently, to stem the shift of oil refining from point of consumption to point of production. In 1981 it published a policy document entitled "Problems Affecting The Oil Refining Industry in the Community"[51] in which it recommended that total community refining capacity should be reduced by one-third by 1990.

Occasionally the Commission has seemed ready to tolerate some measure of protection for domectic refining where other energy policy aims could be secured thereby. We have seen how long it took to secure the removal of the elements of the French oil monopoly designed to promote domestic refining; and the Commission has accepted the United Kingdom landing requirement, and its arrangements for BNOC, both of which may be used – and were in part designed – to secure refining in the United Kingdom rather than the export of oil in crude form.[52] In the sphere of State aids, however, its practice has been consistent, with refusals to approve aid both for the increase[53] and the conversion (to a different product mix)[54] of refinery capacity. It has taken a similar approach where a State has sought to use discriminatory taxation to protect its refining industry.[55]

Aids which correspond with Community objectives in the energy sector, such as diversification of sources of imports, have fared better. The Commission showed more lenience, for example, when notified of a system of aids to be introduced for the West German oil industry. This system allowed for the granting of loans in the form of repayable subsidies of up to 30 per cent of the costs of acquiring crude oil deposits or holdings in

[51] COM (81)534 final. See also COM (83)504 final, in which this general policy goal was reaffirmed by the Commission.
[52] See note 40, *supra*.
[53] *Re investment aids at Antwerp* [1982] 3 C.M.L.R. 138
[54] O.J.1973 C 270/22.
[55] See text at note 58, *infra*.

companies working such fields. Thus the aim was to diversify and guarantee the supply of crude oil to the Federal Republic by encouraging the use of independent resources outside the Community. Such an aim accorded well with the objectives of Community oil policy and hence the Commission allowed the proposed system of aids to stand.[56]

VI. Internal Taxation

Finally, we may refer briefly to the question of internal taxation of energy resources. The EEC Treaty forbids internal taxation which has the effect of discriminating between domestic and imported products; and the European Court has so interpreted the relevant articles as to prohibit also internal taxation which discriminates against exports by burdening them more heavily than domestic sales.[57] The way in which these provisions work is simply shown by another case involving refining, from 1965. The Dutch government sought to protect domestic refining through the levy of a tax of 5 per cent on the selling price of crude oil as well as on petroleum products refined outside the Netherlands. However, this tax was not levied on domestic products. The Commission considered that this infringed article 95, and the Dutch government accepted that there had been such an infringement and agreed to withdraw the tax.[58]

Most internal energy taxation, however, is not discriminatory in this way. General indirect taxation has been harmonised by the adoption of a system of VAT which requires its imposition on imports and remission on exports, of energy as of other products. In the energy sector, specialised taxes are also important, particularly excise taxes on petroleum products. Such taxes apply indifferently to domestic products (where these exist) and to imports, and are therefore fully compatible with article 95. Their level, and system of imposition, vary considerably from State to State, and this constitutes a real barrier to the creation of a single Community market in such products; but the solution for this problem needs to be sought rather in a programme of harmonisation than in straightforward enforcement activity under articles 95–99. Such a programme is now regarded as a priority matter under the new strategy.[59] Discriminatory taxation of energy exports has not hitherto been a problem within the Community (as has been the case, for example, in the United States).[60] Specially designed resource

56 Bull. of the EC 1969, no. 12, p. 28.

57 Case 142/77, *Aedie Metaller* [1978] E.C.R. 1543

58 EEC Eighth General Report, 1965, p. 171.

59 See Energy Policy: Pricing and Transparency, COM (81)539 final.

60 See Williams, "Severance Taxes and Federalism: the Role of the Supreme Court in Preserving a National Common Market for Energy Supplies" (1982) 53 Colo. L. Rev. 281.

taxation is most unusual. Mining operations are subject to the general regimes of income or corporate taxation, which have neither the object nor the effect of discriminating between production destined for export and for domestic consumption.[61] Within the range of resources subject to the EEC Treaty, the most significant special measure of resource taxation is the United Kingdom Petroleum Revenue Tax. This is in the nature of a specialised profits tax, being applicable only to profits from oil accruing to persons participating in oil fields in the United Kingdom, its territorial sea and continental shelf.[62] Profits are assessed on a field-by-field basis according to a complex formula.[63] In this assessment, the destination of the oil sold by the participants in oil fields is of no significance.[64] The assessment is simply based on the proceeds of sale of oil sold crude (the sale price if sold at arm's length, the market value if not) by each participant in a given period. This system effectively excludes the possibility of a discriminatory export regime.

VII. Conclusion

Looking back at Commission intervention (or lack of it) on the basis of the rules applying to the operation of the common market as they affect the energy sector, it could be fair to say that a 'chicken and egg' problem has developed. The Commission has been reluctant to attack national regimes, such as the French oil import monopoly or the British landing requirements, when, in the absence of essential elements of a common policy (such as a common export regime), there have been no effective Community instruments to put in their place. However, the continued existence of such divergent national regimes would seem itself to militate against the emergence of a common energy policy. One reason, perhaps, for the long perpetuation of this state of immobility in the energy sector has been the absence of privately initiated litigation, on the basis of directly applicable Treaty provisions and other instruments, which would permit the Court to rule on certain key issues which the Commission, for reasons already discussed, has not wished to bring

61 For a general survey, see International Fiscal Association, Cahiers de Droit Fiscal International, Vol. LXIIIa (1970) "Taxation of the Extractive Industries", which includes reports on West Germany, Denmark, France, Italy, Netherlands and the United Kingdom.

62 For details, see Hayllar and Pleasance, *The Taxation of North Sea Oil and Gas* (2nd ed., 1981).

63 See Oil Taxation Act 1975, s. 2 and Sch. 3.

64 A minor exception is to be found in the Oil Taxation Act 1975, s. 1091 (a), but since it relates only to gas sold or to be sold under contracts concluded before the coming into force of the Act, should have no effect on future behaviour.

before it. In many other areas such litigation, brought before the Court under article 177, has been the motor for the advancement of the decision-making process within the Communities. In the energy sector, apart from a couple of unsuccessful early attempts to get the Court to rule on the French petroleum monopoly[65], it has until recently been all but unknown. One can only speculate as to the reasons: our guess would be that the oligopolistic structure of most energy markets, the major role played therein by public enterprises, and the high degree of dependence of many energy enterprises on discretionary governmental decisions (e. g. in the allocation of licences and permits), all combine to deter litigation in the energy sector.[66]

65 *Shell Berre, supra*, note 32, Case 20/64, *Albatros* [1965] E.C.R. 34.

66 See Daintith and Hancher, "The Management of Diversity: Community Law as an Instrument of Energy and other Sectoral Policies; (1984) Yearbook of European Law, forthcoming.

Chapter VII

The Community Energy Strategy: An Evaluation

In the foregoing chapters we have sought to assemble the data against which we could judge the claim, implicit in the new strategy, that the energy situations of Member States are too divergent, both with regard to supply and demand situations and institutional frameworks, to warrant or permit the implementation of a fully integrated common policy, centralising energy-related decisions in the hands of the Community. In so doing we have emphasised the role of law in structuring energy institutions and markets, and have postulated that legal systems in themselves might provide additional and independent elements of divergence. We have also raised the question of how far the strategy model of Community action could be compatible with the protection of basic free trade principles within the Community. In this chapter we shall look at these points in turn, concluding with an attempt at a more general evaluation of the capacity of the strategy model to overcome problems of energy policy implementation occasioned by the persistence of these same legal divergences.

I. Divergence

It is hardly surprising that after 24 years of vainly trying to lay the basis of a common energy policy, meeting active or passive resistance from Member States at every turn, the Commission should have formed the view that the divergence of State situations and interests was simply too great to allow for centralised solutions to energy policy problems. The objective examination conducted here lends substantial support to this appreciation. Certainly, we have seen that Member States face a common general problem, in the shape of an urgent need to reduce an excessive dependence on imported energy supplies, and that this has both enabled them to agree, within the Community framework and elsewhere, on a common commitment to work for such reduction, and has induced a broad similarity in the energy policy objectives they have set themselves at the national level, which we have been able to reduce to a unified list. The essential problem of decision-making within the Community, however, resides not so much in the identification of objectives as in the selection of appropriate instruments for their attainment, and here it is clear that the divergences between States, in such matters as resource endowments, energy market organisation, and so on, have caused them to choose combinations of instruments which are so different in type or content as to be incapable of transfer to, or even harmonisation at, the Community level.

Pressing our analysis of these instrumental choices a little further, it would appear that differences in resource endowments may possibly be a less important factor than differences in energy markets and institutional structures. Variations in resource endowment have tended to lead to differences in the content of policy instruments, which can be allowed for as objective circumstances in Community decision-making. Thus Community decisions have been possible in relation to firing of electricity generating stations even though the Dutch were increasing oil-firing (at the expense of natural gas) when other members were moving away from it; and in relation to the sharing of oil supplies in crisis situations, notwithstanding the enormous disparity in domestic oil resources between, say, the United Kingdom and Italy. This is not to say that Community solutions will always be possible: the failure hitherto of attempts to establish a Community coal policy[1] is largely attributable to this kind of difference.

Again, when one looks at the economic structure of energy markets, one does not find differences so profound as to explain fully past problems of centralising or harmonising energy decisions. Patterns of energy *demand*, and the importance of different classes of consumer, vary relatively little from one Member State to another, once geographical differences are allowed for. Privileges of especially powerful consumer groups (like the Dutch horticulturalists) have gradually been brought into line with the observance of general Community principles[2]. Structures of *supply*, in terms of concentration and the presence of public ownership, are remarkable more for their similarities than their differences. The major oil companies are largely present everywhere, with the partial exception of Italy; the gas industry is strongly concentrated in all countries, though ownership pat-

1 See, most recently, Proposals for a Balanced Solid Fuels Policy, COM (83) 309 final.

2 The Commission initiated procedures against the Dutch government on the grounds that preferential gas tariffs for Dutch horticulturists were contrary to Articles 92–93 of the EEC Treaty. The Dutch government argued that the tariffs were fixed by a private contract between Gasunie and the Landbouwschap, but the Commission replied that Gasunie was a type of public sector commercial undertaking, and that the tariffs were only applicable on the approval of the Minister of Economic Affairs. O.J. 1982, L37/31. The case came before the Court of Justice (O.J., 1982 C69/10) but was settled after negotiations in the Council: See Commission Decision of July 22, 1982, O.J. L229/38 and the letter of the Dutch Minister of Agriculture, White Paper, no. 17100, XIV, no. 23. The tariffs were replaced by non-discriminatory agreements. See Written Question of H. Seeler to the EEC Commission no. 1935/81, O.J. 1983, C3/1.

terns vary; the electricity industry is essentially a public undertaking in all countries, though much less concentrated in the Netherlands and Germany than in Britain, France and Italy. In some respects, however, the low levels of concentration in the former countries are compensated for by an advanced degree of interest organisation among electricity utilities, which has for example permitted some systematisation of tariff policy. We should note here the structural differences that remain may be more important in terms of diversity of performance — which is a key concern of the strategy — than in determining the scope for centralising decision-making. Large enterprises may have much greater investment and planning capacities than combinations of smaller ones, even when the latter are strongly organised.

Most important as a source of difficulty for a Community policy of the type hitherto attempted, it seems to us, are those differences in the mode of conceiving and carrying out energy policies which are closely linked to national political choices, administrative practices, and legal structures. While we have drawn attention to the pursuance, in each State, of a more or less common set of energy policy objectives, there is great variety in the way in which these objectives are related to the broader political context within the State. In this sense, energy policy is an essentially ambiguous term. For some, it may be a sectoral element of a general endeavour to eliminate obstacles to the free working of the market; for others, a practical case of the need for more State intervention in strategic sectors. It may be understood to embrace the control of the operations of multinationals; or giving workers in the energy industries co-determination rights; or the management of domestic energy resources in the national interest. These specific understandings reflect political choices about effective modes of government (French dirigisme versus German Sozialmarktwirtschaft, for example) choices which may also be expressed, to some extent, in the market structures just discussed. In this context, the special significance of legal rules and structures lies in the way they normally give permanent shape to the political choices they express and implement.

In our conclusions to Chapter V we have shown, on the basis of a detailed survey of post-1973 national measures, how strongly these have been shaped by the existing legal organisation of national energy industries and by other, more generalised, national legal concepts. These examples show how given modes of doing things, once concretised through legal expression, exercise a powerful attraction for the later policy-maker, even though his objectives may differ sensibly from those of his predecessor. Basic legal structures, like that of the French petroleum monopoly, the standard government-nationalised industry relationship in the United Kingdom, the price control system in Italy, or competition laws in Germany, thus acquire a certain polyvalence. Because they are there, they are adapted to serve a variety of policy purposes, within the energy sector and maybe also outside it. While other means of attaining the same goals are clearly available (as the practice of other States obviously shows), accepting harmonisation or centralisation at the cost of abandoning the national system is extremely difficult. Even a partial departure may be seen as a threat to the integrity and coherence of the system, which may have developed inherent values for those who operate it and are affected by it. The centrality of energy resources to the national interest is not of recent date: there has thus been plenty of time for such national legal structures for energy institutions and markets to develop and ramify, to a greater extent, perhaps, than in most other sectors.

It seems more reasonable to attribute lack of Member State response to Community policy goals to this structural stiffness of their internal arrangements than to simple chauvinism. In areas where structures are newer or more flexible, Member States have shown plenty of willingness to emulate each other's attractive instrumental ideas, even without explicit Community impulsion: the British creation of an "umbrella" energy conservation agency, along the lines of the French one, is a recent case of this type.[3] Conversely, there is strong interest in Member States in combined heat and power schemes, particularly successful in Scandinavia; but the rate of implementation has clearly varied according to structural differences – in allocation of powers between central and regional (or local) governments, in the existence or absence of national electricity utilities with monopoly powers, and so on.

In adopting its "strategy" approach the Commission appears to have accepted, at least in part, that it is unprofitable to try to challenge these established, legalised national preferences about modes of policy implementation. We say "in part" because three of the five priority areas for Community action identified by the Commission in its strategy document involve continuing efforts at co-ordination or harmonisation of national policies in areas where divergences of this type may be of considerable importance: energy pricing and taxation, avoidance of oil market instability, and external relations. This is particularly true of the key area of energy pricing, where even a simple policy of price transparency (as opposed to more ambitious attempts at alignment) involves the disturbance or reformulation of long-established conventions governing relationships between governments and energy enterprises in the field of prices[4]. The difficulties likely to be encountered in this field may be gauged, inter alia, from the fact that the Commission's directive on transparency of relations

[3] The existence of the Community framework may help to focus and accelerate this process: consider comparable U.S. experience analysed in Walker, "The diffusion of innovations among the American States," (1969) 63, Am. Pol. Sci. Rev. 880, esp. at pp. 888–91.

[4] See Chapter IV, pp. 82–92.

between Member States and public undertakings[5], which encountered the most vigorous opposition from some Member States[6] did not even attempt to cover energy undertakings.

II. Free Trade Principles

Outside these three areas, whose selection clearly reflects a continuing concern for the operation in the energy sector of common market principles[7], does the strategy reflect a weakening of commitment to those principles? Our analysis in the previous chapter suggests that even before 1981, energy policy objectives were just as important as free trade objectives (if not more important) in determining the attitude of the Commission to enforcement action in the case of legally dubious Member State practices. This orientation is made explicit in the strategy document. (In this connection the linkage from 1981 to 1985 under a single Commissioner of the Energy Directorate-General, and the Industry Directorate-General which is responsible for internal market questions, should be noted. This link must have facilitated the relating of these two kinds of objective. But note also the continuing independence of the Competition Directorate-General, whose attitudes – in relation, for example, to the policing of article 92 – need not necessarily coincide with those of Energy.) From this it is clear that free trade principles play an instrumental role, in the sense of providing a basis for Commission enforcement powers which can be used to reinforce the collective discipline for which the strategy calls.

There is an important question, which we consider in the next section, about how adequate a basis these principles offer. There is also room for a fundamental difference of opinion about the instrumental approach to the free trade principles on which the common market was founded. It may be argued that this approach is to be taken as a sign of maturity in the Community's policy, as an indicator of the Commission's readiness to concentrate on the real problems that confront the Community and its members rather than making a fetish of market integration for its own sake. On the other hand, one might see a measure of market integration as the single solid achievement in this sector as in others, which could be jeopardised if the Commission invokes its enforcement powers based on those principles only in aid of uncertain energy policy goals. What we have to say in the next section about monitoring and enforcement under the new strategy bears in some measure

5 Commission Directive 80/723, O.J. 1980 L195/35.

6 Cases 188–90/80, *France, Italy and the United Kingdom* v. *Commission* [1982] E.C.R. 2545.

7 See, Community Energy Strategy: Progress and Guidelines for Future Action, COM (83) 305 final, p. 4.

upon this latter argument. Here it might be recalled that there are other avenues – principally the Court of Justice – through which market integration can be defended, and indeed promoted, by interested parties without the intervention of the Commission; but that – as already noted[8] – there has been remarkably little recourse to these avenues in the energy sector, in strong contrast to certain others. Defenders of market integration thus have an unused weapon in their own hands.

III. Monitoring and Performance under the Strategy to Date

For the future, much clearly depends on the success of two key elements of the strategy: Commission monitoring of Member States' actions and policies to see how far these conform to agreed Community objectives and its capacity to secure such conformity where that is found lacking; of monitoring Robert De Bauw has written:

> While this is not a new role – in the past the Commission has presented several reports on the development of national energy policies[9], as requested by the Council Resolutions of 1974 and 1980[10] – what is novel as far as the 'strategy' is concerned is the expressed intention and agreement on the part of Member States that this review should be of a critical nature, drawing attention to the gaps and weaknesses in national policies so that convergence may be assured.
>
> The IEA also undertakes an annual review of the policies of its member countries, which include nine of the ten EC States. While one cannot deny that there may be some degree of overlap between the two, there are important differences in the nature of these reviews.
>
> In the first place, the Commission review is based on specific criteria which reflect the quantitative objectives set by the Community (e. g. that coal and nuclear should cover 75 per cent of electricity generation by 1990). Furthermore there exists a body of Community legislation to ensure the attainment of these goals (e. g. the directive on the limitation of the use of hydrocarbons for electricity generation). The IEA on the other hand, can only make non-binding policy recommendations, while the Commission may have recourse to the various rules of the Treaties, and secondary legislation examined earlier, and has also the potential of creating new legislation. Furthermore the Community has its own finan-

[8] See Chapter VI, pp. 144–145.

[9] *E. g.*, The Energy Situation in the Community, COM (80) 60; Review of Energy Policy Objectives for 1990, COM (81) 64.

[10] O.J. No. C 153/1 of 1975 and O.J. No. C149/1 of 1980.

cial resources (e. g. ECSC and Euratom loan schemes) which it may use to encourage or supplement the action of Member States[11].

Hence we would comment, first, that these various enforcement and incentive powers add little to the advancement of the Community policy unless the monitoring process itself can be effectively carried out. Here, events since 1981 give some cause for concern. In its 1982 "Review of Member States' energy policy programmes and progress towards 1990 objectives"[12] the Commission found it necessary to ask for the provision of a more continuous flow of information from Member States[13] and acknowledged that it needed better indicators of progress towards energy policy objectives in several areas, which would also take account of the different energy policy instruments possessed by Member States[14]. The problem of divergence of instruments here appears in a new guise. The same request for adequate information was repeated a year later, which suggests that the Commission was then still not in a position to perform its monitoring function satisfactorily[15]. More worryingly, the pattern of Council behaviour which proved inimical to the operation of an energy policy appeared to be repeating itself in this new context, in that the Council had already promised, in July 1982, an adequate and timely flow of information for this purpose. Subsequently the situation has in some respects improved, in that the Commission's 1984 report on Member State energy policies refers to information problems only in the investment area[16]; at the same time we should note that it is bringing an article 169 proceeding against one Member State for failure to meet its obligations regarding oil price reporting.[17] Secondly, even if the Commission can accurately ascertain how fast and in what direction Member States are proceeding, there must remain serious doubts about its capacity to make them alter course. Up to now, sweet reason, by itself, has achieved very little for the Commission. Enforcement powers, as De Bauw acknowledges, are needed, and some indeed exist. But their deployment raises two kinds of problems.

[11] "La Communauté Européenne et la Politique Energétique", paper presented to the Colloquium on the Legal Implementation of Energy Policy, held at Florence, September 1982.

[12] COM (82) 326 final.

[13] *Ibid*, paras 35–37.

[14] Para 40.

[15] Energy Strategy of the Community: Progress and Guidelines for future Action, COM (83) 305 final, p. 5.

[16] EC Commission, Review of Member States Energy Policies, COM (84) 88 final, para 22.

[17] EC Commission, first annual report to the European Parliament on Commission monitoring of the application of Community Law – 1983, COM (84) 181 final, para. 109 Annexe B (p. 78).

(i) Does the Commission dispose of a wide enough range of powers? If Member States take positive action which impedes the attainment of common goals *and* is of doubtful legality under Community rules, the Commission should have no problem in intervening. But suppose the problem is one of inaction by a Member State, for example in encouraging energy-saving investments? Or that the State behaviour which is negative from the Community point of view occurs in an area where the common market has not been completed, for example that of energy imports from third States? The Commission is concerned that such imports, for example of natural gas, should not lead to excessive dependence, but it is hard to see what tools it has available (short of securing Council agreement to concrete measures, which appears as difficult in the post- as in the pre-strategy period) for the purpose of translating that concern into action. Where Member States refuse to act, or have limited capacities to do so, the obvious Community action would appear to be to act in substitution, for example in the field of investment, but Member States have so far been reluctant to countenance this kind of substitution.

(ii) Will Commission promotional and enforcement activity operate with appropriate effect on different Member States, given their different instrument choices and legal structures? The strategy involves monitoring and improving *performance*, that is, progress (by whatever route) towards common goals. We have already seen that institutional and legal structures may determine important elements of performance. Considerations of concentration and ownership in the electricity supply industry, State-public enterprise relationships, division of powers between the State and regional and local governments, and of national preferences in the construction of a legal regime for plant siting decisions, can all be invoked in the attempt to explain the different performances of France, Germany and Italy in the introduction of nuclear generation of electricity. In so far as features of such structures impede progress in the achievement of energy policy goals, they are likely also to impede the effective operation of Commission remedies for such shortfalls. One implication, perhaps, of the performance-oriented enforcement inherent in the new strategy is that the Commission try to adopt a highly differentiated approach to the failures of Member States, selecting its remedies (or its enforcement powers) with an eye to the specific legal arrangements through which the Member State concerned has been acting in relation to the policy goal. Securing change in a gentlemen's agreement, of the type favoured in the Netherlands[18] may require an approach quite different from that of securing changes to a complex of formal regulations, such as those within which the French oil

18 For example between the Minister of Economic Affairs, and NAM, Chapter V, p. 117.

industry operates[19]. Sensitivity to this issue, based on the kind of legal and other data here collected, may produce a better return on the Commission's promotion and enforcement efforts.

IV. Conclusion

In a number of respects, the observer of the Community's post-strategy behaviour experiences a sense of déjà vu. The strategy certainly did not exclude Community action as such; rather it identified priority areas for such action, whether in the nature of centralised Community initiatives, as with investment and research and development, or of co-ordination or harmonisation of Member State action, as with pricing and taxation policy, or oil market stabilisation. Since the strategy document the Commission has addressed to the Council a stream of specific proposals for action dealing mainly, though not entirely, with these priority areas[20]. Among other subjects covered, for example, is the possible reform of the supply chapter of the Euratom Treaty, on the Council's table, in one form or another, since 1964[21]. At first sight these documents do not look very different in nature from those that the Commission has produced, with such limited success, at various times in the past, though there is, perhaps, less emphasis on proposals which will fit neatly into the overall Treaty framework, and more of a concern to identify problems and then to propose whatever solutions, whether operative at Community or at national level, seem most appropriate[22]. In this sense the Commission's approach since 1981 reflects the judgement of Robert De Bauw:

> The principal difference between the concepts of strategy and policy is not so much one of substance, but is more a matter of approach and presentation. Common policy involves a body of Community rules and a centralisation of the decision-making process. The strategy, however, is more pragmatic and accepts more that action is better taken at national level, subject always to the constraint that it contributes to a common effort. But Community initiatives are advocated (by the strategy concept) whenever and wherever it seems necessary or more effective.[23]

It has clearly been the hope of the Commission that this new approach on its part would win greater co-operation from the Member States and confer

[19] See Chapter IV, pp. 54–56, and Chapter V, p. 110.

[20] See Appendix 2, for a list of post-strategy Commission proposals to end-1983. More have followed.

[21] For the text of the proposal see O.J. 1982, C.330/4.

[22] Audland, C. "European Community Energy Strategy and its Legislative Implications", in (1983) 1 Journal of Energy and Natural Resources Law, 9.

[23] De Bauw, *supra* at note 11.

a greater chance that its proposals would be accepted by them, as they would be based on demonstrated need, rather than imposed *a priori*. Unfortunately the scales do not yet appear to have fallen from the eyes of national energy Ministers. In a progress report on the strategy issued in June 1983[24], the Commission felt it necessary again to argue the need for a reinforcement of action in the energy sector, and for Community action (particularly in the form of a five-year programme of projects financed by the Community). Its accounts of progress since 1981 in the five priority areas (or rather, of the lack of progress) give no hint of any radical change in attitude on the part of the Council: failure to approve a regulation for Community energy investment incentives; failure to adopt a permanent framework for Community programmes of research and development; failure to adopt a decision on Community procedures for dealing with sub-crisis situations in oil supply; absence of agreement on common tax principles for energy supply. In this period, as so often in the past, the essential legislative achievement of the Council appears to be the adoption of general resolutions and non-binding recommendations, for example on guidelines for national energy investment, and for the construction of gas and electricity tariffs[25]. As the Commission itself never ceases to say, something more than this is needed.

At the present time, therefore, there is ample reason to fear that the element of the strategy which seeks to remove barriers to Community action in the sector by confining proposals for such action strictly to what can only be done, or can be done much better, at the Community level, is going to fail. One can only hope that this fear is ill-founded. But even if it is realised, the elements of the strategy which have most interested us, as lawyers, may remain in operation: that is to say, the attempt to develop a Community discipline for the achievement by Member States of common goals by divergent means. This study has offered evidence of the entrenchment of instrumental divergences in Member States, which amply justifies the decision of the Commission to experiment, in the energy sector, with a new conception of the use of its monitoring and enforcement powers. It has also indicated how strongly events were already pushing the Commission in this direction, even before the formal adoption of the strategy. More time will be needed before we can tell whether the strategy document has marked the beginning of a phase of imaginative and effective employment of the Commission's legal competences in aid of energy policy aims, or simply the abnegation in this sector of its responsibility to protect the integrative achievements of the Community.

24 Energy Strategy: Progress and Guidelines *supra* note 7.

25 See Council Resolution of December 3, 1981, Bull. EC 12–81, pt. 2.1.159, and March 16, 1982, in Bull. EC 3–82, pt. 2.1.110. On gas and electricity prices see Council Recommendation 81/924 on electricity tariff structures, O.J. 1981, L. 337/12; Council Recommendation 83/230 on the method of setting natural gas prices and tariffs in the Community, O.J. 1983 L 123/40.

Appendix I

The Development of an Energy Strategy for the Community

(Communication from the Commission to the Council)

I. Introduction

In the course of recent years the European Council has repeatedly declared the need for the Community to face up to the energy challenge.

This has led to two Council Resolutions – in 1974 and in 1980[1] – setting Community energy objectives whose main features are a reduction in oil dependence through the more rational use of energy and broader diversification of energy supply.

But it has not led to the implementation of an overall strategy comprising action by the Community, Member States and producers and consumers. The inadequacy and inconsistency of the action taken in the wake of these expressions of political will can only be deplored.

Relatively slack demand between 1975 and 1980, combined with weak pricing and taxation policies, reversed the upward movement in real oil prices, leading to a certain complacency and slackening of efforts to use energy more efficiently and to replace oil. The events in Iran, which caused price tensions on the world market, gave rise to a new interest on the part of Governments. The consequent vigilance displayed at a Community and an international level has helped to prevent any new pressures on the oil market in the short-term. But the longer-term problems still await satisfactory solutions. It is inevitable in these circumstances that the scope for a sustained upturn in economic growth will be constrained once again by undue dependence on oil.

In stressing this situation the Commission does not intend to belittle the importance of the political commitments which have been made or that of the measures already adopted at national and at Community level. Its objective is to present – in the context of the follow-up work to its Report

[1] OJ N° C 153 of 9.7.75, p. 1 and OJ N° C 149 of 18.6.80, p. 1.

on the Mandate of 30 May[2] – a framework for action allowing the Community to respond more effectively and without harmful delay to the serious challenges which the energy question raises now and for the future.

II. The Challenges to the Community

1. Despite the success of efforts to reduce energy and oil demand since 1973 the Community is still the single largest oil importer in the world (8.7 mbd in 1980).

More than half of these imports come from three countries (Saudi Arabia, Libya and Nigeria).

The broader international picture is also far from comforting. It would be risky to count on a fall or even a stabilising in demand for energy.

As far as the less developed countries (LDCs) are concerned a marked increase is a real possibility. At the same time world market supplies for oil will be derived from a diminishing number of oil exporters, with Saudi Arabia playing a more and more dominant role.

2. The Community economy has been badly hit by the effects of the doubling of oil prices in 1979. The challenge is to shield it from the risk of further pressure, both by reducing as rapidly as possible the Community's dependence on oil and also by taking effective measures to limit possible causes of increase in the price of its supplies.

To these ends measures need to be taken both on the energy demand side (energy saving and rational use of energy) and on the supply side (diversification). In the latter field efforts must be stepped up, particularly by increasing coal consumption, pursuing vigorous nuclear programmes and by developing renewable energy sources.

3. To bring about the necessary changes will require first and foremost action within the Community itself. But its success will depend heavily on what is done externally. The industrialised countries need to work together if they are to reduce their dependence on oil. Avenues for cooperation with the energy exporting countries to assure stable supplies while respecting their legitimate interests, must be explored. Finally the serious problems faced by a large number of developing countries as a result of their position as oil importers calls for rapid, vigorous and broad action by the world community. The European Community has at its disposal instruments which allow it to give technical and financial help to these countries so as to enable them to develop their resources.

4. But in other ways too the process of change poses new challenges and offers new hopes. The energy transition will have far-reaching consequences

[2] COM(81)300 final.

for Community industriy, offering prospects for the development and application of new technologies to help revitalise the industrial base. This is underlined in the Fifth Medium-Term Economic Policy Programme[3]. The challenge is to maintain the continuity of action required in the face of short-term economic fluctuations. Such continuity is essential both to give confidence and to ensure lasting changes.

III. Forms of Community Action

1. To meet these challenges the first imperative is to ensure more rapid progress towards consistency between energy policies of Member States. All Member States have a common interest in the success or failure of energy policy throughout the Community. Differences of effort and achievement between Member States will not only mean widening divergences in the security of energy supply. They will also adversely affect the level of economic activity in the Community as a whole. Equivalence of effort does not require any substantial centralisation of energy policy instruments; nor does it require the pursuit of uniformity in the diversification of supply, which must vary according to national circumstances. But it does call for collective discipline going beyond mere expressions of common agreement. The policies of each Member State must reflect a willingness to pursue common goals.

Every year the Commission presents a report[4] on the energy policies of Member States in the light of the Community objectives and after consulting national administrations. By drawing attention to progress made and to constraints and weaknesses this report must now become the instrument ensuring consistency. It will be submitted to the Council, together with appropriate proposals and recommendations, after examination by the Medium-Term Economic Policy Committee and the Energy Committee.

2. In the second place specific Community action must be set in train where this is required by the provisions of the Treaty or where it will be more effective than the sum of national measures even when these are properly coordinated. This is true as much for action within the Community as in external relations, where solidarity strengthens collective security of supply.

3. Some action must be supported by financial means, whether from the Community budget or from the Community's lending instruments. Up to now recourse to these means has enabled significant support to be given but this has been limited in relation to the total financing requirements of the energy sector. [...]

The necessary rôle for Community finance is already recognised in some areas, notably research and development, aid to LDCs and aid to certain

[3] COM(81)344 final.

[4] See for example COM(81)64 final.

kinds of investment. There are other sectors, such as technological demonstration and the encouragement of certain categories of investment, where spending is essential to meet common energy objectives and to improve collective energy security. Community financing measures in these sectors should also command general support.

It is of course true that the success of common action cannot be measured in terms of the amount of budgetary finance involved. Many of the objectives described above can and should be pursued through, for example, better coordination of national policies supported by a system of agreed analysis and recommendation. But the financial means available to the Community must be equal to the requirements for action determined by its strategic objectives. The amounts assigned to energy in the Community budget must therefore grow more quickly than in the past, reflecting the strategic priorities.

4. These principles of action will be applied to every sector of energy supply and demand.

It is generally accepted that *coal* should have a more important rôle to play in Community energy supply. The scope for possible reconversion to coal is considerable, especially in industry. Large expenditure is needed throughout the Community in this area and in coal transport, import and storage. The basis therefore exists for a reexamination of Community coal strategy and for common action to ensure greater consistency between the coal policies of Member States, and to bypass the sterile arguments between coal producing and coal importing countries in the Community. In its absence the prospects for coal within the Community will remain uncertain, damaging the morale of the coal industry and adding further uncertainties to the development of new technologies in the coal sector.

The development of *nuclear energy* is vital to ensure security of energy supply and one of the main ways of reducing dependence on oil. The pursuit of vigorous nuclear programmes is an essential element in an economic policy for Europe aimed at overcoming structural problems in the energy sector.

The Community can help to ensure the best possible progress in the nuclear sector not only by exercising its specific responsibilities in the field but also by setting the development of nuclear power within the framework of an overall energy strategy.

Natural gas has become over the past fifteen years an important element in the energy balance of Member States, making a useful contribution to diversification of supply. Maintenance of this trend however poses a number of problems as regards security of deliveries, coordination of investments and coherence in pricing policy.

New energy sources have a great potential for growth but there are problems of cost and of timing. A smooth entry on to the markets of all Member States will not be assured without action ahead of time (in research and technological development). Such action will not bear all its fruit – in the energy and industrial fields – without a Community approach taking account of the different possibilities in each Member States.

Oil is bound to remain a major element in the Community's energy balance and the bulk of oil supplies will come from outside. There must be Community solidarity in measures to guarantee security of these supplies. The pricing of oil products must reflect both the need to reduce oil dependence and the objectives of economic policy.

On the *demand* side structural change is already underway. This must be continued so that consumers can adapt in the best possible economic conditions to the shift from oil to other energy sources.

Agriculture[5] is a special case both on the supply and the demand side. It consumes directly and indirectly large amounts of energy. It has therefore an urgent need for new technologies and additional investment to reduce its energy consumption. But while increases in oil product prices sets new constraints on agriculture, they also offer the possibility of new outlets for products of agricultural origin for use as raw material for energy production. The Community has every interest in promoting progress in both these directions and in using its financial instruments to that end.

Between now and the end of March 1982, the Commission will set out its views in each of these areas in more detail, together with proposals.

IV. Operational Priorities

There are five main priorities for Community action:

(i) ensuring an adequate level of *investment* both in alternatives to oil and in the more rational use of energy;
(ii) the development of a common approach to energy *pricing and taxation*;
(iii) the establishment of measures of Community solidarity to *avoid instability on the markets*;
(iv) the reinforcement of common policies in the fields of *research, development and technological demonstration*;
(v) the further development of common approaches and initiatives in *external energy relations*.

A. Investment

1. Diversifying the sources of energy supply and the more rational use of energy (including energy saving) will require a major investment effort.

2. At the present time energy investment is stagnating around 1.6% of GDP. The most optimistic forecasts of Member States point to a possible

[5] COM(80)800 final.

rise to an average of 2.2% of GDP over the decade. Over the same period the United States expects energy investment to amount to above 4% of GDP and Japan to between 3 and 3.5%. The particular circumstances of these countries are not a sufficient explanation of this difference in order of magnitude. If the Community does not take the necessary decisions its overall level of investment could be too low, adversely affecting its ability to adapt to high energy costs and thereby its competitivity.

3. There is moreover a real risk that the forecasts themselves will not be realised. Action must therefore be taken in relation to every factor liable to influence the level of investment;

- Many decisions are held up by the uncertainty of investors and consumers about future trends in oil import prices and about the energy pricing and taxation policies of public authorities. The action proposed by the Commission on energy pricing and taxation (see ii below) will have an essential role to play in this respect;
- There are risks inherent in the industrial application of new processes such as coal gasification and liquefaction or in the large-scale exploitation of solar energy and other renewable sources. The action proposed by the Commission in the field of technological demonstration (see iv below) is intended to help overcome the constraints on the behaviour of investors in this field.
- Public concern is another factor delaying certain projects. It is felt most clearly about the health and safety risks in nuclear programmes. More recently it has also been expressed in relation to the ecological impact of increased coal consumption.

  The Community has a direct role to play both in presenting balanced information on the advantages and disadvantages of different ways of meeting energy needs and in developing common action to resolve specific problems. Community action in the fields of research on radioactive waste disposal, improving security of supply and safeguarding nuclear materials must be strengthened. The Commission will present proposals very shortly.
- The recession and the risk that it may persist also raise doubts about the profitability of certain investments.

  This factor weighs particularly heavily on the development of investments in the more rational use of energy: in new energy-efficient equipment, the conversion of oil-fired heating and motive power to coal, and the application of new energy technologies in industry. These investments offer the best prospects for the regeneration of Community industry and for the direct and indirect creation of employment and they have the most direct effects in reducing oil imports and helping the balance-of-payments.

4. Two studies completed for the Commission have examined, respectively, the technical feasibility of rapid advances in the more rational use of energy[6] and its investment and employment implications[7], concluding that the scope for and benefits of accelerated investment on the demand side are considerable. The upper limit of cost-effective investment of this kind amounts perhaps to as much as 250 billion ECU over this decade. These investments are delayed however because they involve a large number of decision-makers – households and companies – many of whom are affected in the present economic climate by problems of short-term profitability and access to external finance on acceptable terms.

5. There is already an active debate on how to accelerate these investments, and the Commission is conducting – with the aid of Member States – a detailed survey of the perspectives and problems associated with investment in the more rational use of energy. This survey will enable it to define the most effective ways of stimulating these investments and will serve as a basis for proposals in this area that will follow shortly from the Commission.

In the meantime the Commission will propose that the New Community Instrument should be used more in support of investment in the more rational use of energy with a specific tranche set aside for that purpose. The Commission will also use interest-rate subsidies financed from the ECSC budget to support the same kind of investment in the coal and steel sectors.

Investment in energy saving and in substitution for oil must be encouraged both as a means of reducing the share of oil in total energy consumption and because of its favourable effects on the level of economic activity and employment. The responsibility of the Community in this field is linked to that in the field of medium-term economic policy.

B. Prices and Taxation

1. Through its impact both on energy demand and in the long term on energy investment, energy pricing has a fundamental role to play in the pursuit of energy policy objectives. But pricing policy also has wider implications, affecting industrial competitivity and trade between Member States and with the rest of the world. A common approach to energy pricing is therefore a critical determinant of the coherence of the energy policies of Member States, supporting investment policy and enabling proper judgments to be made about the effectiveness of energy saving measures and the economics of alternatives to oil. Moreover, it is essential to the avoidance of distortions in intra-Community competition and in the encouragement of greater consistency between the pursuit of general macro-

[6] In favour of an Energy-Efficient Society, XVII 235(79)EN.

[7] Investment and Employment in an Energy-Efficient Society, XVII/052/81.

economic or budgetary objectives, on the one hand, and energy policy objectives, on the other. Finally, it is important to the credibility of the Community in its encouragement of sensible pricing practices in the countries with which it trades and competes.

2. The Commission has already underlined these points in a communication on "Energy and Economic Policy"[8], and has developed some of them in its paper on "Oil Taxation"[9]. The Council has also been invited to adopt a recommendation on electricity tariff structures[10].

In a separate communication[11], the Commission has further developed the principles of energy pricing adopted by the Council in a Resolution of 9 June 1980. These principles emphasise the need for consumer prices to reflect in full the cost of development of alternative energy resources and so to encourage investment, even when in the short run world prices for oil are stable or falling.

Within the Community there should be a common market in primary energy. Differences in the prices at which coal, crude oil and gas are made available to the energy industries should be limited to those arising from differences in transport costs. This does not however mean that consumer prices can or should be identical throughout the Community. On the contrary, it is right that prudent investment in energy transformation (refining, transport, distribution and – especially – electricity generation) within individual Member States should be reflected in advantageous consumer prices. However, consumer prices are determined not only by comparative costs, but also by important differences in policy, notably as regards taxation, price control and the financing of public utilities.

Consistency in energy pricing and taxation policies, in accordance with energy supply and demand objectives, requires first of all an improvement in transparency of energy prices and tariffs and a common effort to adapt oil taxation to the aims of energy and economic policy.

C. A Mechanism to Avoid Instability on the Markets

1. The objectives of security and stability of supply apply to all forms of energy and their pursuit is a key feature of Community strategy. They are of particular importance as far as oil is concerned given the dominant role played by oil prices and the less flexible nature of the oil market compared with the past.

2. The lesson of 1979 was that even very limited shortfalls in oil supply over a brief period – and even the risk itself of such a development –

[8] COM/80/583.
[9] COM/81/511.
[10] COM/81/356 and COM/80/322.
[11] COM/80/539.

can have serious and disproportionate effects on oil price movements. A repeat of those events would have damaging consequences. The relative slackness of the market in recent months could mean that this danger will be underestimated even though the rise in the dollar has increased considerably the cost of the Community's imported oil.

The Community would be failing in its task if it did not manifest solidarity in the face of such difficulties. This solidarity would be more difficult to achieve if it were not established beforehand in a period of calm. A mechanism already exists to deal with serious supply difficulties. But it is vital that the Community should arm itself ahead of time with procedures and means to soften the impact of any future oil supply shortfalls, especially on prices.

3. The Commission has accordingly proposed a procedure to handle situations of limited shortfalls on the oil market, together with a series of measures from which the Council could choose the most appropriate in the light of circumstances.

To be effective the set of actions proposed would have to be closely coordinated in a wider framework involving the USA and Japan. But as the preparation of Western Economic Summits has shown – and especially those in Tokyo in 1979 and Venice in 1980 – the Community can helpfully give a lead to the other major oil consumers by virtue of its position as collectively the single largest buyer on world markets.

The Community is more vulnerable than other consuming groups as far as external oil supplies are concerned. It must therefore protect itself against the risk of fortuitous tension on the world oil market. Even if measures to that end are taken only on a contingency basis, agreement on the conditions and procedures under which they would be applied, without prejudice to the precise decisions required by particular circumstances, would be proof of the credibility of the Community strategy.

D. Research and Development; Technological Demonstration

Research and development

1. The logic of action at Community level on energy research and development is self evident. It enables the Community to support large-scale activities beyond the financial reach of individual Member States (e. g. the development of controlled thermo-nuclear fusion); it avoids costly multiplication of effort; and it works as a catalyst in promoting the cross-fertilisation of ideas and the more rapid diffusion of results. In each of these ways, it helps the Community to make up for the natural benefits enjoyed by the USA and Japan.

2. The Community has been involved in support for energy R & D since its inception, first in coal under the ECSC Treaty, then in nuclear fission and fusion under the Euratom Treaty, finally in energy conservation and new energy sources under the stimulus of the first "oil crisis" of 1973/4.

The result is that energy already absorbs some 70% of total funds in the Community's R & D budget. [...] The Community budget provides thereby the equivalent of some 10% of total public support (Member States and Community) for the financing of R & D in the energy and related fields, and the overall effort coordinated within the Community framework is still greater.

3. An increased research effort is needed to help reduce more rapidly the Community's dependence on oil (energy saving and substitutes) and to make it easier for Community industry to adapt to changes in the energy market. This will mean a need for increased financial resources. Community intervention will enable expenditure to produce the maximum possible benefit, to avoid waste of resources and to ensure the widest dissemination of research results.

Against this background the Commission has begun to reorganise its service involved in research and is examining the different programmes. It will make proposals to intensify research on the more rational use of energy and renewable energy sources, not only in its own interests but so as to meet the needs of the LDCs.

It will do the same in the field of coal research to reflect the growing importance of coal.

Technological demonstration

4. The involvement of the Community in coordinating and financing support for projects to demonstrate the industrial and commercial viability of new methods and technologies is more modest than that in R & D and now requires renewed attention. The demonstration phase provides the essential bridge to the full-scale commercialisation of new techniques, thereby supporting industrial as well as energy policy in encouraging the launching of new industries, processes and products.

It has been clear for some time that the Community's pluriannual programmes of support for such projects in energy saving and in alternative energy sources which began in 1979 would be insufficient to meet demand. In 1980 therefore the Commission made precise proposals to the Council involving a doubling of the financial ceilings[12]. The Commission's Reports on the existing programmes underline the positive experience of the operation of the existing Regulations to date. The Commission will take all the steps necessary to ensure effective dissemination of the results of the programmes so as to maximise the benefits throughout Community industry.

5. As a further element in the encouragement of innovation in and through the energy sector, the Commission intends also to help ensure that those

[12] COM(80)567 final.

involved in the development and exploitation of new energy technologies are able to secure the full benefits of the common market, and in particular that markets for high performance but relatively high cost equipment can be fully developed. Particular attention will be paid to the development of common standards so as to avoid the creation of non-tariff barriers to trade.

Innovation is a necessary part of energy strategy. Financial action and coordination at the level of the Community are vital to the achievement of the most effective results in research and development and in technological demonstration. The potential in this field must be better exploited and exploited to the full.

E. External Relations

1. Community energy strategy must inevitably be pursued within a wider international framework involving the other main consuming nations, the energy exporting — and especially the oil-exporting countries, and the oil importing developing countries. The Community alone offers a credible basis for the expression of the interests of Member States vis-à-vis each of these groups, developing relations with each as far as possible in a balanced way and making use of a variety of methods and frameworks for action.

The benefits of Community coordination have already been amply demonstrated in the preparation of Western Economic Summits, meetings of the International Energy Agency (IEA) and most recently in the UN Conference on New and Renewable Energy Sources. The Community must build on this experience, both to enhance Community cooperation in the fields of hydrocarbon supplies, the international coal trade and supplies of nuclear fuels, and, most importantly, cooperation with the developing world.

2. Cooperation among Member States in securing supplies of *natural gas* from outside has been less than satisfactory in the past. It can and should be enhanced. The negotiation and conclusion of new contracts should be pursued within the framework of a common approach to Community requirements and objectives and the Commission has put forward to the Council specific proposals to this end[13].

3. In the fields of *coal* and *nuclear fuels* the aim of the Community must be to develop a framework of relations with the exporting countries which can likewise ensure stable and secure supplies. This cannot be achieved satisfactorily by individual Member States acting alone. The essential need for Community action in securing supplies of nuclear fuels is already well established and has led to the satisfactory conclusion of cooperation agreements with the main suppliers, notably Australia, Canada and the

[13] COM(81)530 final.

United States. This position must be maintained and developed so that new negotiations or renegotiations that may prove necessary in the light of changing circumstances can follow a similar course.

4. The Community and its Member States have already made a substantial contribution to the development of *energy resources in the developing world*, with total aid (grants and loans) amounting to over 700 m ECU in 1980 alone. Of this total nearly one third (over 200 m ECU) was accounted for by loans from the European Investment Bank which is one of the main sources after the World Bank in the provision of loan finance for energy development. In addition to direct support for the financing of energy investment by this means, the Community has also helped with the evaluation and planning of energy supply and demand in a large number of developing countries.

5. The Commission proposes the following approach to intensify energy cooperation with developing countries. Firstly, there must be closer coordination between the aid programmes of Member States and those of the Community. Secondly, more use must be made of the specific means available to the Community both by virtue of the Lomé II Convention and of agreements with non-associated countries.

It should be noted in this respect that Lomé II emphasizes projects involving regional cooperation and increases the aid available to projects developing alternative energy sources in the associated countries.

6. There must be a global approach to energy cooperation with developing countries, taking full account however of the particular situation and priorities of each country concerned and of the nature of its relations with the Community. This approach should cover the following areas in particular:

(a) development of guidelines for aid in energy programming (the evaluation of resources and requirements);

(b) assistance in the form of information required for investment decision-making (project evaluation; specialised techniques, for example in prospecting; R & D, including more recourse to the Joint Research Centre and association between research centres in the Member States; access to data banks);

(c) technical and professional education;

(d) exchanges of information on techniques that might be applied in developing countries, especially as regards the rational use of the energy, and the encouragement of their use in these countries;

(e) extension of the practice of co-financing which has already been used with other institutions such as OPEC, the Arab Funds, the World Bank, etc;

(f) encouraging industry to adapt a constructive investment policy towards LDCs, with recourse as necessary to the possibilities offered by Lomé II in this respect;

(g) encouraging the use of new and renewable sources, especially linked to programmes of rural development and environmental protection.

The Commission will present proposals to the Council covering the whole of this approach.

The Community alone provides the necessary dimension for the expression of the interests of Member States on the world stage. It must establish, with those countries which supply its energy imports, a framework of relations which ensure stable supplies, particularly of coal and natural gas, just as it has already done in the nuclear field in general. Priority must also be given to energy cooperation with the developing countries both to meet their own needs and to help reduce pressure on world oil supplies. To that end the possibilities offered by the Lomé Convention must be fully exploited and efforts must be increased towards the other developing countries, especially those with whom the Community has contractual relations.

V. Conclusions

(a) The adoption of common objectives, the pursuit of these objectives by means of coordinated action by Member States and the acceptance of collective discipline are the basis for the Community policy proposed above. In the absence of such an approach the Community will not be in a position to meet the energy challenge.

The essence of this approach lies in efforts at Community level to anticipate developments. Instead of simply reacting to events in the energy field we must prepare the way, in the best possible conditions, for the changes that are most likely to be required by future developments on the energy markets, while minimising the economic and social consequences of those developments. Such a forward looking approach has the added advantage of supporting the objective of economic revival and increasing employment.

(b) Energy objectives have already been adopted by the Community. This development will remain of use only if the objectives are constantly brought up to date and if there can be a regular examination of how far they are reflected in national policies, followed as necessary by an adjustment of those policies. The first role for the Commission in developing energy strategy is therefore one of guidance and monitoring.

The Commission can also take action on its own account in certain fields: those prescribed by the Treaties; those where no other means exist to meet common objectives; and those where to exploit the Community dimension is likely to bring results that go beyond those that can be achieved by Member States acting alone or even in coordination.

In some cases Community action will require financial resources. These must be adequate for the tasks involved. Various instruments already exist which need to be refined or developed in the light of the Community's needs and other objectives.

(c) There are five priorities in what must be done to reduce the Community's dependence on oil by a better use of all available resources and a broader diversification of supplies. These are: investment; pricing and taxation policy; stability of supply; development of the potential for technological innovation; and relations with third countries. The Member States and the Community have taken a number of steps in some of these fields. But these have been inadequate or uncoordinated. The Commission has already made a number of proposals to increase the Community commitment. Others will follow. Such an increased commitment would be a major step forward in the development of our common strategy.

(d) The Commission requests the Council to approve the strategy described above; to agree on the objectives; and, on that basis, to state its position on the various proposals already put to it and on those that will follow.

Appendix II

Community Communications, Proposals, and Measures 1979–1983

For a complete list of legislation prior to 1979 see:

Community Energy Policy – Texts of the Relevant Legislation 1976 Cat. No. CH 22 761 32-EN-C

and Community Energy Policy – Texts of the Relevant Legislation Supplement No. 1. 1978 (1979) Cat. No. CB 28-79-132-EN-C.

For a list of Communications, proposals and decisions in the field of energy, January 1979 – June 1980, see "Energy Policy in the European Community Perspectives and Achievements" Com (80) 379 final

and CEC Bibliography in Energy, Documentation Bulletin Series B 2/1 (1981).

Principal Communications, Proposals and Measures – post 1981

Energy Strategy

The Development of an Energy Strategy for the Community	Com (81) final 2 October 1981
The Energy Situation in the Community Situation 1981: Outlook 1982	Com (82) 77 final 24 February 1982
The Energy Situation in the Community Situation 1982: Outlook 1983	Com (83) final

Investment in the Rational Use of Energy

Investment in the Rational Use of Energy	Com (82) 24 final 10 February 1982

Proposal for a Council Regulation (EEC) on the payment of financial incentives in support of categories of investment in the rational use of energy	Com (82) 537 final 14 September 1982

Pricing

Energy Pricing – Policy and Transparency	Com (81) 539 final 1 October 1981
Energy Pricing – Developments in Community Policy 1981–82	Com (82) 651 final 19 October 1982
Council Recommendation (EEC) 82/924 on Electricity Tariff Structures	OJ L337, 1981
Council Recommendation (EEC) 83/230 on Natural Gas Tariff Structures	OJ L123, 1983

Taxation

Taxation of Petroleum Products	Com (81) 511 final 11 September 1981

Monitoring Member States' Energy Policies

Review of Member States' energy policy programmes and progress towards 1990 objectives	Com (82) 326 final 10 June 1982

Solid Fuels

The Role of Coal in Community Energy Strategy	Com (82) 31 final 10 February 1982
Report on the Brown Coal and Peat Industries in the Community	Com (82) 649 final
Council Recommendation (EEC) 83/250 on the encouragement of investment in the use of solid fuels in industry	OJ L 140 1983
Communication from the Commission to the Council on Proposals for a Balanced Solid Fuels Policy	Com (83) 309 final 10 June 1983
Commission Decision on the granting of financial support for pilot industrial and demonstration projects in the field of liquefaction and gasification of solid fuels	Com (83) 1124 final 29 July 1983
Proposal for a Council Regulation on Financial Support of the Community in favour of industries producing solid fuels	Com (83) 447 final 8 August 1983
Revised Forecast on the outlook for the Community. Coal Market in 1983	Com (83) 532 final 15 September 1983

Communication from the Commission to the Council in a New System for Coking Coal and Coke for the Iron and Steel Industry in the Community	Com (83) 583 final 6 October 1983
Communication Decision on the granting of financial support for a second series of pilot industrial and demonstration projects in the field of liquefaction and gasification of solid fuels	Com (83) 1507 final 19 October 1983
Council Recommendation (EEC) 83/251 on the encouragement of the use of solid fuels in public buildings and urban heating systems	OJ L 140 1983

Nuclear

An Energy Strategy for the Community: the Nuclear Aspects	Com (82) 36 final 9 February 1982
Proposal for a Council Decision adopting the new provisions relating to Chapter VI, 'Supplies' of the Treaty establishing the European Atomic Energy Community	Com (82) 732 final 3 December 1982
Report from the Commission to the Council on the implementation of the verification agreements considered by Euratom and its Member States with the International Energy Agency	Com (83) 36 final 27 January 1983
Euratom Accord 82/52 on relations between Euratom and Canada, concerning enrichment and reprocessing of nuclear fuels	OJ L 127 1982

Oil

Measures to limit the effects of a limited shortfall in oil supply	Com (81) 533 final 30 September 1981
Proposal for a Council Directive amending Directive 68/414/EEC imposing an obligation on Member States of the EEC to maintain minimum stocks of crude oil and/or petroleum products	Com (82) 41 final 4 February 1982
Proposal for a Council Decision on a Community procedure for the adoption of measures to mitigate the effects of a limited shortage of crude oil and petroleum products	Com (82) 41 final 4 February 1982
Proposal for a Council Directive on the fuel rationing for commercial transport between the Member States	Com (83) 405 final 1 July 1983

Report from the Commission to the European Parliament and to the Council on the Application of Article 10 of Regulation (EEC) 3056/3 on the support of Community Projects in the hydrocarbons sector	Com (83) 571 final 4 October 1983
Commission Decision 83/314 on fuel aids to the Belgian fishing industry	OJ L 169 1983

Natural Gas

Communication from the Commission to the Council concerning natural gas	Com (81) 530 final 1 October 1981
Communication from the Commission to the Council concerning measures to enhance the security of natural gas supplies to the Community	Com (82) final 15 February 1982
Communication from the Commission to the Council on Community natural gas supplies	Com (82) 653 final 15 October 1982
Draft Council Recommendation on the methods of setting natural gas prices and tariffs in Community	Com (82) 603 final 29 September 1982

Research, Development and Demonstration

Communication from the Commission to the Council concerning the review of the energy research and development programme adopted in the Council Discussion of 11 September 1979	Com (82) 124 final 18 March 1982
Proposals for a European Scientific and Technical Strategy Framework Programme	Com (82) 865 final 21 December 1982
Communication from the Commission to the Council. Evaluation of the Community Demonstration programmes in the energy sector	Com (82) 324 final 11 June 1982
Assessment Report on the Community Demonstration. Programmes in the field of energy saving and alternative energy sources	Com (82) 324 final 11 June 1982
Assessment Report on the Community Demonstration. Projects in the fields of energy saving and alternative energy sources (Annexes I, II and II)	Com (82) 324 final 17 June 1982
Proposal for a Council Regulation (EEC) on the granting of financial support for pilot industrial projects and demonstration projects relating to the liquefaction and gasification of solid fuels	Com (82) 555 final 3 August 1982

Proposal for a Council Regulation (EEC) on the granting of financial support for demonstration projects relating to the exploitation of alternative energy sources, energy saving and the substitution of hydrocarbons	Com (82) 458 final 3 August 1982

Norms and Standards

Council Directive 82/885 on the encouragement of combined heat generation	OJ L 378/19 1982
Draft Directive on labelling	Com (80) 108 final

Refining

Problems affecting the oil refining industry in the Community	Com (81) 536 final 30 September 1981
Problems of the oil refining industry: Progress report	Com (82) 360 final 15 June 1982
Problems of the oil refining industry in the Community	Com (82) 304 final 3 June 1983

Substitute fuels

Draft Council Directive on crude oil saving through the use of substitute fuel components in petrol	Com (82) 491 final 29 July 1982

Appendix III

National Plans and Policy Statements

United Kingdom

Fuel Policy, Cmnd. 2798 (1965)
Fuel Policy, Cmnd. 3438 (1967)
Economic and Financial Objectives of the Nationalised Industries, Cmnd. 3437 (1967)
Offshore Oil and Gas Policy, Cmnd. 5696 (1974)
Energy Policy: a Consultative Document, Cmnd. 7101 (1978)
Nationalised Industries, Cmnd. 7131 (1978)

France

Projet de loi (Messmer) of April 2, 1974: see Faberon, Politique et Moyens Juridiques des Economies d'Energie en France, La Documentation Française (1979)
Commission générale du Plan: Rapport de la Commission de l'Energie. Rapport préparatoire du VIIIème Plan
Rapport sur les Principales options du VIIIème Plan, Projet soumis par le gouvernement à l'avis du Conseil Economique et Social (1979), IIIe Partie
Commission de l'énergie et des matières premières, La Relève du Pétrole (1980)

The Netherlands

Energienota, Bijl. Hand. TK 1974–75, 13122 nr. 2
Nota Energiebeleid del II, Bijl. Hand. TK 1979–80, 15802, nr. 6–7
Structuurschema Electriciteitsvoorziening, Bijl. Hand. TK 1974–75, 13488
Aavullend Structuurschema Electriciteitsvoorziening, Bijl. Hand. TK 1975–76, 14363
Bradstofinzetplan Centrales, Bijl. Hand. TK 1979–80, 15891

Italy

Donat-Cattin Plan, approved by Interministerial Economic Council (CIPE), December 1975

Bisaglia Plan, approved by CIPE, December 1977
Pandolfi Plan (second version), approved by CIPE, 1981: see Mondo Economico, July 22, 1981

Germany

Bundeswirtschaftsministerium, Das Energieprogramm der Bundesregierung, September 26th, 1973
Bundeswirtschaftsministerium, Erste Fortschreitung des Energieprogramms der Bundesregierung, November 4th, 1974
Bundeswirtschaftsministerium, Guidelines and key figures for the extension of the Energy Programme (1977), 30 Bundesregierung 269
Bundeswirtschaftsministerium, Third Revision of the Energy Programme (1981) Bundesregierung November 5, 1981
Bundeswirtschaftsministerium, Energy Research and Development Programme of the Federal Republic of Germany, Annual Reports 1974, 1975, and 1976
Bundeswirtschaftsministerium, Energy Research Programme for 1977–1980

Appendix IV

Colloquium on Implementation of Energy Policy in the EEC, 1973–1980: Legal and Other Aspects held on 22–24 September 1982 in Florence

Papers

1. La Communauté Européenne et la Politique Energétique –
   R. De Bauw
2. National Political and Administrative Constraints on Energy Policy: A Comparative Overview –
   N. Lucas
3. The Nuclear Energy Conflict in France and West Germany –
   D. W. Fach and G. Simonis
4. Legal Implementation of Energy Policy: A Framework for Comparison –
   T. C. Daintith
5. Legal Implementation of Energy Policy: Comparative Examples –
   L. Hancher
6. Legal Aspects of Energy Policy in Italy –
   F. Roversi-Monaco
7. Legal Aspects of Energy Policy in France –
   P. Pringuet
8. Legal Aspects of Energy Policy in the United Kingdom –
   M. Forster
9. Legal Aspects of Energy Policy in the Netherlands –
   R. Barents
10. Legal Aspects of Energy Policy in West Germany –
    W. Birner
11. Regulation of the Siting of Nuclear and Conventional Electricity Generating Plants –
    E. Hubert
12. Relations between Oil Companies and Consumer Governments –
    G. Lévy

External Participants

Mr. R. De Bauw, DG XVII Commission of the EEC, Brussels
Mr. N. J. D. Lucas, Imperial College, London
Prof. D. W. Fach, Department of Social and Political Science, University of Konstanz
Dr. G. Simonis, Department of Social Science, University of Konstanz
Prof. F. Roversi-Monaco, Scuola di Perfezionamento in Scienze Amministrative, University of Bologna
Mr. P. Pringuet, Ministère du Plan et de l'Aménagement du Territoire, Paris
Mr. M. Forster, Director, Centre for Energy Law and Policy, University of Southampton
Mr. R. Barents, Legal Secretary, European Court of Justice, Luxembourg
Mr. W. Birner, Ministerialrat im Bundesministerium für Wirtschaft, Bonn
Mr. E. Hubert, Professeur Associé à l'Université de Liège
Mr. G. Lévy, Adjoint au Directeur des Hydrocarbures, Ministère de l'Industrie, Paris

Index

FSC
www.fsc.org
MIX
Papier | Fördert
gute Waldnutzung
FSC® C083411

Kolibri 360 GmbH
Ferdinand-Jühlke-Straße 7
99095 Erfurt, Deutschland
produktsicherheit@kolibri360.de